WILTSH
AIRFIEL
IN THE SECOND
WORLD WAR

David Berryman

COUNTRYSIDE BOOKS
NEWBURY, BERKSHIRE

First published 2002
© David Berryman 2002

All rights reserved. No reproduction
permitted without the prior permission
of the publisher:

COUNTRYSIDE BOOKS
3 Catherine Road
Newbury, Berkshire

To view our complete range of books,
please visit us at
www.countrysidebooks.co.uk

ISBN 1 85306 703 2

*For my parents, Noreen and Geoffrey Berryman, who both
served their country in the Royal Air Force during World War II,
and who each spent a good proportion of their service at
various Stations in Wiltshire.*

The cover painting is from an original by
Colin Doggett and shows three new Spitfires Mark V
passing through Old Sarum airfield whilst on test
from High Post. One aircraft performs a 'touch and go'
landing whilst the others fly overhead.

Designed by Mon Mohan

Produced through MRM Associates Ltd., Reading
Typeset by Techniset Typesetters, Newton-le-Willows
Printed by Woolnough Bookbinding Ltd., Irthlingborough

CONTENTS

WILTSHIRE AIRFIELDS IN THE SECOND WORLD WAR

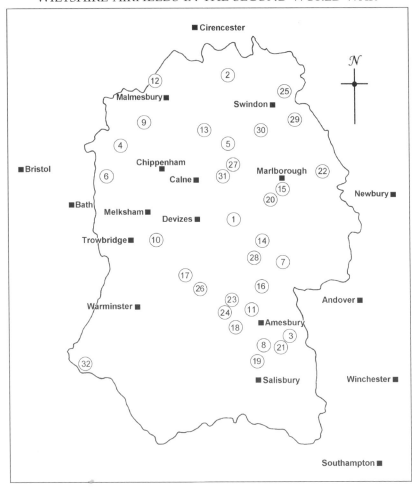

KEY TO AIRFIELDS

1. Alton Barnes	9. Hullavington	17. New Zealand Farm	25. South Marston
2. Blakehill Farm	10. Keevil	18. Oatlands Hill	26. Tilshead
3. Boscombe Down	11. Larkhill	19. Old Sarum	27. Townsend
4. Castle Combe	12. Long Newnton	20. Overton Heath	28. Upavon
5. Clyffe Pypard	13. Lyneham	21. Porton Down	29. Wanborough
6. Colerne	14. Maningford	22. Ramsbury	30. Wroughton
7. Everleigh	15. Marlborough	23. Rollestone	31. Yatesbury
8. High Post	16. Netheravon	24. Shrewton	32. Zeals

ACKNOWLEDGEMENTS

I would like to thank the following individuals and organisations that have assisted me in writing this book:

Terry Heffernan
Dr Hugh Thomas
Roger Day
Peter Amos
Sqn.Ldr Christopher Bartlett, RAF (Retd)
Sandy Beattie
Gradon Carter
Kevin Byrne
Norman Parker
Michael Oakley, Nick Stroud and the team at Aeroplane
Mrs Jean Buckberry, Senior Librarian, Royal Air Force College
    Cranwell
Col Derek Armitage (Retd), Curator Museum of Army Flying,
    Middle Wallop
Wiltshire County Archives, Trowbridge
Royal Air Force Museum, Hendon
Public Record Office, Kew
Salisbury Journal
Salisbury Reference Library
Cambridge University Library (Vickers Archives)
Wroughton History Group
No.56 Squadron, Royal Air Force Coningsby
No.7 Regiment Army Air Corps, Netheravon
The Battle of Britain Memorial Flight, RAF Coningsby
Dstl

I would especially like to thank Nicholas Battle and his team at Countryside Books for their help and encouragement, and my wife Karen, for all her support and hard work in helping me get the manuscript together.

I
SETTING
THE
SCENE

Wiltshire is one of the oldest counties in Britain, having its origins in the 9th century. The county that was described in the Domesday Book of 1086 has changed very little geographically since. It is fitting therefore that one with such deep historical origins should also embrace new activities, and having played a part in aviation from its very early beginnings has had a long-standing involvement in it ever since. The first awakenings of interest in aviation in Britain can in fact be traced to Malmesbury in Wiltshire, when, in the 11th century, the first recorded attempted flight was made. Brother Elmer, a Benedictine monk, made a pair of wings and jumped off the roof of Malmesbury Abbey. Although he broke his legs, the fact he was not killed was probably due to the wings giving him at least some lift and slowing his contact with the ground! His 'flight' is commemorated in a stained-glass window at the Abbey.

The origins of powered flight can be traced to Yorkshire in 1799 when Sir George Cayley, 'the Father of Aerial Navigation', designed the first modern aeroplane. After building a series of models and full-sized unmanned gliders, the climax to his career came in 1853 when the 80-year old Cayley flew his equally aged coachman over his estate in a glider with rudimentary controls. Many followed in the quest for manned powered flight, including the Briton Percy Pilcher, who was on the verge of fitting a small engine to one of his gliders when he was killed in a glider accident in 1899. It was the Wright Brothers who were the first to succeed, at Kittyhawk, North Carolina on 17 December 1903, narrowly beating several other pioneers to the prize.

The first powered flight in Britain took place on 16 October 1908 when Samuel F. Cody flew from Laffan's Plain, Farnborough (subsequently the site of the Royal Aircraft Establishment). A few months later another early aviator, Horatio Barber, began to experiment with an aeroplane of his own from a shed built for the purpose at Durrington Down, Larkhill, in Wiltshire. He patented a design and had it built by the Howard Wright Company of Battersea. It was delivered in June 1909. Barber was joined by two other pioneers, G.B. Cockburn and Captain J.B. Fulton, at Larkhill, and soon the airfield became an important site for British aviation. In June 1910 a major enterprise was started when the British & Colonial Aeroplane Co. (later to become the Bristol Aeroplane Co.) opened a flying school at Larkhill. This aroused great interest, particularly among the military, and a couple of Bristol Boxkite aeroplanes on loan from the British & Colonial Co. were used by the army during the autumn manoeuvres of 1910.

Military aviation had started in Britain in 1878 when the Royal Engineers experimented with balloons. Balloon detachments went to Africa with Army expeditions in 1885. After further use during the Boer War, training in balloon operations regularly took place on Salisbury Plain. The Royal Engineers also experimented with aeroplanes. As a result the Air Battalion was formed on 1 April 1911, with two companies, No.1 operating balloons from Farnborough and No.2 flying aeroplanes at Larkhill. Six Boxkites were delivered to No.2 Company during 1911, and the unit began to recruit pilots. Initially these were confined to officers who had already learnt to fly at their own expense, although the army generously agreed to repay £75 of their tuition fees on their acceptance by the Air Battalion. To formalise the training of military pilots a Central Flying School was set up at Upavon in June 1912. This laid down the foundations for the training of flying instructors in the British military. It was later to set the standards for military flying training across the world.

The War Office wished to establish a specification for military aeroplanes, so in August 1912 held a military trial at Larkhill. The trial was open to all-comers (apart from Government designs), and the prize-winning aeroplane was to be purchased for the army. The competition attracted thirty-two entries from Britain and the Continent. After a series of tests over several weeks the prize went to the Cody Cathedral biplane. Two examples of the Cathedral were bought for the

BE2A and Maurice Farman trainers in front of the wooden hangars at the Central Flying School, Upavon in 1913. (Aeroplane)

army, but both crashed soon afterwards. One was rebuilt and can be seen today in the Science Museum.

Larkhill continued to be the powerhouse of British military aviation over the next few years. The first night flight by a British military aeroplane took place on the night of 15/16 April 1913 when Lieutenant R. Cholmonderley of No.3 Squadron flew from Larkhill to Upavon and back by moonlight. Pupils came from all over the world to train at the Bristol School (the first Chinese national to receive a Pilot's Certificate, for example, was Zee Yee Lee, who graduated at Larkhill on 17 October 1911. He went on to become the Chief Flying Instructor of the Military Flying School in Peking). On the outbreak of War in 1914, 127 out of the 664 British military pilots had been trained at Larkhill.

In August 1914 the newly-formed Royal Flying Corps (RFC) was centred on two major airfields in Wiltshire – Upavon and Netheravon (which had replaced Larkhill). With just seven squadrons the RFC was a tiny force compared with the German Air Service, and so these vital training establishments had to work hard to produce more trained pilots and observers for the front-line squadrons. However, by 1916 there was concern that the output of trained aircrew was not meeting the demand. It was therefore decided to build more training establishments in Wiltshire, with the result that a number of Training Depot Stations (TDSs) were built the following year. Five aerodromes were

9

opened on Salibury Plain alone in 1917. These were Lake Down, Old Sarum, Stonehenge, Boscombe Down and Lopcombe Corner (the latter being just over the Hampshire border). Yatesbury was also built to the north. Together they trained a large number of British, Commonwealth and US aircrew from opening until the end of the war.

Stonehenge was an exception to the others as it was not a flying school, but was used by the School of Navigation and Bomb Dropping as a finishing school for RFC bomber pilots and navigators. The station occupied a large area running north and south of the main Wyle-Amesbury road (the A303), not far from Stonehenge itself (indeed it was even suggested at one time that the stones should be removed as they were a flying hazard!). Day and night training took place there on Avro 504s and DH9s, as well as the giant Handley Page 0/400 bombers. Four sizeable hangars and many other buildings had been erected on the airfield for the school which, at the height of its activity in mid-1918, turned out sixty day- and sixty night-crews every month. The Royal Naval Air Service, that had been formed from the naval wing of the RFC on 1 July 1914, had an out-station at Stonehenge where it, too, trained bomber crews.

A total of nine training establishments was in operation in Wiltshire in 1918, operating well over a thousand aeroplanes, and employing

Stonehenge airfield in September 1918. The aircraft in the foreground are Handley Page 0/400, DH4 and DH9 bombers. (Jack Bruce, via Terry Heffernan)

thousands of personnel. With the Armistice, however, the picture radically changed. The busy airfields fell silent and many were closed down. Old Sarum, Netheravon and Upavon remained open, but the numbers of aircraft, squadrons and personnel were drastically reduced.

During the inter-war years several private airfields, such as High Post and Marlborough, were opened in Wiltshire. One way in which interest in aviation was sparked in the county was as the result of visits by Sir Alan Cobham and his 'Flying Circus' from 1932 onwards. Flying displays included aerobatics and crazy flying, and joy-rides were offered to the public. The official title of Cobham's Circus was the 'National Aviation Day Campaign', and it received widespread publicity wherever it went.

Military flying in Wiltshire too revived in the 1930s. In 1930 Boscombe Down re-opened as a bomber station. A few years later, in 1934, the Government initiated the RAF Expansion Scheme, as it was realised that the strength of European air forces, particularly those of France and Germany, were being increased. To face these fleets of thousands of modern bombers and fighters the RAF could then only muster 850 front-line aircraft. Of these the fastest was the 207 mph, two-gun Hawker Fury biplane fighter, and the most powerful was the

Trainee pilots await their turn to go up. Wiltshire airfields played an important role in the training of aircrew during World War II. (Aeroplane)

11

Handley Page Heyford biplane bomber that could carry a 4,500 lb bomb load at 200 mph. Under the Expansion Plan a series of schemes brought in new home defence fighter squadrons, an increase in the reserves, and more bomber units. Balloon barrages were also established and new air stations were built.

New aircraft types were developed, with the general intention of replacing the RAF's fleet of biplanes with the more modern monoplanes. The Battle and Blenheim replaced the Hind, the Harrow and Whitley replaced the Heyford and the Hurricane replaced the Fury. In Wiltshire this meant that Yatesbury was re-opened as an Elementary Flying Training School (EFTS) and later Radio School, while Colerne, Hullavington and Wroughton were opened as

Airborne troops prepare to board a Horsa glider during a training exercise in Wiltshire in December 1942. (Aeroplane)

Maintenance and Aircraft Storage Units. The result of this preparation was that on the outbreak of war the RAF had in front-line service about 2,000 aircraft (many of them modern monoplanes), with some 2,200 in reserve. The Luftwaffe had meanwhile been expanding too, and had 4,160 front-line aircraft with 1,000 reserves. The Nazis were numerically superior, but the RAF's aircraft were operated by personnel who, in terms of training, courage and spirit, were second to none.

In September 1939 military aviation was once again widespread throughout Wiltshire, and indeed Britain. However, with the outbreak of war all general civil flying was stopped, and only authorised civilian flights were allowed to take place. The vast majority of civilian aeroplanes were then requisitioned for service use.

During the early stages of the war most of the airfields in Wiltshire were too far from the Continent for the conduct of offensive operations, but they were nevertheless ideally situated for training and support. Airfields such as Upavon, Netheravon, Yatesbury, Castle Combe and Hullavington housed flying training units, while army cooperation squadrons were based at Old Sarum and Larkhill. Netheravon later became the centre for airborne forces glider and parachute training. As the war progressed convenient locations were found in Wiltshire for operational units. These included Colerne and Zeals, which flew fighters, and Blakehill Farm and Keevil, which were bases for airborne forces. Lyneham was an air transport base much the same as it is today.

All of the permanent stations were built to a similar plan and pattern and cost an average of £750,000 each. They were usually grass airfields, at least 1,100 yards in diameter. Their most obvious features were massive hangars which fronted onto a large apron of concrete where the daily upkeep and maintenance of aircraft took place. The hangars were up to 150 feet wide, and up to 48 feet high, with large sliding doors at each end. The interior of an average hangar was as large as a football pitch, and one was provided for each squadron. A mixture of workshops, offices, stores and crew rooms surrounded the hangars. Operational buildings erected on the airfield included a watch office or control tower, fire station, met office and briefing rooms. Accommodation was provided, for airmen in brick barrack blocks near the concrete parade ground, and for officers and senior NCOs in separate messes.

The architecture of the pre-war RAF stations bore a striking similarity wherever they were built. This was largely due to the architect who had been appointed by the Air Ministry Aerodromes Board, Sir Edwin Lutyens. He stamped his distinctive style on many

RAF stations, which is still evident today. The main structures are well proportioned neo-Georgian buildings which have been described as a cross between a country house and a hotel. Lutyens' attention to detail was also applied to the smaller buildings and even the guard rooms, which had pillars and curved arches. Few pre-war airfields were built with concrete runways; these were added later. It was not until December 1940 that all new bomber airfields would be provided with them. For the standard three runway layout, linked by a perimeter track, with access to dispersals, up to 40,000 square yards of concrete would have been laid along with 50 miles of pipes and conduits.

The programme of wartime airfield building required an immense input of labour and materials. A typical large airfield took seven months to complete, with a thousand men being employed at the height of the work. The Minister of Labour, Ernest Bevan, was responsible for providing the labour for the airfield building programme, and also for other defence and civilian projects. There was, for example, the need to repair civilian housing, as many thousands of houses had been damaged in air raids but had only had 'first aid' repairs.

To give an idea of the scale of the airfield building programme, in December 1942, 510 airfields were in operation against a target of 670. A further 106 were under construction and 54 were at various stages between site evaluation, land requisition and contractor selection. RAF Works Squadrons and US Army Engineers helped, the Americans working on twelve of these sites.

In addition to operational airfields, dummy ones were also built. Known as decoys, they were designed to draw enemy attacks away from the real airfields. To devise the decoys a special department had been established by the Air Ministry: the Department of Decoys and Deception, which was housed in the Shepperton Film Studios. It was located there in order to tap into the expertise of the British Film Industry, which had been extraordinarily successful in making mock up indoor film sets so that filming would not be interrupted by the unreliable British weather!

There were two types of decoy site: K sites for day decoys and Q sites for night. The Q sites were easier to construct because it was only necessary to reproduce the lighting of an airfield at night and keep it maintained. Ordinary farmland could be used and because the lights were carried on poles the exact nature of the ground did not matter. It didn't have to be level and, in fact, the less that it looked like an airfield the better, to avoid detection during the day. K sites were more difficult to construct as they had to be laid out in every detail to include all the necessary buildings, installations and resident aircraft to convince an attacker that it was the real thing. The decoy sites were extremely successful. Forty were in effect by June 1940 and during that month thirty-six attacks were made on them by the Luftwaffe. As more and more airfields were constructed so too were more decoys until there were about 200 of them all around the country. By the end of June 1941 the Luftwaffe had made 322 attacks on the dummies as opposed to 304 on the genuine airfields.

Other types of decoy site were the Starfish and QL sites. Having noticed how German aircraft were attracted by fires, equipment was designed so that fires could be ignited and controlled remotely from a control bunker. These sites were given the code SF – Special Fire – and this soon evolved into the name 'Starfish'. The QL sites consisted of special lighting effects that were either used on their own or added to Starfish sites to add realism; for example, devices such as 'Hares and Rabbits' were sets of lights on a rig that travelled up and down the site simulating an aircraft taking off or landing and other rigs simulated vehicle lights. As well as simulating airfields some Starfish/QL sites were built to draw German bombers away from industrial targets. A ring of such sites were built around Bristol, including one in the Mendip Hills simulating Bristol Temple Meads Station and marshalling yards together with nearby factories. Military Q sites built in Wiltshire included Pitton to protect Old Sarum, Allington (Hullavington), South Newton and Winterslow (Boscombe Down), All Cannings (Upavon), West Littleton and Monkton Farleigh (Colerne), and Easton Down (Yatesbury). Military Starfish were built at Monkton Farleigh to protect Box Bridge, Lacock (Thingley) and Shipton Bellinger (Tidworth). Civil Starfish were built at Liddington and Barbury to protect Swindon and at Oddstock and Clearbury Down to protect Salisbury.

As well as airfields there were other sites in the county of Wiltshire that had an involvement with aircraft operations. Among these was the RAF ammunition depot at Chilmark, to the east of Wilton, which was given the title No.11 MU to disguise its role. The depot was located in a former underground limestone mine. It had the capacity to store 20,000 tons of aircraft bombs. In the autumn of 1939 a subsidiary site was opened at Dinton in a wooded area two and a half miles east of Chilmark. Chilmark remained an important depot for the RAF until it was controversially closed in 1994.

Other ammunition depots in the county included a complex in the abandoned stone 'quarries' (actually underground stone mines) to the east of Bath. Four quarries were purchased by the Air Ministry in 1936 and 1937, and were used for the storage of aircraft bombs and anti-aircraft ammunitions. Being at least one hundred feet underground, they were invulnerable to air attack, and were linked to the surface by railway tunnels. Some of the depots remained in government hands as stores depots until the 1990s.

Underground factories were established in the stone mines in 1940 under a scheme devised by Lord Beaverbrook, the Minister of Aircraft Production. This followed a number of Luftwaffe raids that destroyed or severely damaged many important factories. A factory was built in Spring Quarry at Corsham as a dispersal factory for aero-engine production by the Bristol Aircraft Company. A British Small Arms factory was also started up, in August 1943, to produce aircraft cannon, and this unit produced over half of Britain's output of Hispano and Polsten barrels. The Bristol factory took a while longer to set up, but by the end of 1943 work was under way on the production of the Bristol Centaurus engine, which was fitted into the Hawker Typhoon and Tempest fighter-bombers. Production carried on until April 1945, when the factory was closed. A total of 523 Centaurus engines had been built there.

Following an initiative by the RAF to find underground accommodation for its Group and Sector Command Centres, early in 1940 Brown's Quarry, a small quarry near Corsham, was converted into a secure underground Command Centre for No.10 Group HQ, Fighter Command. This group was responsible for the air defence of the south-west, and controlled fighter squadrons from Middle Wallop in the east to Portreath in the west. The operations room and control rooms on floors at two levels, accommodating the various controllers, radio operators, staff and planning officers, were built in a single chamber excavated into the rock fifty feet square and forty-five feet high beneath the Rudloe Manor estate. Noreen Berryman, the author's mother, was a member of the Women's Auxiliary Air Force and worked at No.10 Group HQ during late 1943 and early 1944. At least half of the operations staff at the HQ were WAAFs. South-West Control was situated in another part of the quarry nearby, to provide a secure military telephone exchange and teleprinter centre for No.10 Group and other RAF units in the south-west. RAF Rudloe Manor was retained after the war, and the underground facilities were still in use by the RAF until recently.

Wiltshire was also an important centre for chemical defence. The Chemical Defence Experimental Station at Porton Down played an

Chemical warfare training at an RAF station. The station's instructors would have been trained at the RAF Anti-Gas School, Rollestone, using techniques developed at CDES Porton Down. (Aeroplane)

important part in the development of defensive measures against gas and other chemical weapons that the Germans had large stocks of, and could easily have used. Ironically, it appears that one of the main reasons that the Germans did not use such weapons was that Hitler had been gassed during the First World War, and forbade their use. As well as defensive measures, CDES also developed retaliatory methods, and expanded their interest into other areas of chemical warfare, such as the use of smoke as signalling and protective methods. Another important allied location was the RAF Anti-Gas School at Rollestone, where RAF instructors were taught how a unit could defend itself against a chemical attack and still operate effectively.

There were several RAF hospitals in Wiltshire, including Melksham (where there was also located an RAF Technical Training School) and Wroughton, adjacent to the airfield. Melksham was a temporary convalescence hospital, and took medical cases such as appendicitis. Wroughton, on the other hand, had been built as an RAF General Hospital as part of the pre-war Expansion Scheme. However, while still under construction, it was bombed during the summer of 1940 by a passing German aircraft and was finally opened on 14 June 1941. It was later extended and in early 1943 had 319 beds. More extensions were built to cope with the high level of casualties expected following the invasion of Europe. The hospital was put on standby in the spring of 1944 although no-one was told why. The truth soon became known and on 13 June the first D-Day casualties arrived. Having come straight from the battlefront they had only received first aid and were still covered in mud. The casualties were brought in from RAF Lyneham, having been flown in from the advanced landing grounds in Normandy. The treatment system worked perfectly and over the following six months 4,811 casualties passed through the hospital from the Normandy battlefields. Wroughton Hospital remained open after the war and continued to give good service to the RAF and the local community for over 50 years. It was closed by the Ministry of Defence in 1994.

Wiltshire made a significant contribution to the production of aircraft during the Second World War. As well as being the home of the nation's main military aviation research and development establishment at Boscombe Down, the county also housed a Shadow aircraft factory for trainers, bombers and fighters at South Marston, and provided a refuge for the beleaguered Supermarine Company when it was seeking alternative facilities for the production of the Spitfire following the destruction of its Southampton factories in 1940.

Although not one of the 'front-line' counties at the beginning of World War II, the airfields of Wiltshire initially took on the role of training and support, then defence against enemy air offensives. As the war moved on, and the balance of power tilted, this developed into offence and invasion. The flying units of the three services based in Wiltshire were involved at every step of the way, as will be seen from the following pages.

2
BLAKEHILL
FARM

*National Grid Reference (173) SU080915, 2 miles SW of Cricklade,
S of the B4040.*

More than 700 years ago Blakehill, situated 2 miles southwest of
Cricklade in north-east Wiltshire, was part of the ancient Blaydon
Forest, a hunting ground for King John.

In 1943 the Government requisitioned 580 acres of land at Blakehill
to create an airfield. This was to be one of three new airfields (the
others being Down Ampney in Gloucestershire and Broadwell in
Oxfordshire) to be constructed north of Swindon to house No.46
Group, the RAF formation that brought together the tactical air
transport squadrons that were to support the army in the planned
invasion of Europe.

Hedges at Blakehill were grubbed up and the area cleared of trees.
Three tarmac runways were laid down, in the traditional A-shape
typical of many wartime airfields. There was a good reason for this
layout. As aircraft had to take off and land into wind, the A-shape was
the optimum configuration to make best use of the wind direction.
There would be a main runway aligned with the prevailing wind, with
the other two subsidiary runways angled to meet the other common
wind directions. The angles between the runways would differ from
one location to another, depending on local topography and wind
conditions. Several T2 hangers were erected at Blakehill, along with
other airfield buildings, training and administration buildings and
accommodation for personnel.

When the station opened on 9 February 1944, conditions were very difficult initially, as few buildings were actually ready for occupation, and very little road transport was available. Road vehicles were essential in the operation of airfields, for communications, ferrying, maintenance, refuelling and safety duties.

However, these teething problems were eventually sorted out in time for the arrival of the first of the flying squadrons in March. This was No.233 Squadron equipped with Douglas Dakota aircraft. Previously flying Lockheed Hudsons on U-boat hunting missions from Gibraltar, this unit was converted to an airborne forces squadron, towing gliders and dropping paratroops. For the RAF to order such a change in role seems rather strange, but the crews soon adapted to their new Dakotas and to their new duties. During early 1944, many experienced Dakota aircrew were brought back to the UK from overseas to create the backbone of a Dakota force being formed within No.46 Group in preparation for the invasion of Europe. Flight Lieutenant Lew Cody was one of these, having flown Dakotas with No.216 Squadron on airborne operations in the Mediterranean. He was posted to No.233 Squadron at Blakehill Farm and formed a crew that would spend almost 18 months together, and would go on to fly some of the most difficult operations undertaken by the squadron.

The Douglas Dakota is one of the most celebrated transport aircraft of all time. During the Second World War the aircraft served in every battle zone and was the mainstay of the transport squadrons of both the RAF and USAAF.

Training at Blakehill Farm started with the new Dakota and intensified from mid-March onwards as glider towing was introduced, then paratroop dropping. Huge exercises were mounted, involving large formations of transport aircraft on long-range sorties for mass parachute drops of men and equipment of the 6th Airborne Division. Some of these exercises took place at night, with No.233 Squadron flying as many as 22 aircraft for each exercise. Formation flying was practised and the aircraft would stream out over the English Channel before turning in to drop paratroops over the Salisbury Plain training area. With the expected invasion approaching rapidly, these exercises increased. On 24 April 1944 a Corps exercise known as Operation Mush took place as a dress rehearsal for the airborne phase of the invasion. During this build-up period many crews gained experience of cross-Channel operations by flying 'Nickelling' missions over northern France. These sorties involved the dropping of propaganda leaflets and were an excellent opportunity to practise navigation procedures over enemy-held territory. The aircraft were brought up to readiness on 1 June for Operation Tonga, the airdrop phase of Overlord, the overall D-Day operation. At this time No.233 Squadron was joined by a part of another No.46 Group squadron, No.271, deployed to Blakehill Farm because of congestion at Down Ampney, their base in Gloucestershire on the other side of Cricklade.

Following a final briefing on the evening of 5 June, the crews of Nos.233 and 271 Squadrons were among those of the 362 transport aircraft from fifteen RAF squadrons who boarded their aircraft at eight airfields in the south of England that night. The first aircraft to take off from Blakehill Farm were six No.233 Squadron Dakotas towing Horsa gliders at 22:50 hours. They were quickly followed by 24 Dakotas carrying paratroops. The aircraft were routed over Littlehampton to a point off the French coast north of Merville, before turning for the landing area.

Flight Lieutenant Cody and his crew flew Dakota KG448 and were assigned to drop zone (DZ) 'K' near Toufreville, the most southerly of the DZs used. Having crossed the French coast at 00:45 hours Cody homed in on the Eureka beacon positioned by pathfinder paratroops on the DZ and made his run-in at 800 feet. The troops carried by No.233 Squadron were from the 9th Parachute Battalion of the 3rd Parachute Brigade. They had one of the hardest tasks of D-Day, which was to put the Merville Battery out of action. This gun battery was on high ground to the east of the landing beaches, and it was thought that it could seriously threaten the left flank of the beach-head. It was manned by a garrison of 130 men, operating guns that were in thick concrete emplacements protected by minefields, barbed wire entanglements and machine guns.

The CO of 9 Para, Lieutenant-Colonel Terence Otway, having planned the attack in meticulous detail, had arranged for a full-scale replica of the battery to be built on farmland near Newbury in Berkshire. His troops, which included Royal Engineers to breach the wire and clear a path through the minefield, trained remorselessly until they were satisfied that they could take the battery by day or night. The plan was for the main body of paratroops to be dropped by No.233 Squadron's Dakotas to the south of the battery while the emplacements were bombed by RAF Lancasters and Halifaxes, partly as a diversion, partly to destroy the mines and wire. With the paratroops on the ground, eleven Horsa gliders would land the sappers and their equipment so that a way could be cleared through any remaining mines and wire to gain access to the battery. The main assault would then go in, supported by snipers, while three more Horsas were to land on the roof of the battery with troops to attack the gun emplacements from above.

When Lt. Col. Otway assembled his men on the DZ, only 150 of the expected 600 men reported in. The rest had been scattered around the local area, and the main force of Horsa gliders had landed several miles away. Otway gathered his remaining men together, and they headed towards their objective. With the few sappers that he had, a path was cleared through the minefield by hand with bayonets, and although German machine-guns opened up on the sappers as they worked, accurate return fire from the snipers put many of the German guns out of action. Right on time two of the gliders that were to land on the battery roof arrived overhead (the third was still in England, its tow-rope having snapped). Unfortunately, the pilots couldn't make out any landmarks in the smoke and dust now surrounding the area, and both landed some distance away from the battery. The paras went in anyway, and after a short but sharp battle with Sten guns, grenades and fists, found themselves in command of the guns, while the surviving Germans barricaded themselves into rooms underground. Otway put the guns out of action with plastic explosive, then, having lost 60 officers and men in the attack, beat a hasty, but prudent, retreat to the south with his remaining men.

Having successfully dropped their paratroops, Lew Cody and the rest of his squadron turned and set the return course for Blakehill Farm. At the debriefing he learnt that two of the squadron's aircraft had failed to return. Nonetheless, during this huge operation the majority of the paradrop aircraft dropped their troops and supply containers success-fully on or close to their targets.

Once the beach-head had been established the Dakotas flew reinforcement and resupply missions. On 8 June No.233 Squadron flew Operation Rob Roy, a resupply mission to the 6th Airborne Division east of the River Orne near Ranville. Twenty-one Dakotas took off carrying 371 supply panniers containing food, ammunition, fuel and radios. Near the French coast the formation came under intense AA fire from 'friendly' Naval vessels. Two aircraft went down in flames (the lead aircraft and the number 2) but the remainder dropped their supplies successfully.

On 13 June a Dakota from No.233 Squadron became the first allied transport aircraft to land in France after the invasion, landing at a British-controlled airstrip. As well as taking in supplies and reinforce-ments, the aircraft also brought casualties out on the return flight.

RAF Blakehill Farm, like the other stations in No.46 Group, was equipped with a Casualty Air Evacuation Centre (CAEC). These centres were staffed by medical personnel, including female nursing auxiliaries who were trained as Air Ambulance Nursing Orderlies. These orderlies were to fly on the aircraft to look after the patients during their return flight. The first time a significant number of these staff were involved was during the invasion; they were the first female RAF aircrew to fly into the combat zone. The Dakota aircraft were not dedicated air ambulances because they were basically transport aircraft given a temporary additional role. On the outbound flights the aircraft carried ammunition and supplies, and on the return flights carried casualties. As a result the aircraft could not be marked with red crosses. Once having landed at the forward airstrips, the air landing grounds in Normandy, the Nursing Orderlies supervised the loading and securing of their patients, each aircraft being able to carry eighteen stretcher cases and six sitting casualties.

Each casualty would have had emergency treatment in the field for his injuries. During the flight home the sole Nursing Orderly on each aircraft would dispense tea and comfort, or, if necessary, oxygen and morphine. On arrival at Blakehill Farm casualties would be unloaded from the aircraft and taken to the CAEC for assessment before allocation to the appropriate specialist hospital. Casualties with burns were taken to Oddstock near Salisbury. Head injuries went to St Dunstans near Oxford and spinal or serious skin injuries went to Stoke Mandeville near Aylesbury. No.233 Squadron continued to fly these operations for the next couple of months, but in August their mission changed and they were tasked to fly food into the airfield at Orleans for the relief of Paris. The squadron delivered 230 tons of food during this time.

A new flying unit appeared at Blakehill Farm when No.437 Squadron was formed on 4 September 1944 as another Airborne Support Squadron within No.46 Group. This was a Royal Canadian Air Force unit that, like No.233 Squadron, was equipped with Dakotas. Soon both units were making intense preparations for another airborne operation, Market Garden – the capture of the bridges to Arnhem. The airborne part of the operation to capture the three bridges involved was 'Market', and the armoured thrust by ground forces to relieve the paratroops was entitled 'Garden'.

The main plan embraced simultaneous airborne assaults on Arnhem, Grave-Nijmegen and Eindhoven. Arnhem, the most northerly section, was allocated to the British airborne forces, the other two to US airborne forces. Unfortunately there were no landing zones (LZs) close

No.233 Squadron transported supplies to the battle areas following Operation Market Garden. Here Flying Officer Clarkson hands over his cargo of rations to the Royal Army Service Corps in October 1944. (Aeroplane)

to Arnhem Bridge, which made a surprise attack on the bridge difficult to achieve. Not all the troops needed for the attack were to be dropped on the one day, but over a period of three days. A further British landing was to be made at Nijmegen, where General Browning was to set up his HQ, and in the process become the first Corps Commander to be landed by air into battle. D-Day for the operation was 17 September 1944, H-Hour was to be 13:00 hours. As well as paratroops, 38 Hamilcars, 588 Horsas and 4 CG-4As carrying elements of the British 1st Airborne Division, the Polish Parachute Brigade, the 878th US Aviation Engineering Battalion and Airfield Control units were to be landed on four LZs to the north of the Arnhem bridge. Although they landed as planned, the glider troops and paratroopers had too far to march in order to reach their objective, and they became split up on the way to the Arnhem Bridge. Nonetheless the Parachute Regiment was able to seize the bridge, and put out a defensive perimeter to protect it from counter-attack. Divisional HQ was set up at the Hartenstein Hotel, some distance from the bridge, and another

Focke-Wulf FW190s attacked the Dakotas of 233 and 271 Squadrons over Arnhem.
(Aeroplane)

defensive perimeter was established there. Meanwhile, General Browning had flown to Holland in a Horsa flown by Colonel Chatterton, OC of the Glider Pilot Regiment (GPR). Chatterton managed to put his glider down safely, but he came in just off the main LZ and landed in a cabbage patch. Once the glider had come to a halt, General Browning stepped through the doorway, and made his way through the cabbages to collect his troops, with his staff in tow.

No.233 Squadron flew 37 sorties to Arnhem during the first two days (17 and 18 September) towing gliders and dropping paratroops. This was followed by 35 resupply missions, 240 panniers being dropped to the beleaguered 1st Airborne Division in their defensive perimeters. Enemy opposition was intense and included attacks by Focke-Wulf Fw190 fighters as well as flak. Of the eighteen aircraft despatched by the Squadron three were lost.

Most of the aircraft that returned to Blakehill Farm that day were damaged in some way. During the Arnhem operation Dakota squadrons were again involved in casualty evacuation. For this each squadron was tasked with bringing home 200 casualties a day, as well as ferrying supplies to the battlefield on the outbound leg. This meant at least two flights per day into the battle area.

25

Despite the brave and costly sorties by RAF aircrews to drop supplies and reinforcements to the besieged airborne troops at Arnhem, the powerful armoured and infantry forces that the Germans had brought into the area eventually overwhelmed the pockets of lightly armed British troops. A withdrawal was ordered, and during the night of 25 September the remnants of 1st Airborne were ferried back across the Rhine. Of the 10,005 men of the Division landed at Arnhem, a mere 2,163 escaped, the remainder being killed or captured. Although the operation was ultimately unsuccessful, Market Garden really was a considerable achievement. During the first four days of the battle 660 gliders, 95 guns and 544 jeeps and carriers as well as the 10,005 paratroops and glider-borne troops were transported up to sixty miles behind enemy lines. This made the operation the most successful airborne operation up to that date. The fact that the relief column could not reach them within nine days (they were expected to hold out for up to four days), and that they came up against German opposition that was ultimately overwhelming, does not detract from that achievement.

The last major operation to be mounted by the Blakehill Farm Dakota squadrons was the Rhine crossing in March 1945. With the Allied armies poised on the borders of Germany, it was decided to establish a bridge-head on the east bank of the River Rhine, north of Wesel. A

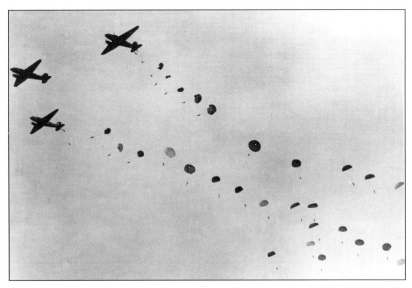

RAF Dakotas dropping paratroops during Operation Market Garden in September 1944. (Aeroplane)

crossing was to be made by 12 Corps of the British 21st Army Group on the night of 23/24 March, and airborne troops were to be landed by parachute and glider the following morning to consolidate the bridge-head. In order to achieve surprise and minimise casualties Operation Varsity, as it was to be known, was to be a 'single-lift' operation with all the participating paratroops, from the British 6th Airborne and US 17th Airborne Divisions, being dropped on the one day.

The British force was to be lifted by seventeen RAF squadrons towing gliders, and the US Ninth Transport Command dropping paratroops. They were to be joined by a US force of transport aircraft and gliders taking off from bases in France. In total the force was to comprise some 1,600 transport aircraft and 1,330 gliders, transporting approximately 21,700 troops. Air superiority was a high priority and numerous fighters, bombers and ground attack aircraft were to fly in support of the force. They were to be escorted by almost 900 Allied fighters on the way to their objectives, while some 1,250 more US fighters were to patrol in German airspace. The actual landings on the DZs and LZs were to be covered by 900 more aircraft of the RAF's 2nd Tactical Air Force. Due to a shortage of army glider pilots, it was decided to draft in RAF aircrew that had been trained, but not deployed. They joined the GPR, and were mixed in with the army pilots into the same wings and squadrons of the regiment. The RAF crews were given as much military training as possible in the time available before the operation. For the operation all participating units were moved forward to jump-off points in East Anglia, and twenty-four aircraft of No.233 Squadron were positioned at Birch Airfield in Essex.

At dawn on March 24, each with a Horsa glider in tow the aircraft took off with 357 troops of the Oxfordshire and Buckinghamshire Light Infantry. This unit was to make up part of a force to take the bridge over the River Isel, to prevent it being blown up by the Germans. One glider, flown by Squadron Leader VH Reynolds, an RAF pilot of the GPR, was carrying the OC of the Ox and Bucks LI, and shortly after having cast off was engaged by a flak battery which continued shooting at them all the way down to landing. The flak battery was near his landing point, and as he flew over it the second pilot engaged the battery with his Sten gun. The troops disembarked from the Horsa, charged the flak battery and quickly took it, capturing 30 prisoners. They later came under fire from another flak gun, which was then stalked by a team of glider pilots. Flying Officer Bailey scored a direct hit on the flak unit with his PIAT gun, killing the crew. No.437

RAF Dakotas at Brussels Airport in October 1944 taking wounded aboard for return to Blakehill Farm. (Aeroplane)

Squadron also took part in the operation, towing Horsa gliders. The landing force received a mixed reception. In some areas there was little enemy opposition, but in others they met determined resistance and suffered heavy casualties. By the end of the afternoon however, most of the airborne troops had taken their objectives, and had linked up with Allied ground troops.

Following the Rhine crossing the task placed on the transport squadrons hardly diminished. Both Nos.233 and 437 Squadrons found themselves flying at maximum effort in order to support the rapid advance of the Allied armies across North Germany. The main commodity in demand was fuel, and daily flights were made from Blakehill Farm to the forward airfields at Selle, Rheine and Luneburg. No.437 Squadron moved to the continent in early May 1945 to provide a shuttle transport service around the Allied bases there. Though continuing transport support missions to the Continent, No.233 Squadron remained based at Blakehill Farm until 8 June 1945, when it moved to Odiham in Hampshire. Earmarked for action in the Far East, the squadron began moving to India in August, but by the time it arrived in-theatre the Japanese had surrendered.

Meanwhile, at Blakehill Farm No.22 Heavy Glider Conversion Unit moved in from Fairford, equipped with Hamilcar gliders and Albermarle tug aircraft. However, the requirement for glider towing had diminished, and the HGCU was disbanded on 15 November 1945.

A month later Dakotas reappeared at Blakehill Farm with the arrival of No.575 Squadron. This unit had been involved in the D-Day, Arnhem and Rhine crossing operations. However, No.575 Squadron's stay at Blakehill Farm was to be short, and it was in fact to be the last major flying unit to be based at the station. At the end of January 1946 it flew out to Bari in Italy.

In December 1945 No.1528 Radio Aids Training Flight arrived at Blakehill Farm with their Oxfords, finding the Station's Blind Approach Beam System, installed the year before, useful for training. Although the unit moved off to Fairford in February 1946, it reformed and returned to Blakehill Farm as No. 1555 RATF in April 1946, but left again the following August.

Closed on 5 November 1946, Blakehill Farm was put on Care and Maintenance. It was not long though before aircraft were back in the circuit. This time they were not from Transport Command, but from Flying Training Command. In December 1948 No.2 Flying Training School started to use the airfield as a Relief Landing Ground. The unit's home base at RAF South Cerney was a grass airfield, so the tarmac runways and radio facilities at Blakehill Farm came into their own for practical training. Piston-engined Provost aircraft from South Cerney continued to use Blakehill Farm well into the 1950s. In May 1952, 2 FTS became the Basic Element of the Central Flying School. However, in May 1957 the CFS re-organised and moved its Basic Element to Little Rissington, and this finally meant the end of flying at Blakehill Farm.

The station remained in Government hands. In 1967 Government Communications Headquarters (GCHQ) set up an experimental radio and monitoring station at Blakehill Farm. Their instruments included one of the country's tallest wooden masts, at some 200 feet high. There was a partial site-clearance in the 1970s, when the runways were torn up to provide hardcore for the building of the M4 motorway. GCHQ moved out in the late 1990s and Blakehill Farm was finally disposed of by the MOD in 2000. The Wiltshire Wildlife Trust hopes to restore the site to become the UK's largest area of reinstated ancient meadowland.

With remaining buildings cleared the only sign of Blakehill Farm's important part in history will be the memorial, standing alone in a meadow, erected some years ago to the members of No.437 RCAF Squadron.

3
BOSCOMBE DOWN

National Grid Reference (184) SU 180398, SE of Amesbury

The name of Boscombe Down is synonymous with excellence in flight testing and development. Originally opened as a training unit during the First World War on downland eight miles north of Salisbury, it later became a bomber station. It was not until September 1939 that flight testing started at Boscombe Down, when the Aeroplane & Armament Experimental Establishment moved there from Martlesham Heath. The task, during those dark days of war, was to test aircraft and their weapons, to ensure that they would perform as safely and effectively as possible. Sixty years on, that task has not changed, and that work carries on today.

During the First World War, as flying in the UK expanded out of all proportion to its pre-war levels, Boscombe Down was established as a training airfield, in October 1917, to give advanced training to Royal Flying Corps pilots in order to meet the high demand for experienced pilots on the Western Front. As well as British pilots, pupils from Australia, New Zealand and the USA were trained at Boscombe Down.

With the end of the war flying at Boscombe Down was curtailed, and the airfield was eventually closed and disposed of. However, the senior officers at the Air Ministry must have had a change of heart, for a few years later the land was re-purchased, and in October 1927 work started to make Boscombe Down into a permanent RAF Station. Some buildings were renovated while others, particularly those made of wood, were replaced with brick ones. New married quarters were

A Handley Page Hinaidi circles behind the Boscombe Down hangars on 24 May 1934, Empire Air Day. (via Terry Heffernan)

built. Officers' and Sergeants' Messes were constructed along with the other many and varied buildings required for operations, maintenance and support, and a new modern hangar was built.

Construction carried on until 1932, although the station was officially opened as part of the Wessex Bombing Area on 1 September 1930. The first squadron to arrive at the new station was No.9 (Bomber) Squadron, with the Vickers Virginia. It was joined in February 1931 by the Porton Experimental Flight, which was to become the longest-serving unit at Boscombe Down. Its work in support of the Establishment at Porton Down was later to be taken over by A Squadron, A&AEE, and this continued into the 21st century. A second bomber squadron, No.10, with Handley Page Hinaidis took up residence at Boscombe Down in April 1931, having transferred from Upper Heyford in Oxfordshire.

During the mid-1930s Boscombe Down became the centre for the expansion of the RAF Bomber Force. This entailed taking one flight of an established squadron to form the basis of another unit. In this way a progressive programme of expansion was achieved around the core of experienced personnel. It is a noteworthy achievement that in the short period of a year and a half, Boscombe Down had taken a very active and invaluable part in the expansion of the RAF Bomber Force by forming four new squadrons. When the squadrons finally left Boscombe Down they went on to equip three further newly-opened RAF Bomber bases.

By January 1938 there were three squadrons at Boscombe Down: Nos.88, 150 and 218 Squadrons, each equipped with the Fairey Battle light bomber. During the Munich crisis later that year, detailed plans were put together to define the roles of service units should they be mobilised. For Boscombe Down this meant the formation of No.75 Wing, comprising the resident Battle Squadrons. Their role on mobilisation was to form part of the Advanced Air Striking Force (AASF) for active service.

The order was given on 23 August 1939 to partially mobilise No.75 Wing. All personnel were recalled from leave and the squadron was put on a war footing. On 1 September the signal to fully mobilise was received with mixed emotions. The wing was to proceed immediately to the Continent with the forward air and sea contingents of the AASF. That evening transport aircraft were loaded with stores and equipment and the squadron aircraft were prepared for their flight overseas. The next afternoon the sixteen Battles of No.88 Squadron took off, moved into formation and headed for France, later landing at Mourmelon-le-Grande, from where they were to operate. The other squadrons followed. Their work was to mount reconnaissance patrols over the German positions. It was on such a mission, on 20 September 1939, that No.88 Squadron scored Britain's first air combat kill of World War II when Sgt K. Letchford, observer aboard Battle K9243, piloted by Flying Officer L.H. Baker, shot down a Messerschmitt Bf109 fighter. The squadron subsequently saw some very heavy fighting and suffered serious losses. It lost most of its aircraft during the combat of the following summer and was withdrawn in June 1940 to Sydenham in Northern Ireland.

As elements of No.75 Wing were leaving Boscombe Down for France the advance party of another unit was arriving at the station. This was the Aeroplane & Armament Experimental Establishment (A&AEE) from Martlesham Heath, Suffolk. The basic role of A&AEE, (which had originated in the 1920s), was to remain throughout its existence, that of the evaluation and acceptance testing of aeroplanes and their weapons.

It was recognised that A&AEE was an important military aviation organisation, but also that its base in Suffolk would be vulnerable to air attacks from the Continent should hostilities start. The War Plan for the Establishment therefore said that on mobilisation the A&AEE should move to a safer location, and this was identified as being Boscombe Down. The move was to pose problems because the Wiltshire airfield was initially not equipped for experimental flying. There were no metalled runways and limited airfield and range facilities. Boscombe Down had been built to accommodate two Bomber Squadrons, so the arrival of 62 experimental aircraft of various types in September 1939 immediately caused hangarage difficulties. The number of A&AEE's aircraft on arrival at Boscombe Down could in fact have been considerably lower, for as the first formations approached their new base, they were fired on by army units on Salisbury Plain, who presumably assumed that these unfamiliar aircraft were hostile!

The A&AEE organisation at Martlesham Heath was recreated at Boscombe Down, and after a lot of hard work Group Captain B. McEntegart, the Commanding Officer, declared the establishment operational on 20 September 1939. Mr E.T. Jones was the Chief Technical Officer and Mr F. Rowarth the Chief Engineer. The establishment was organised into two squadrons – Performance Testing Squadron (or PerT for short) with thirty-seven aircraft, and Armament Testing Squadron (ArmT) with twenty-five aircraft. Each squadron was divided into three flights according to aircraft category: A Flight had the fighters, B Flight the large aircraft and C Flight the twin-engine aircraft.

At the outbreak of World War II there was a line of five hangars at Boscombe Down, four dating from 1918 and the fifth from 1930. The only hard standings for aircraft were between and in front of these hangars. The remaining buildings dated from 1929/30. In 1940 ground defence buildings were constructed. A main runway was laid late on in the war and the only other permanent buildings to be erected during the period were the control tower, the large stop butts for armament testing, and the blower tunnel. The latter was constructed to perform flame-damping tests on engines. Power for the facility was provided by four Rolls Royce Merlin engines. Completed in 1944, it is still in use today.

An early problem was the lack of suitable areas for air firing and bombing. To start with the only facilities available in the vicinity were at Porton, by arrangement with the Chemical Defence Experimental Station, and Larkhill, subject to permission from the Army. As only practice bombs could be dropped at each range their usefulness was limited. Other locations were sought to supplement these facilities and by the end of 1939 A&AEE had obtained its own range. This was at Crichel Down five miles north-east of Blandford in Dorset. Another

Captured Messerschmitt Bf109 AE479. This aircraft was evaluated at Boscombe Down in April 1940. (Aeroplane)

range was opened in early 1940, at Ashley Walk near Fordingbridge, Hampshire.

In May 1940 A&AEE came under a new master with the formation of the Ministry of Aircraft Production (MAP). This was formed to provide for the airborne needs of the British Services, which included not only the actual production of aircraft, but also their development and introduction into service.

On 4 May 1940 the first enemy aircraft arrived for testing at the establishment. This was a Messerschmitt Bf109E that had force-landed in France in November 1939. During her time at Boscombe Down the aircraft was flown by a number of experienced RAF fighter pilots. The Messerschmitt later went to RAE Farnborough, then became part of 1426 (Enemy Aircraft) Flight at Duxford. She gave demonstration flights at RAF fighter airfields, along with other former Luftwaffe aircraft, and may well have returned to Boscombe Down in this role during this period. The flight inevitably became known as the Rafwaffe!

Incidentally, German aircraft designs were rarely given names, but were identified by letters and numbers. Two letters stood for the manufacturer (e.g. 'Ju' for Junkers), while the numbers denoted the actual type. Exceptions to this were the early Messerschmitt designs (Models 108, 109 and 110) which were manufactured by the Bayerische Flurgzeugwerke (BFW) and were designated 'Bf', hence the Bf109. BFW became Messerschmitt AG in 1938 and the company's subsequent designs were prefixed 'Me'.

The first raid by the Luftwaffe on Boscombe Down occurred on 26 June 1940, when a single raider dropped four small bombs on the airfield, but no damage resulted. In the summer of 1940 the Battle of Britain was developing and raids by the Luftwaffe over southern England were intensifying. Because of the vulnerability of Boscombe Down it was decided to place a fighter squadron there to defend it. On 14 August 1940 No. 249 Squadron moved in with its Hurricanes. With the move to Boscombe Down the squadron was to become part of 10 Group, which had its HQ at Rudloe Manor. Its main priority at the new base was to be the defence of Portsmouth and Southampton, along with Boscombe Down itself. The squadron was in action on the afternoon of its arrival for, at 17:00 hours, it was scrambled. Radar stations on the coast had reported two large formations of aircraft. Twenty minutes later twenty-seven Junkers Ju87 Stukas of Stukageschwader 1 (StG1) and twenty more of StG2 were seen heading for Portland while a dozen Ju88s of Lehrgeschwader 1 (LG1) and fifteen more from II Gruppe escorted by Bf109s of Jagdgeschwader 27 (JG27) and JG53 with Bf110s of LG1 and ZG76 (Zehrstoerergeschwader 76) were sighted approaching the Isle of Wight. Interceptions were made by defending fighters over Southampton and the Solent, but the German formations forced their way inland making their way into Hampshire towards RNAS Worthy Down and the RAF airfields of Odiham and Middle Wallop. Meanwhile No.249 Squadron had been ordered to patrol at 15,000 feet over RAF Warmwell, Dorset. The six Hurricanes of B Flight encountered 11 Ju88s escorted by some fifty Bf110s heading for Middle Wallop. Without hesitation the B Flight pilots went into the attack on the escorting Bf110s, and shortly afterwards were joined by Spitfires of No.609 Squadron from Warmwell. A fierce dogfight then developed to the south of Salisbury. Flight Lieutenant Barton and Pilot Officer Meaker of No.249 Squadron each claimed a Messerschmitt shot down, both of which came down near Romsey, while three pilots of the Squadron (Flying Officer Parnall, Pilot Officer Beazley and Sergeant Davidson) jointly claimed a third.

Flight Lieutenant Barton attacked and damaged another Bf110. This was later shot down by a No.609 Squadron Spitfire. Despite the attacks by the RAF fighters the raiders were able to reach Middle Wallop. This airfield was still under construction and the freshly dug chalk around the new hangars was easy for the enemy bomber crews to spot. Two hangars were hit, with two Blenheims destroyed and five damaged. A little damage was also caused to Worthy Down and Odiham. The raiders from LG1 lost 8 JU88s in this action while their escorts, ZG76, lost a dozen Bf110s. In the confusion a Blenheim was attacked by a Spitfire in mistake for a Ju88, but fortunately the aircraft managed to make it back for a crash landing at Middle Wallop.

Two days later, on 16 August, a dozen of No.249 Squadron's Hurricanes led by Flight Lieutenant Barton were sent off from Boscombe at 13:05 to bolster defences over the south coast. Shortly after having arrived on station at about 18,000 feet over Southampton, enemy aircraft were sighted and Red Section of A Flight was sent to investigate. Red Section was led by 23 year old A Flight Commander, Flight Lieutenant James Nicholson (Red 1 in Hurricane P3576), and this was to be his first experience of air combat. Pilot Officer Martyn King (Red 2 in P3616) and Squadron Leader Eric King (Red 3, P2870) made

Battle of Britain Memorial Flight Hurricane Mk II in the markings of Flight Lieutenant James Nicholson VC at the Boscombe Down Battle of Britain Air Display, 1990. (Peter James)

up the rest of the section. As they got closer to their intended quarry, twelve Spitfires appeared and engaged the enemy fighters. Nicholson decided to leave them to it, and turned his section round to rejoin the squadron. Climbing back to patrol height with the sun behind them, Red Section were caught in the classic fighter trap. They were bounced by German fighters (probably Bf110s but possibly Bf109s) which came from above and behind and attacked out of the sun. All three aircraft of Red Section were hit simultaneously. Red 1 and 2 were critically damaged. Squadron Leader King's Red 3 was hit badly in several places but he was able to evade his attackers and nurse his aircraft back to make a safe landing at Boscombe Down. Pilot Officer King managed to get out of his stricken aircraft and open his parachute. However, as he drifted down to about 1,500 feet above the ground his parachute canopy collapsed, possibly due to damage from a cannon shell during combat, and he fell into a large tree, then into the garden of No.30 Clifton Road, Shirley. He died in the arms of Fred Poole, who lived nearby and had rushed over to where Martyn King lay on the lawn.

Flight Lieutenant Nicholson's aircraft caught fire after being hit when the fuel tank ignited and the cockpit became a mass of flames. As he was struggling to bale out, a Bf110 – possibly his attacker – overshot his burning Hurricane. Nicholson dropped back into the cockpit, pushed the throttle forward, chased the Bf110 and opened fire. He continued to fire as the flames lapped around him, and only after he lost sight of the Messerschmitt did Nicholson attempt to abandon the Hurricane. He managed to get free of the aircraft and pulled his ripcord. Nicholson could well have shot at the Bf110C of III/ZG76, which was later reported to have crashed off the Isle of Wight that afternoon. The combat had taken place at 13:45 hours, just 40 minutes after the 249 Squadron pilots had left the relative tranquillity of Boscombe Down. Baling out was not the end of Nicolson's traumas that day, for as he drifted down on his parachute in great pain from his burns, the pilot was hit by gunshot from the ground. A Sergeant of the Local Defence Volunteers had opened fire on Nicholson, taking him to be a German. When the severely burned and bleeding airman lying on the ground was found by the gathering spectators to be an RAF pilot they attacked the LDV Sergeant, who was saved from even more serious injury by the arrival of a policeman. Nicholson was taken to the Royal Southampton Hospital, where he went into intensive care. He was later moved to the RAF Hospital at Halton, which specialised in the treatment of burns, then to the Palace Hotel, Torquay, which had been requisitioned as an RAF convalescent hospital. Whilst at Torquay, on 15 November, Nicholson learnt that he had been awarded the Victoria Cross. It had been his first and last combat in the Battle of Britain. James Nicholson was the only RAF fighter pilot to receive the Victoria Cross during the Second World War. He later reached the rank of Wing Commander, but was killed in a Liberator crash in May 1945.

Patrols by No.249 Squadron continued for the rest of August. At the end of the month it was ordered to move to North Weald in Essex to relieve No.56 Squadron, which had been in the thick of the fighting over London. On 1 September, No.56 Squadron moved to Boscombe Down to reform and rest, and was to spend most of the autumn of 1940 at its new base. The squadron's pilots spent their first few days practice flying. However, they were soon to be involved again with the Luftwaffe when one flight was diverted from its practice to intercept an enemy raid reported as coming in from the south, but they did not make contact. The next few days were to be fairly quiet, and on 13 September an interception of a different kind was made when two of No.56 Squadron's aircraft were sent off to track down a couple of barrage balloons that had broken their moorings and made a bid for freedom!

From mid-September onwards, the weekly routine for the squadron seemed to be flying training for a few days, then being sent off to intercept a raid. On 14 September, one such interception resulted in Flight Sergeant Higginson shooting down a Dornier Do17 into the sea 40 miles off Bournemouth. The squadron's first casualty while operating from Boscombe Down occurred on Sunday 15 September 1940 (the day that saw the fiercest fighting of the battle, and that was later to be marked as 'Battle of Britain Day'). During dog-fighting practice not far from the airfield, Sergeant J.R. Tweed was flying Hurricane P3660 when he went into a flat spin coming off the top of a loop. The aircraft went out of control and crashed one mile north-west of High Post airfield, killing the pilot. He is buried in the Abbey Church of St Mary and St Mellor in Amesbury. The squadron flew operations from Boscombe Down for the next two months, intercepting German raids and getting involved in several large dogfights. German raids gradually moved more to the south-east, and by December 1940, No.56 Squadron had been moved back to North Weald.

It was during the Battle of Britain that another battle was being fought, later to be known as the 'Battle of the Beams'. This episode represented one of the first instances of electronic warfare on an appreciable scale, and Boscombe Down was to become one of the centres of this conflict. The story effectively started at a Cabinet meeting on 21 January 1940, when the Prime Minister, Winston Churchill, received some shocking news. Dr R.V. Jones of Air Intelligence reported that the Germans were preparing to use a device that would enable them to bomb Britain by day or night whatever the weather. As the basis for this work they utilised the Lorenz Blind Landing System, which had been developed for the safe landing of aircraft at night or in bad weather and which was already in use both in Britain and on mainland Europe. The Lorenz system was adapted into the Knickebein (Crooked Leg) blind bombing system and the more sophisticated X-Gerat (X-Apparatus) system, which would guide bombers by electronic beams to their targets. It was the Knickebein system that was first revealed to the RAF. Following the revelations to the Prime Minister, Downing Street ordered that action to deal with the Knickebein problem should be a priority. Then someone at the Air Ministry realised that the Blind Approach Training and Development Unit (BATDU) at Boscombe Down had personnel already trained and experienced in beam flying. Its Ansons were supplemented with longer-range Whitley bombers and it was decided to use the unit to investigate the German beams. Flights were made from Boscombe Down and from Wyton in Huntingdonshire, where a detachment was based.

BATDU's first task was to identify and plot the Knickebein beams on particular band-widths. Avro Ansons fitted with radio receivers were used for this. The first beam was identified on 21 June 1940 by Flight Lieutenant Hal Bufton (pilot) and Corporal Dennis Mackey (Special Wireless Operator) on a flight from Wyton. In September 1940 the BATDU became the Wireless Intelligence Development Unit (WIDU). Towards the end of that month the Germans realised that their beams were being interfered with. Initially they used counter-measures, such as shortening transmission times and changing frequencies partway through a raid. They also made more use of X-Gerat (codenamed 'Ruffian'), which was not so easy to counter.

Flights to investigate the Ruffian beams then became a priority. Undertaken during periods of enemy activity, and often under hazardous conditions, these flights provided vital information to assist the investigation of this complex system. Trying to pinpoint the beams at night to the high level of accuracy needed for this work was an exacting task. Temporary transmitters were built to combat Ruffian, which operated on a different frequency from Knickebein. Eventually, by November 1940, enough transmitters (codenamed 'Bromide') were in operation to cause the Germans problems. Once they realised that

Ruffian was being jammed, the Germans again started using counter-measures. To reinforce the jamming, WIDU started using direct offensive action against the actual beam transmitters. On the night of 14 November two Whitleys set out to attack the Cherbourg transmitter during the large-scale German raid on Coventry. Despite having to avoid AA fire and barrage balloons at least one hit was scored and both Knickebein and Ruffian ceased transmission for a while that night. Attacks continued during November and it must have been apparent to the defenders that the bombers would be using their own beams to guide them in. More AA guns were installed along with searchlights and the squadron was unable to score any further hits.

The WIDU achieved Squadron status on 10 December 1940 when it was re-titled No.109 Squadron. More attacks on enemy transmitters took place in early 1941 by Whitleys, but in February a Striking Flight was formed especially for this task with four of the Wellingtons. The exact positions of the Ruffian transmitters at Morlaix were pinpointed in May 1941 and on 6th and 11th attacks were made. These were successful and after the second attack the station did not transmit for six days.

On the night of 4 November 1941 Wellington Ic T2565 of No.109 Squadron took off from Boscombe Down on a mission over occupied Europe. Its task was to investigate the origin of Luftwaffe radio and radar beams so that the transmitters could be attacked. A specialist technician, Howard Cundall, was aboard. He was a civilian volunteer and had been given an RAF commission as a Pilot Officer in case the aircraft was shot down and he should be captured. Some two hours after leaving Boscombe Down things started to go wrong. The aircraft was hit by AA fire. The oil pressure of the starboard engine dropped and fell to zero, whereupon the engine seized and the propeller came off. Fuel and loose equipment were jettisoned but the aircraft continued to lose height. When it was down to 5,000 feet the captain ordered the crew to bail out. They all landed safely and dispersed. German troops arrived in the area and, finding no crew in the wreckage of the Wellington, began to search the local area. Cundall stayed at large until 18 November, when he was captured near Mont St Michel trying to steal a boat. The Germans did not realise what a prize they had in Cundall, who not only knew what the British knew about German air defences but also had a wealth of knowledge about the British air defences. There followed four years in a prisoner of war camp, during which time Cundall made a wireless transmitter in his prison hut. He later gleaned further information on German defences and night fighter tactics from other captured aircrew and sent this back to the UK by radio and in coded letters.

On 19 January 1942 No.109 Squadron was divided into three flights and dispersed. The HQ and Wireless Development Flight moved to Tempsford, Bedfordshire, the Wireless Reconnaissance Flight to Upper Heyford, Oxfordshire, while the Wireless Investigation Flight (Radio Countermeasures) remained at Boscombe Down. The squadron was to reassemble at Stradishall in April 1943, where it was to develop Oboe, a British blind-bombing system, as a navigational aid for Bomber Command. It later became one of the first units of No.8 Group, the Pathfinder Force, responsible for pinpoint navigation in order to find and mark targets for the main bomber force, and received Mosquitos and Lancasters to drop target markers.

Because of its blind-landing equipment, Boscombe Down was designated as a Diversion Airfield. This meant that aircraft that were lost or in trouble would be able to pick up the landing beacon signals and find the airfield. These crews made a safe landing at Boscombe Down, often in bad weather conditions. Initially Wellingtons and Whitleys appeared at the airfield, but as the bomber offensive intensified the big four-engined Stirlings and Lancasters arrived. Eventually over 850 bombers were to find sanctuary at Boscombe Down during the war. Many of these were damaged and needed to find the nearest friendly airfield. Others diverted because of the weather or obstructed runways at their home bases, or because they were low on fuel or just simply lost. Crash-landings were not unusual, and Salisbury hospitals received many injured aircrew.

On 30 December 1940 the High Altitude Flight was created as part of A&AEE. The unit was formed to carry out investigations into the problems associated with the operation of aircraft at a height of over 30,000 feet. This was not only because the factors affecting high flying aircraft were not properly understood, but it was known that the Germans had aircraft capable of high flight. Initial aircraft of the HAF were a pair of Spitfires and four Hurricanes. Bombers, such as the Wellington, Fortress and Mosquito, were also used, and later the Mustang supplemented the fighters.

Although the Germans must have known about the importance of Boscombe Down, they never really treated the establishment as a target. A couple of raids did take place in 1940, but these were light. However, during March and April 1941 some heavier attacks did occur. These were made early in the morning, and each time involved the dropping of a dozen or so high explosive bombs. Hangars were hit,

Vickers Wellington V under construction, showing the pressure cell for the crew compartment in the forward fuselage. (Aeroplane)

two aircraft were destroyed and another forty damaged, but fortunately no-one was injured.

Another new unit appeared in April 1941, and this was the Wellington Flight, formed to test the new pressurised versions of the Vickers Wellington bomber, the Marks 5 and 6, which were specifically designed to fly at high altitude. The design was based on the standard Wellington, but was fitted with a pressurised cabin inside the fuselage structure. It was intended that No.109 Squadron should be equipped with the type for Pathfinder work. However, the aircraft was not a popular one, being difficult to operate and with a disappointing performance. On 12 July 1942, on a routine test flight near Derby, one of the prototypes was lost. While flying at a height of 32,200 feet a propeller blade broke off, puncturing the pressure cabin and fatally injuring the pilot. The aircraft dived towards the ground out of control, and during the descent its structure disintegrated. The crew of five were killed. Production and further development of the design carried on for a while, but eventually the project was brought to a halt. The Wellington Flight was disbanded, and its aircraft transferred to the HAF, where the last one was kept on until December 1943.

In order to test aircraft in the intensive way that they would be used on operational squadrons and obtain information on their reliability in service, the Intensive Flying Development Unit was formed at Boscombe Down on 15 November 1941. This remained a fairly small unit, usually having no more than two of each aircraft type that was undergoing testing at any one time. The aircraft were usually early production airframes, flown and maintained by operational air- and ground-crews from the appropriate Service. The aim was to fly at least 150 hours on each aircraft, in order to have enough data to be able measure the type's reliability. The IFDU continued its work throughout the rest of the war, and was still in operation at the end of 1945.

Testing was also required on aircraft already in service, e.g. when modifications had been made as the result of a change in role, and on aircraft considered 'rogues' by their operating unit. This all meant that a lot of aircraft were always on-site. Well over 1,400 aircraft of various types came to Boscombe Down during the war years, some for type testing, others for longer-term trials on systems or weapons, or to support other trials. At any one time it was probable that if an aircraft was in service, a representative of that type could be seen at A&AEE. Enemy aircraft too were present. As well as the Bf109E tested at Boscombe Down in 1940, other captured German aircraft passed through the establishment, either for evaluation or to assist with trials. These included the Focke-Wulf Fw190 fighter and the Junkers Ju88 and Heinkel He111 bombers.

Test piloting was a skill developed at Boscombe Down. Britain pioneered test flying in the summer of 1915, when it set up the Experimental Flight within the Central Flying School at Upavon in Wiltshire, but up to the beginning of World War II test flight duties were undertaken by a small band of largely self-taught test pilots. They were employed by the manufacturers for both prototype and production flying, and by the Services for evaluating new aircraft and testing weapon installations and modifications. By the end of 1942, however, with new types arriving from the factories, the constant modifications to existing aircraft and the arrival of new US types ordered under lend/lease meant that the workload at Boscombe Down had become critical. More trained test pilots were needed and they just weren't available, so the idea of a school for test pilots was proposed. The Air Ministry felt that Boscombe Down would be a fitting location.

In 1943 the Test Pilots Training Flight was set up at Boscombe Down with its main aim being 'to improve the breed of test pilots and thereby to ensure a high and consistent standard by which aircraft may be judged'. The first Commandant of the Flight was Wing Commander Sammy Wroath, previously OC of A Squadron A&AEE. Half a dozen huts on the south side of the airfield were acquired as the Flight's first HQ. Then the first three aircraft arrived – a Halifax I, Master III and a Hurricane I. The first trial course was started on 16 June 1943 with 18 students – mainly RAF, with two naval officers. The standards were high and academically demanding, but fifteen graduated. More aircraft arrived for the flight as the first course progressed, and Sammy Wroath was able to borrow aircraft from other parts of the A&AEE to provide a good cross-section of types for the students to fly.

Although the accent was on the flying the importance of the academic side of test flying was also stressed. When No. 1 course completed in 1944 the fifteen graduates were posted as test pilots to the research establishments or to the company factories. With the concept of test pilot training proven, the Test Pilot Training Flight became the Empire Test Pilots School, the only such school in the world at the time and a notable first for Britain. The title 'Empire' was used for a series of schools in the RAF to show that they were staffed by and for the benefit of airmen from all over the British Empire. The ETPS is the only school left that retains its original title, perpetuating this wartime RAF tradition. The school left Boscombe Down in October 1945 as the establishment was getting too congested, but returned in 1968, and is still in residence.

During the war the pressure on test pilots was high. Men's lives depended on their work so it was imperative that as soon as the tests were completed the results were written up. A&AEE test reports were often contested by manufacturers who did not take criticism easily. Often however, the test pilots were proven right, as in the case of the Handley Page Halifax. Several early Halifax Is were lost in accidents, and it was only after an A&AEE crew were lost that the reason was found, which was the flawed design of the tail. Eventually the manufacturer accepted this and redesigned the entire tail unit, resulting in the Halifax becoming a perfectly acceptable and reliable aeroplane.

Busy airfields like Boscombe Down always present air traffic control problems. The possibility of collision was ever present and this was compounded during the war period by the variety of aircraft types in use and the type of flying being performed. Added to this was the fact that there was another airfield in close vicinity to Boscombe, at High Post, only two miles to the west. Lancaster BIII JA894, an aircraft of No.617 Squadron, was carrying out low level runs to measure air speed indicator system pressure errors on the morning of 10 September 1943.

As the Lancaster turned in for a fourth run at the western end of the airfield it collided with Oxford EB981 from 7 Flying Instructors School at Upavon, approaching to land at High Post. All six people aboard both aircraft were killed. However, it is worthy of note that this was one of only two collisions in the Boscombe Down area during the entire war time period (the other being between a Brewster Buffalo and Handley Page Hampden during a photographic sortie). During the Second World War a total fifty-eight personnel (nine of whom were civilian) were killed flying from Boscombe Down, in thirty-two aircraft accidents.

Machine guns fitted to British aircraft were originally of .303 calibre, the traditional size of the British Army's rifles and machine guns. Because of their fairly small size, these weapons were not particularly effective unless they were harmonised to give a concentrated cone of fire, usually being set to converge at a range of 200 yards. The Germans favoured the larger-calibre cannon, which gave heavier firepower and greater range. To combat this, suitable cannon for British aircraft were sought. The ultimate British aircraft cannon was the 57mm Molins Gun, which was an airborne version of the British Army's famous six-pounder anti-tank gun. This weapon was fitted into a Mosquito, and successfully trialled at A&AEE. Later 12 aircraft were to be modified as the Mosquito F.B.Mk.18, and used by No.248 Squadron against surfaced U-Boats.

The largest gun to be carried by an RAF aircraft was the 75mm cannon fitted to the North American B-25G Mitchell. One of these aircraft was evaluated at Boscombe Down in 1942, but not adopted for operational use. When the gun was fired into the stop-butts the round passed through the back wall and hit a Whitley bomber loaded with Pathfinder flares. The firework display was impressive!

A lot of work was carried out on special weapons, such as the Bouncing Bomb. This weapon had been the brainchild of Barnes Wallis, of Vickers Ltd, who had designed the Wellington bomber. The idea was that if a bomb could be rotated in the opposite direction to that of the aircraft that was carrying it, when dropped onto a lake, it would bounce across its surface for some distance. On contact with a dam wall, the bomb would run down the face until a hydrostatic fuse detonated it at a pre-determined depth. The bomb, later to be codenamed 'Upkeep', was designed specifically for breaching the Ruhr dams. It consisted of a cylinder 50 inches in diameter and 5 feet wide, weighing 9,150 lbs. Avro Lancaster bombers were modified to carry Upkeep, which was slung across the bomb bay, with its doors

Stars of the 1954 film 'The Dam Busters' posing with a Lancaster during filming include Richard Todd, who not only immortalised Guy Gibson in the film, but played a real-life role himself as a paratrooper during the Second World War during the D-Day landings. (Aeroplane)

removed, between two V-shaped arms. Electro-hydraulic equipment was fitted to rotate the bomb at 500 rpm before it was dropped.

A special unit, Squadron X (later to be numbered as No.617 Squadron), had been proposed to make the Upkeep attack, which was codenamed 'Operation Chastise'. Wing Commander Guy Gibson was put in command of the unit, which was formed on 24 March 1943 at RAF Scampton in Lincolnshire. It started training three days later on conventional Lancasters, while the operational aircraft were being modified. Final trials of the weapon were also being mounted at this time. These took place off Reculver and Chesil Beach to test the weapon over water, and over land at Ashley Walk. One aircraft, ED825, was based at Boscombe Down to undertake handling trials and general development. No.617 Squadron's training was intense because of the precise conditions required for the attack. They were told that release of the weapon had to take place at 240 mph, at a height of 150 feet.

One major problem was that of being able to position the aircraft accurately from the dam at the time of release, in order to hit the dam wall in the correct way so that the bomb would work. Wing Commander C.L. Dann, Supervisor of Aeronautics at Boscombe Down, gave this a lot of thought, and came up with an effective way of measuring the distance to the dam wall. Basing his calculations on the known distance between the two sluice towers, he put together a simple wooden sight. This had a peep-hole at its base through which the bomb-aimer looked. When two nails fixed at each end of the sight lined up with the two towers, the aircraft was at the correct release point. There remained the problem of fixing and maintaining a specific height over the water, which was critical to the effectiveness of the weapon, so that it would bounce across the water. After trying and rejecting several different gadgets, the Director of Scientific Research at the MAP, David Lockspeiser, devised an effective method using spotlights. One spotlight (Aldis lights were actually used) was fixed precisely in the centre of the fuselage, set at an angle of 40 degrees to starboard and slanting forward, while a second light was placed 20 feet forward of the first, to port of the fuselage centreline, shining at an angle of 30 degrees to starboard. The lights were positioned to coincide at a height of 150 feet, and were later re-adjusted when the release height was reduced to 60 feet. The 'Spotlight Altitude Calibrator' system, as it was later officially known, was fitted to the squadron aircraft.

Due to the loss of one of the squadron aircraft right at the end of training, the Boscombe Down trials Lancaster ED825 was quickly flown up to RAF Scampton on the afternoon of 16 May and given the squadron code 'AJ-T'. That night 'T for Tommy', flown by Flight Lieutenant Joe McCarthy, RCAF, left with the eighteen other aircraft to take part in the raid. At the briefing shortly beforehand, the actual targets were revealed for the first time (most of the crews thought it was to be the Tirpitz). The plan was that nine aircraft would attack the Mohne Dam, five the Sorpe, while the remaining five were to act as an airborne reserve, attacking other dams as appropriate. The force took off from Scampton and headed South. They crossed the English Channel at low level (so low in fact that one aircraft hit the sea, lost its weapon and returned to base). Despite staying low for the rest of the operation, five aircraft were shot down before reaching their targets. Another turned back after being badly damaged by flak. The Mohne Dam was attacked and breached, so those aircraft with un-dropped weapons flew on to the Eder Dam 40 miles away, and breached that one too.

Other Lancasters attacked the Ennepe Dam, but were unable to breach it. Three aircraft were shot down after the attacks, making a total of 8 lost out of a force of 19 despatched. The losses were grievous, but unfortunately not surprising in view of the hazardous nature of this audacious mission. Considerable damage was caused to the dams, and large areas were flooded. Electricity supplies to the Ruhr were cut off, disrupting production in the arms factories. Although it was not long before the Germans stabilised the situation, the effect on morale more than outweighed any material effects on the ground. It was a blow to German morale, and a terrific boost to the British, who were short of good news at the time. Guy Gibson was awarded the Victoria Cross for his leadership, determination and valour, and his Dambusters became heroes overnight.

In parallel with the development of the high capacity bombs was that of the deep penetration bombs, which were of medium capacity but great weight. These bombs were aerodynamically shaped, with fins offset to impart a spin to the bomb as it fell. As a result, great accuracy was achieved, and when dropped from 18,000 feet their speed was supersonic on impact and they drilled deep below the surface of the ground before exploding. Development resulted ultimately in two versions, the 12,000lb Tallboy, and the 22,000lb Grand Slam. The aircraft chosen to drop the Tallboy was the Avro Lancaster, due to its large, unobstructed bomb bay and its ability to carry extremely heavy loads. Minimal modifications were needed to the aircraft in order to carry the bomb. Initially a number of inert weapons were dropped at

22,000lb 'Grand Slam' Bomb on display at RAF Coningsby. (Author)

Ashley Walk to test the aerodynamics of the bomb casing, and these were followed by six live drops. Tallboys were first used operationally just after D-Day in a successful attack on the Saumur railway tunnel which blocked all rail traffic from the south of France to the Normandy front. Their most famous use was in the attack by Nos.9 and 617 Squadrons on the battleship Tirpitz, when it was sunk in Tromso Fjord in Norway on 12 November 1944.

A larger version of Tallboy was developed, and this was Grand Slam. It was a formidable weapon, the ultimate in iron bombs. At 22,000lbs, there was only one Allied aircraft capable of carrying such a weapon – once again, the Lancaster. The first aircraft to be modified to carry Grand Slam arrived at Boscombe Down in October 1944. After a series of trials dropping inert weapons on the range at Ashley Walk, a live bomb was dropped. Amongst the observers that day was the bomb's designer, Barnes Wallis. After the bomb impacted he counted nine seconds before the ground errupted. The blast was minimal, but local inhabitants felt the vibrations from this 'Earthquake Bomb' as he called it. A crater 130 feet in diameter and 30 feet deep was created. The following day came the first operational use of the Grand Slam, on the Bielefeld Viaduct. This structure carried an important rail link between north Germany and the Ruhr, and had been attacked on many occasions by the USAAF and RAF with 500lb and 1,000lb bombs. The piers could not be destroyed, and any damage to the spans was quickly

50

Fifth production de Havilland Vampire Mk I, TG278. The Vampire jet was tested at Boscombe Down from April 1944. (Aeroplane)

repaired by German Army engineers with steel girders, keeping the trains running. On 14 March 1945 one Lancaster, PD112, flown by Sqn/Ldr C.C. Calder from 617 Squadron, dropped one Grand Slam on the viaduct. The bomb brought down seven piers of the structure, which was put out of use for the rest of the war. In all, 854 Tallboys were dropped during World War II, and 41 Grand Slams. Targets included

U-Boat pens, and V3 'Terror Weapon' sites, which were giant, multi-barrelled guns with their workings deep underground.

The Avro Lancaster was extensively tested at Boscombe Down, from the first examples of the Mark I to the final wartime version, the Mark VII. During this time a total of forty-six Lancasters were trialled at the establishment. As the European war ended, the question of operating the Lancaster against the Japanese in the Far East was being addressed by A&AEE. The maximum range of standard service Lancasters taking off at 68,000lbs all up weight (with 14,000lbs of bombs) was 1,660 miles. At the time USAAF Boeing B-29 Superfortresses were carrying a 10,000lb bomb load over 3,250 miles to attack Japan. To operate over similar distances Lancasters would have had to have been modified considerably to carry a greater fuel load. Two Lancasters were fitted with 1,000 gallon tanks faired in between the flight deck and the mid-upper turret position, the actual turret being deleted. They were known as the MkI (FE), (Far East), and were delivered to Boscombe Down for handling trials. The trials were successful, and it was calculated that the aircraft would be able to carry a bomb load of 6,000lbs for a distance of 3,540 miles. In the event, USAAF B-29s dropped their atomic bombs, and the war ended before the long range Lancaster could be put into service.

The first British production jet fighter was the Gloster Meteor, which was tested by A&AEE staff at the Gloster Company's airfield in February 1944. The first jet aircraft to actually appear at Boscombe Down was the de Havilland E6/41 Spider Crab, later to become the Vampire, in April 1944. It could be said to be Britain's first true jet fighter as its shape was the result of its power plant, rather than in the case of the Meteor, its engines being modified to fit the airframe. The Vampire was the first allied jet fighter to exceed 500 miles per hour in level flight.

In the six years that the war lasted aircraft speeds doubled, operational ceilings increased by 50% and maximum take off weights trebled. The techniques and facilities needed at the end of the war had to match the complex requirements of the aircraft that were to be tested. A second runway was built at Boscombe Down along with new airfield aids which modern aircraft required for safe operation. New buildings were constructed including a new hangar, the Weighbridge Hangar, taking its name from a requirement to be able to weigh aircraft under cover. The record of Boscombe Down in the Second World War is a proud one, and there can be no doubt that A&AEE contributed much to the advance of military aviation during that time. Many

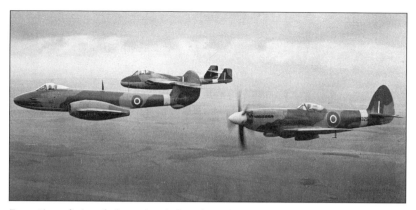

Formation of aircraft flown by A Squadron A&AEE in 1946. A Meteor III leads Vampire 1 and Spitfire 24. (Aeroplane)

changes to the organisation and facilities of Boscombe Down have occurred over the years, including recent name changes to the establishment. However, its job in support of the armed services continues, and, despite initiatives to take the organization into the private sector, the need for Boscombe Down's basic task remains unchanged, and that will continue for many years to come.

4

CASTLE
COMBE

National Grid Reference (173) ST855768, ¹/₂ mile SE of village

Named after the picturesque north Wiltshire village, Castle Combe aerodrome is situated a half-mile away to the south-east from its namesake on a low plateau beside the river valley of the By Brook.

Castle Combe first saw regular use as an airfield in the spring of 1941, when it was opened as a practice landing ground for No.9 Service Flying Training School (SFTS) based at RAF Hullavington. This school was an intermediate instruction unit, and its student pilots would fly their Hawker Hart and Hawker Audax biplanes the few miles across country from their base to practice landings, taxiing and take-offs from what was then just a large grass meadow. Roughly triangular in shape, the field lay between the villages of Castle Combe, Yatton Keynell and Long Dean, and was bounded by roads to the north and west, and to the south-east by the scarp of West Yatton Down. The airfield was used more and more by visiting aircraft, and so it was decided in May 1941 to upgrade it to Relief Landing Ground status. This meant that basic flying facilities were provided, along with accommodation for a modest operating staff.

No.9 SFTS had a varied fleet of aircraft, and during the summer of 1941 its Hawker Hurricane Mark Is and Miles Master Mark Is were often to be seen flying circuits around Castle Combe. This training also continued at night, with illumination of the grass runways being

54

Hawker Hart trainers were flown by 9 SFTS from Castle Combe. (Aeroplane)

provided by goose-neck flares. However, as with many grass airfields, operations at Castle Combe were particularly subject to the weather conditions, and flying often had to be curtailed because of water-logging of the grass surface.

The SFTS was re-designated No.9 (Pilots) Advanced Flying Unit on 14th February 1942. This was to reflect the fact that it had been given a new role, that of providing advanced flying training for British and Commonwealth pilots arriving in the UK from overseas, having been trained under the Empire Air Training Scheme. It was particularly important to get these newly-qualified pilots acclimatised to the conditions in which they would be conducting their operational flying – that was, not in the wide open blue skies of Australia and Canada, but in the congested grey skies of northern Europe! As well as RAF and Commonwealth air force pilots, the unit was also tasked with training Fleet Air Arm pilots. Therefore, in addition to its other types, the unit was now operating Fairey Swordfish and Fairey Albacore torpedo bombers, Blackburn Roc dive-bombers and Supermarine Walrus amphibians in which to fly the naval pilots. North American Harvards and Airspeed Oxfords were also taken on strength to increase the type experience of the students.

With the airfield at Castle Combe growing in importance, work

Naval pilots were taught at 9(P)AFU in Fairey Swordfish aircraft, although not necessarily to drop torpedoes! (Aeroplane)

started on upgrading its facilities. Flying operations buildings were constructed, along with more accommodation and ground instructional facilities. Domestic buildings were constructed, some of them on dispersed sites in the countryside away from the airfield.

On the main base at Hullavington in March 1942 the Empire Central Flying School was formed, with the task of standardising flying training procedures throughout the RAF and Dominion air forces. Because of the increased pressure on accommodation and airspace at Hullavington, it was decided to move the flying operations of 9(P)AFU to Castle Combe on a permanent basis (although the unit's headquarters was to remain at Hullavington). No.9(P)AFU was to remain at Castle Combe until they moved out of the area, which was at the end of July 1942, when they were transferred to RAF Errol in Scotland.

No.9(P)AFU were replaced at Castle Combe by No.3 Flying Instructors School (Advanced). This unit was formed at Hullavington on 1 August 1942 with Miles Masters, Miles Magisters, Airspeed Oxfords and North American Harvards. The school's job was, as indicated by its title, to train flying instructors. As with its predecessor, the HQ Flight was located at Hullavington, while flying training actually took place from Castle Combe, where its aircraft were based.

Flying started on 8 August, but the weather deteriorated as autumn came on, with the rain and waterlogging severely curtailing the flying programme. This led later to the need for lengthy extensions to the training courses to make up lost time. Ground conditions became so bad at Castle Combe in early 1943 that the unit's instructors and pupils found themselves having to commute daily to Colerne and Charmy Down near Bath for flying. More work on the airfield surface took place after this, in an attempt to improve operating conditions. Steel Sommerfeld tracking was laid to make up two runways, and a tarmac perimeter track was built. The opportunity was also taken to improve other facilities and eight hangars (seven Blister and one T-1) were built at this time to provide cover for the aircraft.

Flying resumed once again at Castle Combe after a few months, and by May 1943 it was in full swing. However, barely was the first course completed when the school was informed that it was to move, following the decision to relocate No.15 (P)AFU to Castle Combe from Ramsbury. Therefore No.3 FIS(A) had to move to Lulsgate Bottom near Bristol in early October 1943, but it was not until the end of the month that the Oxfords of No.15 (P)AFU arrived. The main reason for this time-lapse appears to have been to cater for more surface treatment at Castle Combe as waterlogging remained a problem.

Supermarine Walrus amphibians were flown by 9(P)AFU at Castle Combe. (Aeroplane)

Flying resumed with the arrival of the Oxfords, and continued throughout the winter despite the indifferent weather. Problems with the airfield at Long Newnton (another training airfield not far away in Gloucestershire) resulted in the temporary transfer of some flying to Castle Combe in January 1944 and consequently more disruption to the resident unit's training programme. Tragedy struck a few months later when on 13 March 1944 a fully loaded Stirling bomber force landed at Castle Combe. Its bomb load exploded causing substantial damage to the airfield buildings. For three days flying was suspended while temporary repairs were made.

Unfortunately problems with the surface of the runways at Castle Combe persisted during the remainder of 1944 and flying continued to be restricted by bad ground conditions. More repairs took place and by March 1945 the airfield was just about serviceable again. It was about this time that the Long Newnton satellite was closed and the aircraft transferred to Castle Combe, but this level of flying did not carry on for long as the end of the war in Europe was in sight. In May 1945 No.15(P)AFU transferred to Babdown Farm, where they were to disband the following month. All flying now ceased at Castle Combe and the station personnel moved out. The airfield was put on Care and Maintenance pending a decision on its future.

The empty station was later reoccupied for a couple of years when from July 1946 to June 1948 it was used as accommodation for Polish ex-service personnel under the care of No.2 (Polish) Resettlement Unit, part of 27 Group RAF Technical Training Command. In June 1948 the airfield once again became vacant. It was put once more onto Care and Maintenance, and it was disposed of in September 1948.

However, it was not long before the roar of engines was once more to be heard at Castle Combe. The airfield was purchased as a motor racing circuit. Regular race meetings were held throughout the first season and continue to this day. Many of the airfield buildings remain, converted to new uses to meet the demands of motor-sport. The control tower now houses racing control and many of the former operations and technical buildings are now workshops and offices. The airfield perimeter track formed the basis of the actual circuit, the tarmac surface running round the ends of the former runways being almost purpose made for a racetrack. The occasional light aircraft or helicopter still flies in, particularly on race days, maintaining a link between Castle Combe and its wartime aeronautical past.

5
CLYFFE
PYPARD

National Grid Reference (173) SU070755, 3¹/₂ miles S of Wootton Bassett

Situated on the edge of a scarp slope to the south of Clyffe Pypard village, this airfield was situated on flat farmland to the north-west of the Marlborough Downs. The site is equidistant between Lyneham to the north-west and Wroughton to the north-east.

Rudimentary facilities were available at Clyffe Pypard when it opened in September 1941. The first, and in fact the only, unit to operate from the airfield was No.29 Elementary Flying Training School, which formed on 13 September. The school was operated by Marshall's Flying Schools, employing civilian staff to maintain the aircraft, and as flying instructors. Equipped with Tiger Moths and Magisters, the role of the EFTS was to teach its students to fly, and to take them up to just beyond solo standard. The student pilots arrived from Initial Training Wings, where they had been given their basic training, which was an introduction to service life. At the EFTS they would be given a thorough grounding in various subjects in the classroom, such as navigation, radio communication, propulsion, airframes and photography, as well as having practical flying lessons. In the early stages of the war the course lasted six months, but because of the pressure to supply pilots, in the summer of 1940 this was reduced to five months. The following year this was brought down to four months, and furthermore it was made clear to the schools that even this period could be shortened if favourable weather conditions allowed the required amount of flying time to be completed earlier. Throughout the short course the students' performance was monitored, and their aptitude for single or muti-engined flying would be noted. Having gone solo, usually after about ten hours of flying time under instruction, the pupil pilots would spend their time improving and refining their flying skills, by both day and night. This stage of training included forced-landings, formation-flying and aerobatics. Those pupils that passed (there was a 30% failure rate) were then posted to one of the seventeen Service Flying Training Schools (SFTS) for advanced training. Which SFTS they went to depended on their performance at the EFTS, and this would ultimately decide their eventual posting to either Fighter, Bomber or Coastal Command.

Four landing strips varying between 1,050 and 1,333 yards were marked out on the grass at Clyffe Pypard. A ten-foot wide concrete taxiway was laid all around the perimeter of the airfield with turning points every 600 yards, to ease aircraft ground movements and wear and tear on the grass. Some hangarage was available, and eventually the airfield was to have four Bellman and fifteen Blister hangars in which the aircraft could be sheltered and maintained. A bomb store was later added in the northern corner of the site. Hutted accommodation had been provided for 510 servicemen and 200 civilians, and an HQ and offices had also been built.

No.1 Course of No.29 EFTS started on 15 September 1941 with

Pupils prepare for another training sortie in their Tiger Moths. (Aeroplane)

seventy-one students, most having come from No.7 Initial Training Wing at Newquay. Soon the air was full of Tiger Moths and Magisters, with the instructors and their students hard at work. In order to relieve the congestion at Clyffe Pypard the Satellite Landing Ground at Alton Barnes was transferred from the CFS to No.29 EFTS at the end of 1941. It was upgraded to Relief Landing Ground (RLG) status, and Blister hangars were erected there to increase No.29 EFTS' aircraft storage capacity. A link trainer building was later built, and night flying equipment was also installed at Alton Barnes to increase the school's facilities.

In January 1942 blizzards hit the area, and the airfield at Clyffe Pypard was covered in snow-drifts up to three feet deep. An emergency runway was bulldozed through the snow, but little flying took place until the end of the month. Fleet Air Arm (FAA) as well as RAF pilots were trained at No.29 EFTS, and in May 1942 the school's courses were increased in size to cater for army students as well. The first contingent of forty-five members of the Glider Pilot Regiment came to the school for powered flying training before moving on to fly gliders. This pre-glider training for the army continued for the rest of 1942.

On 3 June 1942 No.29 EFTS was upgraded with an increase in size by one-third. Its four training flights were increased to six, the extra two being accommodated at Alton Barnes. As more courses moved through, the school settled down to a routine. Magisters and Tiger Moths continued to provide the mainstay of the school's fleet, but at some stage Fairey Battles were used, probably for the more advanced flying training, as well as Avro Ansons. Another type that made an appearance was literally by accident on the night of 18 October 1942, when Liberator AL538, on a delivery flight from Prestwick to Lyneham, crash-landed at Clyffe Pypard. The aircraft ended up on the eastern edge of the airfield, but fortunately the crew survived. Another unexpected arrival in 1942 was that of Stirling BK667/H of No.15 Squadron, which came down near the airfield after engine failure following damage on a raid to Saint Nazaire. Five of the crew had already bailed out during the return flight, but the remaining crew survived.

From 21 November 1942 No.29 EFTS started to use another RLG to increase its flying training capacity. This was Manningford, which, like Alton Barnes, had been used by the Central Flying School. Grading courses were introduced at No.29 EFTS in addition to its other training from December to assess the flying standards of pilots and instructors

Fairey Battles were used by 29 EFTS to train its pupil pilots. (Aeroplane)

and rate their need for further training or experience.

Training courses continued uneventfully at Clyffe Pypard through-out 1943 and into 1944. In October 1944 Grading courses for FAA pilots were also introduced at No.29 EFTS. The school quietly got on with its job into 1945. With the end of the war, courses were reduced in number, but the school and the airfield remained open, despite widespread closures and reductions elsewhere in the RAF. On 7 July 1945 all No.29 EFTS aircraft were withdrawn from Alton Barnes, and the airfield was put under Care and Maintenance, although the school continued to use Manningford for another year.

The training of RAF and FAA pilots continued at Clyffe Pypard after the war, the training fleet by then consisting entirely of Tiger Moth IIs. Eventually, however, with so many other units still operating and other airfields available to the RAF with better accommodation and facilities, it was decided to close No.29 EFTS and its airfield. The school was disbanded on 5 November 1947, and absorbed by No.21 EFTS at Booker in Buckinghamshire.

Today little can be seen to show that this Wiltshire field played an important part in training aircrew of all three Services during World War II.

6
COLERNE

National Grid Reference (173) ST803715, 4 miles NE of Bath

One of the last Expansion Scheme airfields to be built, Colerne was originally planned as a Maintenance Unit. Lying just inside the Wiltshire border with Somerset, the airfield is located on a plateau which is edged to the south and east by the valleys of the Rivers Lid Brook and By Brook, tributaries of the Somerset River Avon.

Colerne was still under construction in the autumn of 1939, and when war was declared that September, construction was hastened. In the process some of the planned buildings were not completed, or were modified in view of the impending hostilities.

When the airfield was opened by No.41 Group, RAF Maintenance Command, on 1 January 1940, it was still not complete, and the three tarmac runways were not to be finally finished for another year. No.39 Maintenance Unit was formed at Colerne on 18 May, as an Aircraft Storage Unit, and was to be the only occupant of the new station for the next few months. Aircraft were delivered to the MU, usually by air, from the manufacturer's works, then prepared for temporary storage or delivery to a user unit.

Fighter Command took an interest in Colerne at this time, as it was creating another sector within its No.10 Group, which had its headquarters at nearby Rudloe Manor. It was decided not only to use Colerne for fighter operations, but also to form an HQ for the new sector there, and this was created in September. The first fighter unit to arrive was No.87 Squadron on 28 November, with their Hawker Hurricane Mk.Is. As well as its main role as day fighter defence, its B Flight was also involved in night fighting. On its arrival at Colerne the

Boulton Paul Defiant night fighters were flown by the Colerne squadrons from 1941. (Aeroplane)

squadron went over entirely to night fighting. Its Hurricanes were therefore painted black overall, and were fitted with flame-damping exhausts. The runways at Colerne were still not complete at this time, which limited No.87 Squadron's flying. Detachments were therefore sent a few miles to the east, to the newly-completed airfield at Charmy Down, built as a satellite to Colerne, in order to keep the whole squadron flying. When suitable accommodation then became available at Charmy Down the whole squadron moved there.

In early 1941 Colerne was used for fighter squadron training. No.256 Squadron with Defiant night fighters moved there on 6 February, before moving on 26 March to Squire's Gate near Blackpool, exchanging places with another Defiant squadron, No.307 (Polish) Squadron. This unit was an RAF squadron formed in the UK from Polish Air Force personnel. It flew night patrols from Colerne, and on 12 April 1941 had its first confirmed victory, when a German bomber fell to the guns of Sergeants Jankowiak and Lipinski in Defiant N3315. At the end of April, No.307 Squadron moved to Exeter.

Colerne's runways were finally completed in the spring of 1941, and the first unit to arrive after the new aerodrome opened came on 27 April. This was another night fighter squadron, and a former Auxiliary Air Force unit, No.600 (City of London) Squadron equipped with a mixed complement of Bristol Blenheim I and Bristol Beaufighter II aircraft. It was under the command of Wing Commander George Stainforth, the notable Schneider Trophy pilot.

No.600 Squadron was still in the process of re-equipping with the new Beaufighter when it relocated to Colerne. On arrival in Wiltshire, the squadron immediately mounted patrols to cover Bristol, but later ranged generally over the south west. The squadron got off to a good start when they brought down a Ju88 near Shepton Mallet a few days after they arrived. Over the following months, No.600 Squadron intercepted a steady number of Ju88 and He111 intruders.

Another former Auxiliary squadron had arrived at Colerne in April. This was No.501 (County of Gloucester) Squadron, a day fighter unit on the Hawker Hurricane. Once at their new base, No.501 started to escort daylight bombing raids on targets in France. One of the first of these was on 17 April, to escort a force of eighteen Blenheims in an attack on Cherbourg.

When they learnt that they were to re-equip with Spitfire Mk.Is, it was with mixed feelings that No.501 Squadron's pilots said goodbye to their Hurricanes. No.501 took over its Spitfires from another squadron and began working up for offensive activities in their new aircraft.

Once they were declared operational on the Spitfire they initially flew convoy escort patrols, then went on to Rhubarbs (a code-name for low-level strikes against ground targets in occupied Europe), Road-steads (attacks on ships, at sea or in harbour), with the occasional Ramrod (operations against a specific target, but also intended to provoke enemy fighters into battle). Night interceptions were added to the squadron's duties, a task for which the Spitfire was not ideally suited. However, to prove that the aircraft could be viable in the role, Squadron Leader A.H. Boyd scored the squadron's first night victory on a patrol over Portsmouth. Shortly after this, on 25 June, No.501 Squadron left Colerne and moved to a new base at Chilbolton in Hampshire.

A British Overseas Airways Corporation repair unit had been set up at Colerne earlier in 1941, using hangars on the north side of the aerodrome. Although established to repair and maintain aircraft operated by the airline, the unit also undertook the assembly of fighter aircraft. Eventually the unit's work was taken over by RAF personnel and in March 1942 it became No.218 Maintenance Unit. Assembly work continued but this later changed to special installation work, such as AI Radar equipment into night fighters.

The Poles returned to Colerne on 18 June 1941 when No.316 (City of Warsaw) Squadron was moved in with their Hurricanes on transfer from Pembrey in South Wales. The squadron was employed on convoy patrols in the Bristol Channel and they took part in Operation

Defiant target tug of No.286 Squadron. The squadron was based at Colerne for most of the wartime period. (Aeroplane)

Sunrise escorting Hamden bombers on a raid, claiming a Bf109E destroyed, and fighter sweeps over the Channel. In August they provided withdrawal cover for Bomber Command Fortress Mk.1s on their early raids on the Continent. Later in August 1941 No.316 Squadron moved on to Culmhead.

The German night raids of 1940 had shown up several inadequacies in Britain's nocturnal air defences. Many ideas were tried to make up for this. One of these was the 'Turbinlite'. This was an aircraft-mounted searchlight, devised by Wing Commander W Helmore. The idea was that a twin-engined aircraft would carry Airborne Interception (AI) Radar and a large searchlight mounted in the nose. It would be accompanied by a fighter aircraft known as a Satellite. Once the detection aircraft picked up a contact on its radar it would close in and illuminate the target. The Satellite would then move in for the kill once it was positively identified as an enemy aircraft. Ten Turbinlite flights were formed, two at Colerne. The first of these was No.1454 Flight, which formed on 4 July 1941, partnered with 87 Squadron; the second was No.1457 Flight, formed on 15 September 1941 and paired with No.247 Squadron. The scheme was not a success and ended in January 1943 when all ten Turbinlite squadrons were disbanded, the personnel and aircraft being reassigned to other duties.

On 22 December 1941 a squadron arrived that was to be much in evidence at Colerne over the next three and a half years. This was No.286 Squadron, an anti-aircraft co-operation unit. No.10 Group Anti Aircraft Co-operation Flight had been formed at Filton near Bristol in May 1941, and on 17 November of that year the flight became No.286 Squadron. Its duties were to provide target facilities for units of all three Services in the south west. The author's father, Geoffrey Berryman, served with No.286 Squadron. Having been with No.18 Bomber Squadron at Great Massingham during the Battle of Britain, Geoff was posted to No.286 Squadron at Filton on 9 July 1941 (when it was still No.10 Group AAC Flight) as a Corporal Fitter II (Airframes). He later moved with the squadron to Colerne. Promoted to Sergeant, he stayed with the unit until 5 December 1944 when he was posted overseas to join No.70 Bomber Squadron in Italy. The main equipment of No.286 was initially the Westland Lysander, later replaced by the Miles Martinet. Other aircraft flown by the unit were the Airspeed Oxford, Boulton Paul Defiant and Hawker Hurricane. As well as general maintenance to keep the aircraft flying, Geoff Berryman and his crews were responsible for repairs and modifications to the squadron's aircraft.

Another Spitfire squadron appeared at Colerne in January 1942. This was No.417 Squadron, whose personnel were largely Canadian, and it was established as a unit within the Royal Canadian Air Force (RCAF). On moving to Colerne the Squadron was re-equipped with the Spitfire Mk.Vb. On 12 February 1942, No.417 Squadron was called to readiness due to suspected movements by German warships in the Channel. The

De Havilland Mosquito night fighter takes off into the dusk for another patrol. (Aeroplane)

ships were later found to be the battleship Scharnhorst and the battlecruiser Gneisnau, and they made their famous 'Channel Dash' into the Atlantic without being spotted by Allied ships or aircraft.

A further arrival in 1942 was No.264 Squadron. This was another night fighter unit flying the Boulton Paul Defiant and it had in fact been the first squadron to receive the type. However, by the spring of 1942 the Defiant had reached the limit of its effectiveness as a night fighter, and No.264 Squadron was re-equipped with the de Havilland Mosquito NFII. This was a fearsome aeroplane, equipped with four 20mm Hispano cannon under the forward fuselage, as well as four .303 machine-guns in the nose. It was fitted with the AI MkIV, the state-of-the-art AI radar. By 8 June the squadron was operational with its new aircraft, and later on in the month intercepted and damaged a Dornier Do217 over Weston-super-Mare. As the resident night fighter squadron at Colerne, No.264 mounted night patrols to defend the airfield. The squadron's first kill with the Mosquito came on the night of 30/31 July 1942, when a Ju88A-4 was intercepted. Night operations continued over the next few months, but little action took place during this time. In December they went over to day operations in the Bay of Biscay, and later shipping reconnaissance over the Western Approaches.

The weather during the winter of 1942 was extremely wet, and at one stage twelve of the squadron's Mosquitoes were under repair at No.39 MU due to water damage to the wings and fuselages, which were particularly vulnerable, being made of wood. Intruder missions were started in January 1942, targeting enemy shipping, and a detachment was sent to Bradwell Bay in Essex to undertake similar missions over the North Sea until April. Detachments had earlier been flown from Trebelzue and Portreath in Cornwall, and at the end of April the whole squadron moved to Predannack in Cornwall, to be closer to its assigned operational area.

A number of other units spent time at Colerne during 1942. These included No.263 Squadron, flying the Westland Whirlwind. It was the first squadron to be equipped with this revolutionary aircraft – the first twin-engined, single-seater to enter service with the RAF. No.263 Squadron arrived at Colerne on 28 January 1942 for night fighter trials; however, the trials were not a great success. By August the Whirlwinds had been fitted out as fighter-bombers, and the squadron spent the next month attacking enemy airfields in France and shipping in the Channel and Western Approaches, both roles that the aircraft was far more suited to. No.263 Squadron moved to Warmwell in Dorset in mid-September.

Hundreds of Hurricanes went through No.39 MU Colerne. This type, the Mark IID fitted with 20mm underwing cannon, was also flown from the station by No.184 Squadron. (Aeroplane)

Unusual visitors in September 1942 were the Lockheed P-38F Lightnings of the 27th Fighter Squadron, 1st Fighter Group, 12th Air Force, USAAF. They spent almost two months at Colerne before leaving for North Africa.

December 1942 saw the appearance of No.184 Squadron, formed at the station as a fighter-bomber unit with Hurricanes. Originally with the 40mm cannon-armed Hurricane Mk.IID (specially developed for attacking tanks, and nicknamed 'the flying can-opener'), the Squadron worked up and started exercising with local army units, taking part in Exercise Spartan. Before long No.184 was receiving the Hurricane Mk.IV, the last production version of the aircraft. In March the squadron moved to Chilbolton in Hampshire, where it was to start cross-Channel rocket-armed intruder operations, although it was to re-visit Wiltshire shortly afterwards, for a joint operations exercise held at Zeals.

No.175 Squadron arrived at Colerne on 8 April 1943. This was another Hurricane unit, which had been formed at Warmwell a year before. Having been involved in attacks on enemy shipping and convoy patrols, No.175 came to Colerne to re-equip and collected its new Hawker Typhoon Ib aircraft from No.39 MU. Having fully converted to the type, the Squadron worked up at Colerne before moving off to Lasham in Hampshire to start training for rocket operations.

In early 1943 No.456 Squadron was a RAAF Bristol Beaufighter unit flying patrols over the Irish Sea from its base at RAF Valley in North Wales. In mid-March 1943 it started converting to the Mosquito II, and sent a detachment of these aircraft to Colerne, to start intruder patrols over France. The whole squadron then moved to Middle Wallop in Hampshire, from where they stepped up their operations, mainly against the French railway network. They also flew night intruder sorties against Luftwaffe airfields in France. These attacks were codenamed 'Flower', and were mounted on German night fighter airfields during raids by the main bomber force. These operations continued when the squadron returned to Colerne in mid-August 1943. Ranger patrols were also flown, usually by Mosquitoes in pairs, attacking specific targets such as power stations. A Ranger Flight was formed at Colerne, which operated as a separate unit. An Instep patrol on 21 September found eight Ju88s, destroying one and damaging two more. In November No.456 Squadron moved to Fairwood Common.

They were replaced by No.151 Squadron, which was returning to Colerne to be re-equipped by No.39 MU with a later version of the Mosquito, the NFXIII. The squadron had been flying night intruder operations over the Continent and the Western Approaches, and these continued from their new base with their new aircraft. Shortly afterwards they claimed a Messerschmitt Me410 twin-engined night fighter, and in January 1944 claimed the first He177 to be shot down over the UK.

The He177 was one of the largest bombers to be operated by the Luftwaffe. Designed as a long-range heavy bomber and ship-killer, the aircraft was powered by four engines paired together in two cowlings. Although the project had been started in 1938, the aircraft was plagued with problems which protracted its development – 31 prototype or pre-production aircraft either crashed or were destroyed in engine fires. At last, on the night of 21 January 1944, the He177 was finally being used in anger. Its first operation was to be as part of a mixed force of 92 bombers and fighter-bombers loaded with incendiaries to be used in dive-bombing raids over England as retaliation for RAF bomber raids on German towns and cities. This was to be the first of a series of revenge raids on Britain code-named Operation Steinbock, and dubbed the 'Baby Blitz' by the RAF. After taking off from their base, the He177 crews climbed as high as possible while still in German-controlled

Heinkel HE177 of KG40 captured by the allies. One of the unit's aircraft was shot down by a Colerne Mosquito on 21 January 1944. (Aeroplane)

airspace over the Continent, then flew over the Channel in a shallow dive at some 400 mph. The main bomber force was led by the Pathfinders of KG (Kampfgruppe) 100, one of the Luftwaffe's elite units, also flying the He177. As they flew over southern England heading for their target, London, the Heinkels dropped Duppel (Window) to confuse the radar defences. Nonetheless, they were detected, and several of the attackers were shot down that night. The first He177 to be lost was from 1/KG40, and was shot down by Flying Officer H.K. Kemp and Flight Sergeant J.R. Maidment in their Mosquito NFXII HK193 of No.151 Squadron from Colerne. The Heinkel crashed at Whitmore Vale near Hindhead in Surrey, and was completely destroyed apart from the tail assembly. The bomber was just one of the dozen downed by Mosquitoes during the raid, which cost the Luftwaffe 21 aircraft altogether.

Another successful patrol followed for No.151 Squadron six weeks later, when one Ju88 and three Ju188s were claimed on one night. The squadron also took part as escorts in shipping attacks and in March 1944 moved to Predannack to be nearer its area of operations.

When No.151 Squadron moved, it was replaced at Colerne by a detachment from No.219 Squadron, flying the Mosquito MkXVII. Almost immediately the new unit scored, when on 27 March Squadron Leader Ellis destroyed a Ju88 of 3/JG54 over Yeovil. Regular night patrols were flown over the Channel, and as far afield as Holland. The Colerne detachment later re-joined its parent squadron, and from May 1944 was involved in 'Anti-Diver' patrols against V1 flying bombs.

The next unit to provide night fighter cover from Colerne was No.488 Squadron, which flew in from Bradwell Bay in Kent to take over from No.219 on 3 May 1944. Flying the Mosquito NFXII and XIII, No.488 was a Royal New Zealand Air Force Squadron, and was part of the Second Tactical Air Force (2 TAF), the RAF formation that had been formed to take part in the invasion of Occupied Europe. From Colerne the squadron mounted patrols covering the military assembly areas being established as part of the build-up to the invasion. After a week or so the squadron moved to Zeals to continue its work there in less congested airspace, but was to return to Colerne later.

Having taken part in a steady flow of aeroplanes to enable squadron re-equipment as well as providing the occasional single aeroplane to replace those lost in combat or accidents, by early June 1944 No.29 MU was working all-out to prepare stocks of aircraft in readiness for the heavy losses expected during the invasion. On D-Day itself, and over the following weeks, it was very quiet at the MU, as the losses were not as great as had been feared.

On 13 June 1944 No.604 (County of Middlesex) Squadron arrived at Colerne. This was the first of three Mosquito night fighter squadrons to form 147 Wing, 85 Group of 2 TAF. On 28 July the other two squadrons of the wing arrived, these being Nos.410 and 488 Squadrons from Zeals. From Colerne the three Mosquito squadrons of No.147 Wing continued to roam the night skies over France with great success. Without doubt the highlight of this period was the night of 29/30 July, when Flight Lieutenants G.E. Jamieson (Pilot) and N.E. Crookes (Radar Operator/Navigator) of No.488 Squadron flew a sortie over Normandy. Patrolling between Caen and Lisieux in MM466, they intercepted and destroyed three Ju88s and one Do217, all in the space of 20 minutes, using only 360 rounds of cannon ammunition!

The first of these squadrons to leave Colerne for the Continent was No.604, departing on 6 August 1944. On arrival at Landing Ground A8 at Picauville it became the first Allied night fighter squadron to become based in France. In the last few days before leaving for the Continent the squadron shot down three Ju88s. Nos.410 and 488 Squadrons remained at Colerne until the autumn, performing night patrols against enemy intruders, and also Anti-Diver patrols by day and at night.

One of these intruder missions took place on the evening of 9

August, when Flying Officer Doug Robinson (Pilot) and Warrant Officer Nat Addison (Navigator/Radar Operator) of No.488 Squadron took off from Colerne in Mosquito NFXIII MM439 to patrol over France. They orbited to the south of Caen, where they identified a Ju188. As they came up behind it, the German bomber started jinking and trying to confuse the Mosquito's radar. Robinson gave the Junkers four bursts of cannon fire, after which its port engine caught fire. The bomber then went into a steep bank and flew into the ground, exploding in a fireball, with its bombs still on board.

In January 1945 the station and the Royal Air Force entered a new era when the first permanent jet fighter squadron was established at Colerne, and No.616 (County of Yorkshire) Squadron arrived to be based there with its Gloster Meteors. During this time it exchanged its Meteor Is for the more advanced MkIII version. No.616 had been issued with the Meteor I at Culmhead, in Somerset, in July 1944. The squadron was flying its Spitfire MkVIIs on armed reconnaissance over the Continent in preparation for D-Day when it learnt that it was to become the first Allied jet fighter squadron (and in the event the only RAF jet fighter squadron to become operational during the Second World War). Culmhead was an opportune location because of its isolation, which was perfect for the secret training of squadron personnel on the new jet aeroplane. After a month at Culmhead the squadron was sent to Manston in Kent to act as a forward defence against the German V1 flying bombs then being launched over south-east England. On the second day of patrols at Manston one of the Meteor pilots spotted a V1 and brought it down, in the first jet-versus-jet combat in history. Twenty-four minutes later another Meteor brought down a second V1, and by the time the V1 threat petered out at the end of September, there were thirteen V1s on 616's scoreboard. The first operational German jet, the Messerschmitt Me262, was of particular concern to the Allies, especially to the Americans, who were flying their bombing missions over Germany in daylight. No.616 were asked to help the USAAF develop defensive tactics against jets. Five Meteors were detached to Debden to assist. They flew against formations of B-17 Fortesses and B-24 Liberators protected by fighter screens. Some useful lessons were learnt which the USAAF were able to put into practice. From Manston the squadron moved to Colerne.

Once at Colerne No.616 prepared for operational deployment across the Channel. The pilots rehearsed their tactics and flew combat exercises against each other and other aircraft, including the most advanced US high performance fighters of the day, the North

American P-51D Mustang and the Republic P-47D Thunderbolt. Transition from piston engines to jets was not easy because of their different characteristics – jets had a flatter and slower climb, a greater speed in level flight and in a dive, a slower acceleration from speeds below 300 mph, but a greater acceleration from speeds above 300 mph, and they lost speed slowly because of their lack of propellers and other in-built drag. No.616 had to break new ground, and write the textbooks on flying and operating the new jets.

To gain operational experience it was decided to send a flight of Meteors to the Continent. On 4 February 1945 the flight arrived at Melsbroek (B.58) to join 2 TAF. Its duties were to act as defence against Me262s, but as the Meteors were not to fly over enemy territory for fear of capture, opportunities for combat were severely limited. Melsbroek was in fact bombed by Arado 234s, the first operational German jet bombers, on 19 March, but the Meteors were not scrambled in time to catch them. The rest of No.616 Squadron joined the detached flight at the end of March 1945, by which time they were at Gilze-Rijen (B.77) in the Netherlands. Together the Meteors went on the offensive with armed reconnaissance missions in support of the ground forces. Shortly before No.616 Squadron left Colerne on 22 February 1945, No.29 Squadron arrived. This was another night fighter unit and, shortly after arrival at Colerne, exchanged its Mosquito XIIIs for the most potent version of the Mosquito, the NF30. This had more powerful engines and an advanced A1 radar. From Colerne, the squadron flew intruder missions to the Continent, and on one of these on 24 April 1945, Warrant Officer Dallinson shot down one Me262 jet fighter and damaged another.

To assist with the establishment of more Meteor squadrons, it was decided to set up a conversion unit to train fighter pilots, most of whom would have been experienced on the Spitfire, on the new type. On 8 March 1945 No.1335 (Meteor) Conversion Unit was established at Colerne. It flew early versions of the Meteor for conversion training as well as Oxfords and Martinets to provide experience in twin engine and continuation training. The unit performed its task at Colerne until August 1945.

Meanwhile, on 28 March 1945, another jet fighter unit was created at Colerne when No.504 (County of Nottingham) Squadron exchanged its Spitfire MkIXs for Meteor IIIs. Preparation for this had been made in January 1945, when six of the squadron's pilots had been posted to Glosters for conversion training. With Squadron Leader M. Kellet, DFC, a Battle of Britain veteran, in command, April and most of May

74

A line up by 74 Squadron of its Meteor Mark IIIs, which it received at Colerne in May 1945. (Aeroplane)

were spent in training, culminating in practice Ramrods and Rodeos. The squadron was declared operational just too late to see any action, but detachments were made in July to Lubeck in Germany, where they flew some impressive formation displays.

No.74 Squadron became the third RAF jet fighter squadron, on 11 May 1945, when it arrived at Colerne to convert to the Meteor III. By then the war had actually finished in Europe, and No.74 flew its Spitfire IXs in from Drope (B.105) in Germany. With No.504 Squadron it formed the first jet fighter wing in the RAF, the Colerne Wing.

With the war over, a rationalisation of RAF squadrons took place. No.504 Squadron was one of those to be disbanded; its aircraft and personnel passed to No.245 Squadron, which was reformed that same day at Colerne, as part of the Colerne Wing.

Both No.74 and No.245 Squadrons continued to fly their Meteors from Colerne as part of the Air Defence of Great Britain (ADGB – the post-war RAF UK air defence organisation) throughout the rest of 1945 and into the summer of 1946. No.245 Squadron was the first to depart when, on 2 June 1946, it moved to RAF Bentwaters. In October 1946 No.74 Squadron also moved, when it took up its peacetime station at Horsham St. Faith as part of the ADGB.

RAF Colerne was then transferred from Fighter Command to

Maintenance Command, as No.39 and No.218 MUs were still in residence. With the end of the war came a rationalisation of the RAF's equipment as well as its squadrons. As the result of this process thousands of airframes, vehicles, engines and spares were identified as being surplus at RAF stations and MUs all over the country. This vast quantity of material had to be disposed of, and those items that were not of immediate value for export were sold at auction. Hundreds of surplus aircraft and parts were in store at Colerne at this time, available for sale by sealed bid. Several sales took place as the aircraft were disposed of in stages, and a tender form dating from December 1946 shows four Avro Lancastrians (a transport conversion of the Lancaster), twenty Miles Martinet target tugs and twenty Miles Master trainers being put up for sale at No.39 MU. The airfield itself was little used over the next five years, apart from the ferrying and test flying of aircraft, or for storage. One of No.39 MU's tasks during this time was to prepare surplus Spitfires for export to overseas air forces. No.218 MU was closed down in February 1948, but replaced a few months later by No.49 MU, which moved in from Lasham. This unit was to remain at Colerne for the next 14 years, while the original occupant of the station, No.39 MU, was closed in October 1953.

Operational flying resumed again on 1 February 1949 when No.662 Squadron, an Air Observation Post unit, was re-formed at Colerne to fly the Auster AOP6. The level of flying increased in June 1952 with the return of Fighter Command in the form of No.238 OCU, flying Bristol Brigands for night fighter navigator training. The OCU left for North Luffenham at the beginning of 1957. At that time Colerne was taken over by Transport Command, who moved in two Hastings squadrons. A third appeared in May 1959.

As the Colerne Wing these squadrons flew all over the world on Transport Command routes, as well as providing tactical support for the army. One squadron was disbanded in 1961; the other two remained until 1967 when they converted to the Lockheed Hercules and moved to RAF Lyneham. While the Hercules squadrons were being formed Colerne became the maintenance base for the type. A new Hercules squadron, No.48, was formed there in October 1967, but it soon left for the Far East. Hercules engineering continued at Colerne until sufficient room had been created at Lyneham for the Hercules technical organisation to be collocated with the flying squadrons, leaving Colerne empty. No.49 MU had continued with its storage and modification work but was disbanded in 1962.

RAF Colerne was closed in March 1976, having been listed as being no longer required in the 1975 Defence White Paper. The station's aircraft museum, which had been set up in 1964 and was a large thriving concern, was closed and the collection broken up. A good number of the aeroplanes went on to form the basis of the RAF Museum, and some went to other museums, although several were scrapped on site.

The former RAF Colerne was taken over by the army, who now occupy it as Azimghur Barracks. Nowadays it is the home of the Junior Leaders' Regiment, Royal Logistic Corps. Much of the aerodrome and its buildings are complete – the Royal Navy use one or two of the hangars for storage. The airfield itself is still operational, and an RAF unit still operates from it. This is the combined Southampton University Air Squadron and 3 Air Experience Flight, which flies the Grob Tutor aircraft. This unit trains university students to solo standard and provides flying opportunities for members of the Air Training Corps and Combined Cadet Force (RAF). For many Air Cadets their first flight in one of UAS/AEF trainers at Colerne is a thrilling experience and the start of a life-long interest or even a career in aviation; in this respect the former RAF Colerne still has a role to play in the future of aviation, and in doing so provides an important link to the past.

7
HIGH POST

National Grid Reference (184) SU145365

The aerodrome at High Post was founded by local businessman Mr. F. Dorian Webb and opened in May 1931 as the Wiltshire Light Aviation and Country Club. A hangar was built and a clubhouse completed in October. In 1936 a new building, designed by Salisbury architects Bothams and Brown, was constructed beside the main Salisbury-Amesbury road. This comprised offices, an observation tower, radio room and a fully-licensed hotel with a restaurant. It was a modern, stylish building that drew praise from the columns of *Aeroplane Magazine*. The Wiltshire School of Flying, which included the Wiltshire Flying Club, taught people to fly in its Piper Cubs at High Post, and the Royal Artillery Aero Club also flew from the aerodrome. Both clubs participated in the Government's Civil Air Guard (CAG) scheme (the aim of which was to encourage more civilians to qualify as pilots) and maintained CAG sections.

With the outbreak of war in September 1939, all unessential and unauthorised civil flying was stopped, and the aircraft at High Post were stored away in the hangar. All was quiet at the aerodrome until the first Service unit to be based at High Post arrived in June 1940. This was No.112 Squadron of the Royal Canadian Air Force, which was due to be equipped with Westland Lysanders in the Army Co-operation role. The unit was from the City of Winnipeg, and had arrived in Britain at the end of May. Initially sent to Old Sarum, it was decided to move the unit to High Post, where there was more room, before its aircraft arrived. The squadron's personnel set up a tented camp at the airfield. As this was at a time when an invasion was expected any day, following the fall of France, priority was given to the digging of defences and the camouflaging of the aerodrome buildings. The comfortable High Post Hotel was taken over as an Officers' Mess, and, having settled into their new base, the Canadians awaited the arrival of their aeroplanes. The squadron's first three Lysanders landed on 23 June. They were followed by three DH Tiger Moths for training and communications, and four more Lysanders. With a full complement of aircraft, No.112 Squadron started training. Their aircraft flew over Salisbury Plain, practising reconnaissance and artillery observation, and they took part in live shoots on the Larkhill Ranges. German raiders had been seen in the area, and although they were training, the squadron's aircraft were always armed and fully-crewed, particularly after an unarmed Hawker Hart Trainer from Netheravon was shot down by a German intruder on 21 July.

Several aircraft from the Special Duty Flight came to High Post in early August 1940 for towing trials with two Scott Viking sailplanes. The SD Flight was a special trials unit attached to the Air Ministry Research Establishment at Swanage in Dorset. It used a variety of aircraft in its work, and seems to have been particularly involved in radio, telecommunications and radar work. Unfortunately on 3 August an accident occurred when one of the Vikings crashed. Its wingtip had

Westland Lysanders were flown from High Post by 112 Squadron. (Aeroplane)

touched the ground when its pilot had been trying to avoid the other glider. In early September one of No.112 Squadron's Tiger Moths was involved in another crash, this time to the north-west of the airfield.

On 13 November 1940 No.112 squadron moved to RAF Digby in Lincolnshire. With the move of the Canadian squadron other units started to use High Post as a convenient training airfield. These included No.1 Flying Training School at Netheravon, with its Harts, Hinds, Harvards and Battles, and the Central Flying School at Upavon with Masters and Oxfords. They used High Post for navigation and aerodrome circuit training.

On 20 November the aircraft of the two High Post flying clubs were wheeled out of their hangar and taken to nearby Old Sarum, having been impressed by the Government for the war effort. The Piper Cubs of the Wiltshire School of Flying were flight-tested, then issued to D Flight, the Air Observation Post evaluation unit of No.1 School of Army Co-operation. They had been moved at this particular time to make room for the Supermarine Company, which needed the hangar for the assembly of Spitfire aircraft that were being manufactured down the hill in Salisbury.

The company took over the airfield in December 1940, and started to make use of the rudimentary facilities there. The main building was a hangar that was just large enough to take three Spitfires, although it was a tight fit. Sliding doors positioned at one end of the hangar were just big enough to permit the aircraft's propellers to clear at the top. One side of the hangar had a brick-built lean-to extension which housed toilets and other rooms converted into an armoury in which to store and secure the cannons and machine guns that were to be fitted into the aircraft. There was a canteen but this was over half a mile away across the airfield, almost at the boundary fence with the Wessex pyrotechnics factory that was situated next door to the airfield. The canteen was in the Flying Club's old wooden clubhouse. Though the facilities in the clubhouse were basic, the workers could always be assured of a blazing fire in the hearth and a warm meal, particularly on cold winter nights.

Soon the main assemblies started to arrive at High Post, having been produced in the Wilts and Dorset Bus Garage and several other garages and car showrooms in Salisbury, some of the sub-assemblies embodied in them having been manufactured in Trowbridge production units. The main assemblies were brought up from Salisbury by low-loader or 'Queen Mary' aircraft transporter trailers. To ease handling, the wings

80

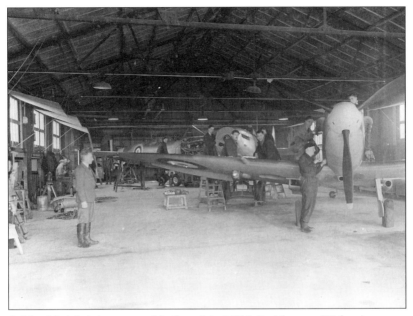

Spitfire Mark Is being prepared in the original High Post hangar. (Vickers)

were mounted on trolleys and the fuselages in cradles. They would be unloaded by hand on arrival at High Post, then moved into the main hangar. The wings were fitted to the fuselage by sheer muscle power, each one being lifted from its trolley onto the backs of a dozen or so men, who shuffled them into position beside the fuselage, which was on trestles, until the fixing attachments were aligned and the bolts were secured. Once both wings were in position the hydraulic pipes were joined to enable the undercarriage to be operated. With the wheels down and locked the men would get under the wings again, this time lifting the entire aircraft off its trestles and onto its undercarriage. The engine cowlings, fillets, guns, propeller and spinner would then be fitted. After a final touch-up of camouflage paint the aircraft would be ready for its initial engine run before its first test flight. In this way six Spitfires were completed per week at High Post with the staff working two and a half days of shifts on each aircraft.

During the engine running and in preparation for test flying a ground handling party would be made available. Their tasks included making any adjustments to the engine or airframe that may be required and lying over the aircraft's tail plane while the pilot ran up the engine to check its performance. Once it was ready for flying the aircraft

81

would be moved away from any buildings that might have a magnetic effect and the aircraft would be 'swung' to check its compass. Each aircraft was slightly different magnetically, and a compass deviation card would be completed for each one and placed in a holder in the cockpit so that the pilot could easily refer to it when calculating his compass reading. A final once-over by Supermarine's Inspector would be followed by a further check by the MAP Aircraft Inspection Department (AID) Inspector. Once both were happy the relevant documentation would be signed and the aircraft would be cleared for flight test. A test pilot would then take the aircraft up. Sometimes this would be an RAF pilot resting from operational flying, but more often than not it would be a company test pilot such as Jeffrey Quill. The test procedure would consist of a measured and smooth routine to examine the aircraft's flying qualities and characteristics, testing the performance of engine and airframe, rather than aerobatics or otherwise pushing the aircraft to the limit. Should any problems be found, the aircraft would be landed for rectification or adjustment before the programme went on. Once the aircraft had passed its checks and the test pilot was satisfied, he would sign a form to that effect and the AID Inspector would officially take the aircraft on charge. It would then be put to one side to await collection by a ferry pilot for delivery to a Maintenance Unit. The first completed Spitfire to fly from High Post was Mark I X4497, a photographic reconnaissance development aircraft, on 12 January 1941.

Cyril Russell was involved in the production of Spitfires at Woolston, Trowbridge and High Post and later wrote about his experiences. He particularly remembers being tasked with the production of components for Mark V Spitfires for Malta. A batch of aircraft were being prepared to be sent out by aircraft carrier, and had to meet a tight deadline. For 48 hours the High Post team worked straight through with minimal breaks – a valiant effort that met the target.

High Post continued to be used by locally-based training aircraft for landing and take-off practices or navigation exercises. The Supermarine staff did not seem to mind this as long as it did not impair their test flying programme. This did happen from time to time, however. On one occasion a heavy landing by a student pilot caused one undercarriage leg of his Oxford to collapse, but the errant pilot managed to bring the aircraft to a halt without causing too much damage or injury to the crew. The airfield had to be closed, however, while the aircraft was recovered. A much more serious accident occurred on the morning of 10 September 1943 when Lancaster BIII

JA894 of No.617 Squadron was flying circuits over Boscombe Down while carrying out low level runs to measure air speed indicator pressure errors. Unfortunately its fourth circuit coincided with the approach of Oxford EB981 from No.7 Flying Instructors School, Upavon, that was coming in to land at High Post. The aircraft collided and all six people aboard both aircraft were killed.

In March 1944 the Supermarine Flight Test Centre was moved to High Post from Worthy Down, near Winchester, to join the Salisbury area production flight test unit there. A new hangar had been built at High Post, along with offices and workshops to accommodate the Supermarine production and development test pilots and the technical staff. The main runway was extended to 2,500 yards in April 1944, and this then ran across the Upper Woodford-High Post road. The road was diverted into the fields around the end of the new runway, and the course of the original road was closed off by means of barriers made up of materials that included three scrap Hawker Tomtit fuselages (possibly remnants from the flying club).

The first formally-trained test pilot to join Supermarine at High Post was Lieutenant Pat Shea-Simonds, RNVR, who had attended No.1 Course of the Empire Test Pilots School along the road at Boscombe Down. After graduating from ETPS, and before joining the staff at High Post, Shea-Simonds was sent on attachment to the Fairey Company. There, while flying an Albacore biplane torpedo bomber, he had to force-land in unusual circumstances – the engine fell out! He managed to get the aircraft down in one piece, and when a replacement engine was fitted, he flew the Albacore out of the field and back to the factory. He was awarded the MBE for this feat.

As Chief Test Pilot, Jeffery Quill had between ten and twelve test pilots on his staff at High Post. As well as undertaking development flying on new variants and types such as the Spitfire Mark 21, the Spiteful and Seafang (the proposed replacements for the Spitfire and Seafire), the pilots test flew production aircraft at Keevil, Chattis Hill and South Marston as well as at High Post itself. The pilots flew out from High Post in a taxi aircraft (usually a Dominie) to the other airfields as required, returning to base later to write their reports for the unit's technical office, and to compare notes with one another. Personalities at High Post included Flight Lieutenant Andy Andrews, who was later shot down and killed in a Spifire XII; Flight Lieutenant Les Colqhoun, a Photographic Reconnaissance pilot; Squadron Leader Titch Havercroft, ex-ETPS instructor; Flight Lieutenant Geoffrey Page, a Battle of Britain pilot, Lieutenant Commander Mike Lithgow, RN, a graduate of the ETPS who later went on to become a Test Pilot after the war with Supermarine and de Havilland, and Lieutenant Frank Furlong, RNVR, who had been a well-known jockey before the war, and had won the Grand National in 1935.

The Wiltshire School of Flying had been re-established at High Post on 16 April 1946, and started flying Austers and a Magister. The Royal Artillery Flying Club also re-appeared at the airfield. However, due to the close proximity of Boscombe Down, which was expanding in size and traffic, Supermarine were already considering moving their activities to a quieter location. By this time, they were flying the final developments of the Spitfire, the Marks 22 and 24, which were powered by the ultimate version of the Rolls Royce Griffon. A jet-powered version of the Spitfire, known as the Attacker, was also flown from High Post. To accommodate this high level of activity, an alternative airfield was found by the company at Chilbolton, and they gradually moved their flight test operation across. The Supermarine Flight Test Centre at High Post was eventually closed on 31 May 1947. The two flying clubs decided that the airfield was untenable, and they too moved out in June 1947 to the well-established airfield at Thruxton. High Post airfield then closed.

Exterior of the flight test hangar at High Post. Several Marks of Spitfire can be seen, including Mark Vs, an HFIX, several PR19s and a Sea Otter. The hangar was moved to Boscombe Down after the war. (Vickers)

Aircraft inside the High Post flight test hangar include a Spitfire with contrarotating propellers, a Mk IX and a Seafire Mk XV. A couple of Sea Otters can be seen in the background. (Cambridge Collection)

Today there is little to show that there was an airfield at High Post, or that it played such an important part during the Second World War. The large hangar built for the Flight Test Centre in 1944 was moved to A&AEE Boscombe Down during the 1950s for the use of A Squadron, and is still in use there. The Upper Woodford-Highpost Road was re-opened after the war, but the diverted road still exists, and can be seen making its way across the fields. The High Post Hotel remains in place, and has been extended over the years. Today it is a popular Salisbury night-spot. The flying club hangar that was originally used for the assembly of Spitfires is also still in place. It was used by Stevens Tobacconists as a cigarette factory for several years after the war, and today, with offices built at one end, is still in use, with the Apsley Engineering Company.

8

HULLAVINGTON

National Grid Reference (173) ST900810, 5 miles N of Chippenham

Opened on 14 June 1937, the construction of RAF Hullavington had been started the previous year as one of the eleven stations around the country that made up the second phase of the RAF Expansion Scheme. Like many RAF stations, although located not far from a large town (Chippenham in this case, five miles to the south), it was named after the nearest village. Situated on flat farm land not far from the Fosse Way, the airfield lies to the north of the village of Stanton St Quintin and just south of the village of Hullavington, which itself is on the edge of the valley of the Gauze Brook, a tributary of the Wiltshire Avon.

With the expansion airfields it was realised that the requirement for a large number of domestic, technical and instructional buildings for similar purposes at a number of different stations could be simplified if a range of standard designs could be used. A simple Georgian style was chosen due to the fact that so many aerodromes were situated in rural locations. At Hullavington further refinements included the use of carefully selected bricks and roofing tiles characteristic of the region. To add to the effect Cotswold stone was specified to face the buildings. Hullavington was designed as a permanent flying training station, but almost as soon as building work had started, it was decided to expand the plans to include an Aircraft Storage Unit (ASU) to hold reserves of aeroplanes in order to back up the flying squadrons.

This policy was to apply to many stations of this phase of the Expansion Scheme as an economy measure, as it was found that by co-locating the ASUs with other units, common buildings and facilities such as messes and headquarters could be shared.

The first unit to arrive at the new base, on 10 July 1937, was No.9 Flying Training School (FTS), on transfer from RAF Thornaby on Teesside. This unit was equipped with the Hawker Hart, a graceful single-engine biplane originally designed as a two-seat light day bomber by Hawker's Chief Designer, Sydney Camm. A year later a second unit appeared. This was No.9 Maintenance Unit (MU), formed at Hullavington on 8 July 1938 as the resident ASU. By the time the war started nine ASUs were functioning around the country, and others were subsequently opened throughout the war. The task of the ASU MUs was to receive and store aircraft, either as new ones on delivery from the manufacturers, or on transfer from other units. They were then to equip, maintain, store and issue aircraft as appropriate in response to requests from the ASU HQ at No.41 Group. The units were designed to hold at least 400 aircraft each and an idea of the storage capacity of the airfield can be gained from the fact that it was provided with 28 hangars, most of which were in use by the ASU. Initially not many aircraft were in residence, so the MU hangars were used for the storage of MT vehicles. However, as more and more aircraft arrived on the unit space became a problem and they had to be stored in the open at the mercy of the elements. In February 1939 the unit was renumbered No.10 MU.

In the spring of 1939 the biplanes of No.9 FTS were supplemented by a more modern design when Avro Anson trainers arrived on issue to the school. This aircraft was originally designed as a twin-engined light passenger aircraft and was purchased by the RAF as a land-based coastal maritime reconnaissance aircraft. A trainer version was developed for the training of navigators, wireless operators and air gunners, and the design was later chosen as one of the main aircraft types for use in the Empire Air Training Scheme.

Squadron Leader M Llewellyn-Thomas recounted his experiences on what started off as a typical night flying exercise at No.9 FTS in 1939. He was to take off for a five-hour solo cross-country flight from Hullavington on a triangular route to Bath and Bristol before returning to base. Take off, he said was easy – he pushed the throttle of his Audax forward and accelerated down the flare path of kerosene lamps into the darkness. After circling the airfield he re-crossed it and checked his compass to ensure that he was flying on the correct heading. He gently climbed to 3,000 feet, flying at an airspeed of 120 knots. He reached Bath, recognising the City as a scattering of lights around a luminous core. However he noticed that there was no horizon, then realised that he was flying under solid cloud. He timed his turn for Bristol and had

Hawker Audaxes of 9 FTS take off from Hullavington in 1939. One of the school's Ansons can be seen in the background beside the partially-built hangar. (Aeroplane)

just set off on his pre-calculated course when it started to rain. The rain got heavier and soon a torrent of water swamped his windscreen and goggles, swirling around and drenching the pilot in his open cockpit. Looking down he could not see the ground. With the aircraft now being buffeted about and lightning starting to appear, he decided to abandon his course to Bristol and head back to Hullavington. He later checked his watch and calculated that he should have been somewhere near his base. However, now flying in low cloud he could not tell where he was. He started a square search flying five minutes per leg, but found nothing. Eventually letting down slowly through the murk he could still see nothing through the rain. Now flying on his reserve fuel tank (meaning that he had 15 minutes of flying time left), apparently at 1,200 feet, he suddenly realised that his altimeter was set at Hullavington's barometric pressure, and that he could be even lower. He fired his Holt's flare, an emergency lighting flare mounted under the port wing, to see if he could discern the ground. In the brilliant light he could see trees flashing past 100 feet below his wing-tip, so he quickly pulled the nose up to gain some height. With five minutes flying time left he was just contemplating baling out, when he saw a red light. It was an airfield identification light. He turned towards it and circled. After circling several times he could not make out the landing area, and there was no green flare from the control tower signifying that he had been seen and was authorised to land. Then he spotted car headlights! They were stationary and pointing along the grass. He did a split-S turn and side-slipped in to land along the headlight beams. He later found that he had arrived at Tern Hill in Shropshire, which had closed for the night. The headlights were from a car belonging to the Adjutant, who was just heading home when he heard the Audax circling, decided he was in trouble, and headed to the airfield to light the way home. The Adjutant gave the student pilot a lift to the Officers' Mess, for a hot bath and dinner!

The declaration of war brought mobilization of the services and the initiation of the various war plans. As it was felt that the bomber bases of East Anglia were vulnerable, many of the squadrons based there were withdrawn and redeployed to other bases. On 1 September 1939 ten Bristol Blenheims of No.114 Squadron arrived at Hullavington on dispersal from RAF Wyton in Huntingdonshire. Seven further Blenheims arrived six days later, this time from No.139 Squadron also at Wyton. This unit had mounted the first RAF operation of World War II over Germany a month earlier, when one of its aircraft flew on reconnaissance over the

German Baltic naval ports. Both squadrons stayed at Hullavington for a few weeks until it was realised that the Luftwaffe were not mounting widespread raids on the East Anglian bases, and they returned to RAF Wyton.

In the meantime, on 3 September, No.9 FTS had become re-designated No.9 Service Flying Training School (SFTS), a name change which reflected a change in role from the basic training to the intermediate training of aircrew. Airspeed Oxfords were added to the school's fleet. Training continued during the winter of 1939 but it was heavily affected by the weather, which was generally deteriorating, getting wetter and colder.

More and more aircraft were arriving at No.10 MU at this time. Space was becoming a problem, even in the open. Supplementary sites had been acquired for the MU, dispersed in the countryside around the main site, but even these were becoming full. Additional fields near the dispersed sites were requisitioned in an attempt to cope with this but these too were filling up towards the end of 1939. Security was an ever-present problem, with relatively few staff being available to guard the large numbers of aeroplanes scattered over such a large area.

As the winter of 1939/40 wore on the weather got worse and temperatures dropped. Flooding and subsequent freezing caused many difficulties for both the SFTS and the MU. Some personnel were still living in tents due to a shortage of accommodation at the station, and they suffered particular discomfort. Working conditions outside were hard, and flying was severely restricted. Many flying courses had to be extended and a backlog of students developed.

In spring 1940 invasion was a serious threat, with German forces only a few miles away across the English Channel and Luftwaffe units now based on French airfields within easy striking distance of Britain. Defensive measures all across the country were stepped up. On airfields such as Hullavington trenches and gun pits were dug and concrete pillboxes were constructed. Anti-aircraft defensive armament was installed, mainly in the form of Lewis machine guns, supplemen-ted with 20mm Hispano Cannons. On 14 May 1940 Training Command issued an Operational Order to Hullavington to convert a number of its Ansons and Audaxes to carry bombs for possible deployment as an anti-invasion force. Shortly after this, responsibility for the station changed. The rapid expansion of the RAF during this early war period led to Training Command being sub-divided into Flying Training Command and Technical Training Command with effect from 27 May 1940. Flying Training Command became responsible for the selection and training of all aircrew, and took over responsibility for RAF Hullavington.

The Germans made their presence felt at Hullavington the following month. During the night of 25 June, while night flying training was in progress, Luftwaffe raiders attacked the airfield. Five bombs were dropped, but they landed off the aerodrome without causing any damage. Air raid warnings were given throughout the area during July, with the result that the night flying programme was constantly interrupted. In an effort to catch up on night flying training Babdown Farm was actuated in July 1940. This airfield had been established as a Relief Landing Ground for Hullavington, being three miles west of Tetbury just across the county border in Gloucestershire. When night training was scheduled the aircraft were flown over from Hullavington to Babdown Farm late in the afternoon. At the end of the training session all personnel and aeroplanes returned to Hullavington, usually in the early hours of the morning. Babdown Farm was successfully used by RAF Hullavington in this way until the end of the war.

In supplementing airfield defence consideration had been given by the air staff to the camouflaging of aerodromes. A Camouflage Section was formed within the Directorate of Works at the Air Ministry to take this on. It was difficult to hide such a large installation, but the aim was to blend the aerodrome into its surroundings so that an enemy pilot was unable to recognise the aerodrome for what it was before he was almost past it. This made any attack difficult if not inaccurate. Techniques were developed to reduce the conspicuousness of buildings and roads, and to break up the airfield into a pattern more closely resembling the surrounding countryside. Buildings were painted in brown, black and green shadow shading, while bold division lines were painted on the roofs and sides of hangars to break up their outlines. The appearance of the landing grounds was disrupted by the marking of hedgerows in black bitumen to simulate field patterns. Hullavington was chosen as the site for many of these trials. The shine from concrete and tarmac surfaces was a problem, but this was toned down by the application of slag or stone chippings onto the surfaces. At Hullavington tests had been carried out in 1939 with another type of treatment, which was an open textured bituminous surface coating. This was such as success that it was adopted for all ASU hard-standings and dispersals and became known as 'the Hullavington System'.

In an attempt to protect the airfield and the local area against air attack, and to supplement the ground defences, an Air Defence Flight

A Hurricane Mk IIA and two Spitfire Mk IIs of ECFS on training sortie over Wiltshire in the autumn of 1942. (Aeroplane)

was formed in July 1940 with three Hawker Hurricane fighters supplied for the purpose. The Hurricanes were flown by instructors from 9 SFTS. It was rather unfortunate that the pilots had just landed their Hurricanes from a local air defence patrol on 14 August 1940 when a German raid came in on the airfield. Heinkel He111s dropped 16 bombs on the station, killing four airmen and wounding another ten. One of the hangars was badly damaged and a fuel bowser was hit on the airfield. The bowser exploded, badly damaging several Harts and two of the Hurricanes.

Despite the interruptions, the work of No.10 MU carried on throughout this period. Flying training also continued at Hullavington. More aircraft arrived for No.9 SFTS, either to update the types operated (such as the Miles Master), or as replacements for aircraft damaged in accidents. By February 1941 the school had 56 Masters and 16 Hurricanes on its books, the latter being flown by the more advanced pupils. Although the training was still interrupted by air raid warnings, only two raids were actually made on Hullavington during 1941. On 27 February an He111 appeared in the area on a low-level daylight raid. It headed straight for Hullavington then bombed and strafed the airfield. A Hurricane and Handley Page Hampden were damaged, but gunners on the ground returned fire, claiming three hits on the Heinkel before it flew off. German bombs were dropped on Hullavington again later in the year but this time not intentionally. A German aircraft was flying nearby, when it was picked up by an RAF night fighter. In his efforts to escape the German pilot jettisoned his bomb load. Hullavington happened to be beneath, but fortunately only slight damage was sustained by a few dispersed aircraft.

On 14 February 1942 No.9 SFTS was re-designated again, this time to No.9 (Pilot) Advanced Flying Unit ((P)AFU). This was to reflect another change in role for the unit, which was to provide advanced flying training to newly-qualified pilots arriving in the UK following training under the Empire Air Training Scheme. The main purpose of this training was to accustom these inexperienced pilots to European flying conditions, having been trained as they had in the sunshine and blue uncluttered skies of such places as Australia and South Africa.

A major event occurred at Hullavington in 1942 when a new unit was set up. This was the Empire Central Flying School (ECFS), and it came into being on 14 March. This new school was formed by Group Captain Down and many of his staff who had moved across from Upavon, following the closure of the Central Flying School there. The role of the ECFS was to pool the vast experience gained within the worldwide RAF flying training organisation and to achieve a standardisation of procedures. To achieve a commonality of approach the ECFS started training instructors who had been selected for staff positions at the Flying Schools. The ECFS consisted of several squadrons, which undertook other work apart from training. These included the Handling Squadron, which produced Pilots Notes (guidance on flying a particular aircraft) for every new type coming into service.

Students came from all over the world for courses at the ECFS, and Course No.1 included attendees from the USA, Canada, Australia, New Zealand and South Africa. Most of the flying training was on the Harvard and Oxford, but a variety of other types were also made available to each course. Visits were made to front-line squadrons, and the students sometimes flew on operational sorties! Subjects covered in the classroom ranged from navigation and engine management to signals and gunnery. Some of the students' most important work was in fact done on the ground, as they were often tasked with the writing of training instructions. Several *Air Publications*, such as the *Syllabus of*

Flying Training and the *Handbook of Advanced Training*, were based on input from ECFS student syndicates.

Because of the demands of the ECFS at Hullavington it was decided to move the (P)AFU flying operations to nearby Castle Combe in their entirety. In place of No.9 (P)AFU a new unit was formed at Hullavington on 1 August 1942. This was No.3 Flying Instructor's School (Advanced) (FIS(A)), which was equipped with Miles Magisters, Masters, Oxfords and Harvards. As its title indicates this unit was responsible for the advanced training of flying instructors. As with the (P)AFU the new unit's HQ Flight was located at Hullavington, but because of the presence of the ECFS, the majority of its flying took place from Castle Combe, where its aircraft were actually based.

The work of both No.10 MU and the ECFS continued without incident for the rest of the war time period. After July 1942 there were no more enemy raids and no more incidents to speak of. Towards the end of the war twenty-two MUs were in operation as ASUs including No.10 MU Hullavington, which by this time had become a long-term storage unit with over 1,000 aircraft of various types in store. When the hostilities finally came to an end it was the role of these units to deal with the vast numbers of aircraft they now had in store. Some aircraft were declared obsolete, and were dismantled and sent to one of the

Line up of aircraft from the ECFS in December 1943. From the front those that can be seen are a Hotspur, Mosquito, Typhoon, Spitfire, Proctor, Tarpon (Avenger), then Anson, Oxford, Tiger Moth, Lancaster, Magister, Wellington, Turbinlite Havoc, Mitchell, Master, Stirling. (Aeroplane)

'reduce-to-produce' plants that had been set up. The Air Ministry also required certain aircraft to be stored for possible future foreign sales, for civilianisation as transports for airlines or for sale to private owners and flying clubs.

During World War II the ECFS produced a great number of highly-qualified flying instructors who went on to have far-reaching effects on the flying training programmes of the Allied nations. It also revised and refined a number of theories on flying instruction that evolved into *Air Publication 3225 – the Instructors Handbook*, which became the bible of modern RAF flying training. The Pilots' Notes produced by the Handling Squadron enabled countless Allied pilots and units to make far more effective use of their aeroplanes. With the end of the war, economy became the watchword, and flying training units were closed down in wholesale fashion. The RAF wanted to retain the ECFS, but the Commonwealth air forces could no longer afford their contributions to keep it up. However, the school was not allowed to disappear. It was re-named the Empire Flying School in April 1946, and continued on for a few more years in this guise. Its main task was to introduce all-weather flying into the RAF, and it was able to base this activity on the important work undertaken by the Day/Night Development Unit of the ECFS during the war. The school remained at Hullavington until July 1949, when it was absorbed into the RAF Flying College at Manby.

In 1945, No.10 MU had over 1,000 aircraft in store. The end of the war meant that the vast majority of these would have to be disposed of. These included US aircraft which, under the terms of Land/Lease, were simply returned to the USA. However, there was a shortage of transport aircraft and the RAF were allowed to retain Dakotas for an indefinite period. A number of Harvards were similarly retained, and wheeled into store at No.10 MU.

Flying training continued at Hullavington for some years after the war. No.1 Air Navigation School moved in from Topcliffe shortly after the ECFS left, with Anson T21s and Vickers Wellington T10s, later replaced by Vickers Vallettas, Varsitys and Miles Marathons. The school stayed until July 1954, when it was disbanded due to the recommencement of navigator training in Canada, this time under a NATO scheme. In 1954, No.2 FTS arrived with Jet Provosts and this unit was replaced by the Air Electronics School, then No.2 ANS, both with Varsitys. Meanwhile, No.10 MU continued to store aircraft at Hullavington until December 1959, when it was closed down. When No.2 ANS left in 1965 active flying ceased at Hullavington. A number of non-flying units were then accommodated in turn there including

L-type hangar at Hullavington in 2002, with its turf covering still in place. (Author)

the NATO Codification Centre, the RAF Balloon Unit, the Parachute Support Unit and No.1 Parachute Training School. The last RAF unit to be based at Hullavington was No.4626 (County of Wiltshire) Aero Medical Evacuation Squadron, Royal Auxiliary Air Force. In October 1991 it was announced that under the MoD Options for Change Report, RAF Hullavington would close.

However, in 1993, No.9 Supply Regiment, Royal Logistic Corps, was looking for a home following its return from Germany. It was moved to Hullavington, where it made use of the former RAF accommodation and hangars. The regiment is still in residence at Hullavington, which means that this prime example of an RAF Expansion Scheme airfield has been saved from demolition and preserved for some time to come. The airfield itself is still serviceable, and is used regularly by visiting Army Air Corps helicopters and Hercules tactical transports from RAF Lyneham. In fact aeroplanes bearing the RAF roundel still fly from Hullavington. The aircraft are gliders of two Air Cadet units, Nos.621 and 625 Volunteer Gliding Schools. The schools provide glider training to the next generation, the cadets of the Air Training Corps, and in doing so, they maintain an important link between the past and the future of aviation at Hullavington.

9
KEEVIL

National Grid Reference (173) ST922571, 4 miles E of Trowbridge

RAF Keevil was planned in the early 1940s as a station for the training of fighter pilots. A site for the airfield was selected on agricultural land to the east of Trowbridge in north-west Wiltshire, to the south of the small village of Keevil and east of the larger village of Steeple Ashton. Land from several farms in the locality was requisitioned and work started on construction in mid 1941. As building took place the plans were revised because of a change in the RAF's training requirements and the aerodrome was actually completed for use by a bomber operational training unit. The airfield was therefore built to Class A (Bomber) Standard and was provided with three long wide runways aligned to cover the prevailing winds, the longest one being 6,000 feet in length. Fifty-one panhandle dispersals were built, each one leading off the perimeter tracks around the airfield.

In the event, when it opened on 15 July 1942 RAF Keevil found itself neither in Fighter Command nor Bomber Command but in Army Co-operation Command. Plans had changed once again, and the airfield was to be used in the build-up of airborne forces for a future assault on Europe. A small party of RAF personnel under the command of a Squadron Leader had arrived to open up the station and get the administration working. Ground defence was set up by No.4157 Anti-Aircraft Flight, RAF Regiment. To start with, however, Keevil was not needed for its newly assigned role, as airborne forces were still being built up at the time.

The main Keevil airfield had been provided with good aircraft storage facilities in the form of two T2 Hangars and nine Extra Over Blister Hangars. The usual operational and administrative buildings that an aerodrome needed were also provided and eventually domestic accommodation was also built, for 2,540 personnel.

It was not until September 1942 that the first operational units to use Keevil arrived. This was not as originally planned, as these units came from the US 8th Air Force! These first units were the 4th, 7th, 8th and 51st Troop Carrier Squadrons of the 62nd Troop Carrier Group (TCG), equipped with the Douglas C-47 Skytrain. The force had come to Britain to take part in Operation Torch, the invasion of North Africa, and shortly after its arrival at Keevil the 62nd TCG had become part of the US 12th Air Force, which had been newly formed for the operation. Intensive training with British and US paratroops took place over the next few weeks to prepare the group for its impending task. In early November 1942 the C-47s of the 62nd TCG left Keevil for Cornwall, which was to be their jumping off point for Gibraltar, the mounting base for the invasion. Operation Torch was a resounding success, and the 62nd TCG was to remain in the Mediterranean for the duration of the war.

It was not long before US aircraft reappeared at Keevil. Three weeks after the 62nd TCG departed for North Africa, the US 67th Observation Group (OG) took over Keevil as a satellite. This group was based at Membury, an airfield located just across the county border in Berkshire. They had several aircraft types on strength including Spitfire V aircraft transferred from the RAF, along with Douglas Havocs, Bostons and a few Piper L-4B Grasshopper light liaison aircraft. The 67th OG had been moved across the Atlantic to become the main tactical reconnaissance element of the US air forces being built up in the UK. Its role was to provide low-level armed visual and photographic reconnaissance in support of US ground forces. The main part of the group to use Keevil was the 153rd Observation Squadron (OS). More Havocs and Bostons arrived for the unit in the spring of 1943. These were fitted with cameras and the 153rd OS moved over to a predominantly photographic role. There followed a more active period of sorties over the French coast, with the squadron's Bostons, Havocs and Spitfires sometimes taking part in sweeps with other USAAF and RAF squadrons. At other times they would operate in pairs or as individuals, mainly in the combat photographic role, which involved flying at low level to capture the required images of targets at close range.

The new airfield at Keevil was seen as an ideal location from which to assemble and flight test the Spitfires that were being manufactured by the dispersed Supermarine production units in Trowbridge. All

Spitfire assemblies manufactured in the town were being sent to Salisbury for incorporation into aircraft assembled there. In the spring of 1943, the Ministry of Aircraft Production (MAP) started to build a purpose-built hangar at the Steeple Ashton end of Keevil airfield. This was to be used for the final assembly of the main components and the rigging of the airframes for flight. When it was completed in the summer, the hangar could accommodate a dozen Spitfires. Its double doors opened out onto a concrete taxiway that linked the site with the main airfield. On one outside wall of the hangar rooms were built to accommodate offices for the foreman, MAP Aircraft Inspection Department inspectors, Rolls-Royce representatives, and an armoury. A stores was built at the opposite end of the hangar to the main doors. A Coles crane enabled the assembly of the main airframe components. Good lighting and ventilation meant that the Keevil hangar was a pleasant place to work. A canteen and boiler house were also constructed, and off to one side, away from the effects of the metal hangar, was a compass-swinging platform.

Some forty experienced workers that went to work at Keevil when it opened in August 1943 were joined by just over one hundred other workers, sent there from all over the country under the Ministry of Labour's Directed Labour Scheme. Accents from Wales, the north of England and the West Country could be heard at Keevil, in addition to local ones.

Each aircraft would usually be given at least ten test flights to check out its basic handling, instrument readings and overall performance. Any shortcomings would be noted, and, if serious, the aircraft would immediately be brought back and 'snagged' for examination by the technicians. When each aircraft had been given a clean bill of health it would be put to one side to await collection and delivery to the RAF. The aircraft were moved around by pilots from the Air Transport Auxiliary who were often female (see Wroughton). They would fly the aircraft to one of the Maintenance Units to be officially taken on charge by the RAF. The first aircraft to be delivered from Keevil was Spitfire MK VIII JF900, on 21 August 1943.

With the build up of US forces in the UK, it was decided to officially transfer the running of Keevil over to the USAAF. An official handover ceremony was mounted at the station on 23 August 1943, attended by high ranking officers of the RAF and USAAF. A guard of honour and trumpeters were provided by RAF Andover for the occasion and a USAAF colour party and US Artillery Band from Devizes were also in attendance. Keevil became known to the Americans as Station 471.

A new US unit appeared at Keevil on 20 December 1943, when personnel of the 363rd Fighter Group started to arrive. However, towards the end of January 1944 the group started to move out of Keevil to its designated operation base at Rivenhall in Essex. The last elements moved out in early February.

It was shortly after this that a shuffle round of other 9th Air Force Units began, following a decision to move its fighter units nearer to the south coast. Following the departure of the 153rd Keevil was transferred back to the RAF. The official handover took place on 10 March 1944 at a parade of USAAF, RAF and Glider Pilot Regiment (GPR) personnel. Once again the RAF Ensign flew from the station's flagstaff and No.38 Group took over responsibility.

The shuffle-round of squadrons that caused the Americans to give up Keevil and No.38 Group to take over was prompted by the imminence of the invasion of Europe. The first RAF residents at Keevil were Nos.196 and 299 Squadrons, who flew their Short Stirling aircraft in on 14 March 1944 from Tarrant Rushton and Stoney Cross respectively. These squadrons were in the Airborne Forces support role and were accompanied to Keevil by Nos.1 and 2 (Horsa) Glider Servicing Echelons.

Soon after arrival at Keevil the two Stirling squadrons got to work. Training resumed immediately at their new base and on 18 March their first exercise took place when twenty-five Stirlings towing Horsa gliders flew down to the coast then cross country to Brize Norton. That same evening, Flying Officer Henry Hoysted, an Australian pilot with No.196 Squadron, and his crew undertook the RAF's first mission from Keevil. They made a supply drop to a group of the Special Operations Executive (SOE), set up by British Intelligence to undertake undercover work in support of the Resistance in Europe. This type of mission was to become regularly undertaken by the Keevil squadrons, and usually involved just one or two aircraft flying low across enemy territory to a pre-arranged Drop Zone (DZ).

Sergeant Bill Higgs, from Hilperton near Trowbridge, was a glider pilot based at Keevil at this time. He and his fellow pilots underwent gruelling training exercises during this time, in preparation for the invasion. 'It was practise, practise, practise,' he recalls, 'but we didn't know what for.' The keys to success in any glider operation were accuracy and timing. The aircraft should navigate with accuracy and arrive over the Landing Zone (LZ) at close intervals in order to capitalise on the element of surprise and concentrate their force into a specific area. This is what the training was all about, and competitions

Horsa gliders lined up at Keevil in preparation for the D-Day operation. (Aeroplane)

were often held to see who could spot-land the most accurately. A triangular area was marked out to resemble their LZ, which, although they did not know it at the time, was to be to the north-west of Caen in Normandy.

In addition to the exercises, the aircrews maintained their skills by flying cross-country navigational exercises. These took place all over southern England, although a popular route seems to have been to Cornwall, with Penzance and St Ives being frequently mentioned in RAF Keevil's Operations Record Book as 'targets'.

At the end of March the aircrews were given lectures in escape and evasion. This was because by now both squadrons were taking part in the occasional operation over occupied Europe during the build-up to D-Day. Over the next few weeks navigation training continued, along with paratroop and supply container dropping and glider towing practices. This included practising the marshalling and take-off of the tugs and gliders in the shortest possible time. Fighter affiliation training also took place, when the Stirlings' crews practised defence against attack by enemy aircraft. Such training had its risks with inevitable casualties. During April two Stirlings crashed, one crash resulting in the deaths of six RAF crew and twenty-nine paratroops.

On 1 June 1944 an unusual visiting aircraft came in, when an Avro York made an emergency landing at Keevil. It was discovered to be a VIP aircraft carrying three officers from the staff of General Smuts who were on their way to Northolt from Gibraltar. This was at a time when there was a buzz of excitement in the air as most people realised that something was about to happen. The Station Commander and the two Squadron Commanders, Wing Commander Alexander of No.196 Squadron and Wing Commander Davis of No.299 Squadron, were called to a conference at HQ 38 Group at Netheravon early on the morning of 2 June. On his return from the briefing later that day the Station Commander called together the Squadron Adjutants, Radar Officers, Intelligence and Armament Officers for their first briefing on Operation Overlord, the invasion of France. At 14:00 hours that afternoon a ban was imposed on movement outside the camp, forbidding the exit of any personnel on any pretext, on pain of being shot. The following day aircraft captains, navigators and bomb aimers were briefed on Operation Tonga, the British airborne element of Operation Overlord, which was to take place during the night of 4 June. On the evening of 3 June, all aircraft were applied with special markings – these 'D-Day' stripes were black and white, and were painted on wings and fuselages to identify them as being Allied aircraft.

Detailed briefings now began to take place. Accurate scale models of the Normandy Drop Zones (DZs) had been made, together with films that were made to simulate the flight and approach to the target. Bob Rose, now a retired Wiltshire Police Chief Inspector from Devizes, was a Staff Sergeant Glider Pilot based at Keevil at the time. He recalls how during his flight over to Normandy he felt that he had been there before. 'The film was just how it really looked. It was uncanny.'

Keevil's two Stirling squadrons were to be part of a much larger airlift by 38 Group to take paratroops of the 6th Airborne Division to the eastern banks of the River Orne. Nos.196 and 299 Squadrons were to drop their paratroops on DZ 'H', an area of approximately two and a half square miles running from Ouistreham and Caen. The troops' objective was to hold the two bridges across the River Orne and the Caen Canal, and protect the eastern flank of the main invasion force landing by sea. During the afternoon of 5 June, after a 24-hour delay due to bad weather, the troops of the 12th Battalion, 6th Airborne Division started to arrive at Keevil and were given their briefings. Final preparations were made as the paras checked their kit and the aircrews went through their procedures. The ground crews checked their 'kites' and ran up the engines in final tests. The scenes around the aircraft before take-off were memorable. Forty-six Stirlings were lined up in sequence at one end of the main runway and the troops were busily engaged in fitting their parachutes, helped by willing ground crews.

Stirlings are lined up on the runway at Keevil in the last minutes before take-off on Operation Overlord. (via H. R. Smith)

There was a tremendous spirit and enthusiasm, with the troops aching to get into action and put all their training into practice.

The first aircraft took off from Keevil at 23:19 hours on 5 June and it was followed by a further forty-five, the last one leaving at 23:59. They successfully dropped a total of 806 paratroops on the DZ near Caen. One unusual parachutist was Leonard Mosley, a *Daily Sketch* reporter, who dropped with the paratroops from 'C for Charlie' of No.299 Squadron, and who later wrote some despatches from the front line. The operation was not, however, without cost. One aircraft was lost from No.299 Squadron, and several other aircraft were hit by flak, although without serious damage. One aircraft from No.299 Squadron, Stirling IV EF267, named 'The Saint' by its crew, was piloted by Pilot Officer Den Hardwicke. He was to fly twenty-one troops of No.225 Parachute Field Ambulance to France together with nine equipment containers. Taking off from Keevil at 23:55 hours on the 5th, they were due over the DZ at 00:50 hours on the 6th. Despite flying through low cloud the pilot picked up a landmark on the French coast and was able to drop the troops and their equipment in the right place.

Having dropped their paratroops the Stirlings returned to Keevil in the early hours of 6 June. While the aircrews tried to get some sleep the ground crews worked hard to refuel, rearm, maintain and make running repairs to the aircraft. They were then lined up at one end of the runway ready for the next operation later that day to take more troops to Normandy. At 13:00 briefings took place for the second part of the airborne operations for D-Day. This was Operation Mallard, which involved taking the troops of 6th Airlanding Brigade as reinforcements to the beach-head, and to sustain the airborne troops already there holding the bridges over the River Orne and the Caen Canal.

The re-inforcements were to be carried in thirty-six gliders from Keevil, eighteen to be towed by No.196 Squadron and eighteen by No.299 Squadron. The troops of the 2nd Battalion, Oxfordshire and Buckinghamshire Light Infantry mounted up and shortly afterwards the force took off. This went well, with the exception of one glider which had to be cast off twice on the runway, due to imperfect trim. Another aircraft, flown by Flight Sergeant Rowell, had one engine fail after take-off. The rest of the stream, led by Wing Commander Davis (OC of No.299 Squadron) towing Captain Morrison flying the first glider, flew on towards the French coast at an altitude of 1,000 feet with fighter cover overhead provided by thirty squadrons of allied aircraft.

According to No.299 Squadron Operations Record Book, the spectacle on reaching the French coast was inspiring to a high degree. The coastline was bathed in early evening sunshine which enhanced the rich greens and yellows of the fields and the sombre grey of the old Norman villages. The ships of the enormous invasion fleet were lying just offshore, with landing craft plying between them and the beaches to disembark their loads of men and equipment. The Battleship HMS Warspite could clearly be seen bombarding German positions with its sixteen inch guns. The Stirlings flew inland and released their gliders at the appointed location, LZ 'W' west of the Caen Canal, at 21:30 hours. After dropping containers and tow ropes over the DZ nearby, they turned for the coast. According to one of the pilots the area looked like fairyland, with the gliders landing in quick succession as the multi-coloured parachutes carrying the containers wafted lazily to earth. However, this illusion was shattered by anti-aircraft fire coming up from isolated pockets of German resistance. Many Stirlings were damaged by these guns although at least one was put out of action by one of the Stirling gunners, Flight Lieutenant Ellis, who fired the four Browning guns from his tail turret in the leading aircraft flown by Wing Commander Davis. One of the Stirlings flown by Flying Officer Clarke of No.299 Squadron was, however, fatally hit and went down in flames, crashing into the sea close to the Warspite. The ground battle

Jeep being loaded aboard a Horsa Mk II. (via DGB)

had been a close thing for the British troops, as the Germans had the upper hand and were about to overrun the LZ when the reinforcements arrived in the nick of time. Although the area had been covered with 15-foot poles with wire stretched from one to the other, causing most of the gliders to crash land, there were few casualties. The reinforcements regrouped and, together with the remaining paratroops, pushed the Germans back.

After the excitement of D-Day operations, life at Keevil settled down to more of a routine. Regular operations continued throughout July and August in support of the SOE and the Special Air Service (SAS). On 20 July twenty-four aircraft took off on special operations to drop SOE and SAS personnel and equipment. Twelve people were dropped by each aircraft. Another big operation took place on the night of the 5 August when 34 Stirlings took off for Eastern France carrying troops and supplies in support of SOE and SAS missions. Unfortunately on this occasion two aircraft were lost, both being shot down near Aunay, between Baden and Vannes, probably by enemy fighters, who were seen in the area.

More aircraft arrived at Keevil from Maintenance Units during August to make up for losses, and more gliders arrived as part of the build-up for the next major operation – Market Garden, the attack through Holland to Arnhem. Soon the airfield was covered in aeroplanes, with over 50 Stirlings and 130 gliders present in early

September. The object of Operation Market Garden was for British and US airborne forces to secure the bridges over the Lower Rhine and River Waal, to enable an armoured thrust to be made across the bridges into Germany. Almost 12,000 men of the 1st Airborne Division and the Polish Independent Brigade Group, together with various attached units, were to be taken by the British element of the transport force. This was to be a maximum effort by No.38 Group to get as many aircraft as possible up in the air to take part. Six Stirling squadrons from the Group, including Nos.196 and 299 Squadrons, along with hundreds more Allied transport aircraft, were to take part. Both of the Keevil squadrons were to tow Horsa gliders, with No.196 Squadron flying 23 Stirling/Horsa combinations, and No.299 Squadron flying 25.

The date was set for 17 September 1944. Take-offs started at 10:30 hours, and as the aeroplanes struggled into the sky local people came out to watch the aircraft depart. Someone said that St.Mary's Church in Keevil village seemed like Eros in Piccadilly Circus as the dozens of aircraft flew over. Soon all 48 combinations were airborne and heading for the Netherlands. Opposition was light as the Stirlings approached their LZs, there being little AA fire from the ground. Those few German aircraft that were in the air were kept well away from them by the massive Allied fighter escort. All of Keevil's aircraft returned safely, the operation having taken just over four and a half hours for each crew.

The next day (the 18th) saw more action, as a re-supply operation was mounted. The Keevil squadrons put up 22 Stirling/Horsa combinations each. Once again the flight across was mostly uneventful. Opposition from the ground was heavier on this day, and although none of the Stirlings were shot down, over 30 were damaged by flak.

The third day, September 19, saw more determined German resistance. This time the tugs were to release their gliders over one LZ, and the re-supply aircraft were to drop their containers in another area, on a DZ one and a half miles away. Because of the increased level of ground fire the force was routed in a different way to avoid sending the aircraft over enemy territory. Nevertheless some flak was experienced on the route in and, flying along the corridor at low level, several Stirlings and Dakotas were shot down. Ground fire intensified as the aircraft got closer to the landing areas. The Stirling pilots had been briefed to fly in vics of three, at a height of 500 feet, in order to concentrate the supply drops. With murderous flak now coming up at them a number of aircraft received heavy damage.

As the pilots pressed on towards the designated DZs, they flew over ground markings made by the airborne troops showing where they wanted the supplies to be dropped. However, the aircrews were under strict instructions to ignore any such markings, as they were assumed to be spurious ones made by the Germans to misdirect the drop. What the RAF crews did not know, of course, because the airborne forces radios were not working, was that the designated DZs were now held by the Germans. A total of thirteen Stirlings were lost that day, including three from No.299 Squadron (one flown by the CO, Wing Commander Davis), and one from No.196 Squadron. Virtually all of the supplies dropped at such high cost fell straight into enemy hands.

On the 20th another re-supply drop was mounted, with seventeen aircraft from No.196 Squadron and 16 aircraft from No.299 Squadron taking part. By this time it was realised that the DZs had been overrun. Corrections were made and on this day all of the containers dropped reached the airborne troops, who were by now in desperate need of them. The flak was again heavy, and several aircraft were lost to German fighters.

Re-supply missions to the Arnhem bridgehead continued for the rest of the following week. Eventually it was realised that the British paratroops were in an untenable position and their withdrawal back across the Rhine was ordered. This was achieved on the night of 25 September. In the operation to re-supply 1st Airborne Division, the RAF lost 44 Stirlings with 105 aircrew killed. No.196 Squadron lost eleven Stirlings on these sorties, and No.299 Squadron lost fifteen.

In late September 1944 it was announced that Nos.196 and 299 Squadrons, together with the Servicing Wing, were to move to Wethersfield in Essex, which had just been handed back to the RAF by the 416th Bombardment Group of the USAAF. Many bases in eastern England had become available with the move of USAAF Units to the Continent, and by moving to the east transit times to the European mainland for the RAF squadrons would be reduced. The move started in early October. Due to the lack of available road transport the bulk of the technical equipment was packed into gliders to be flown to their new base. The two Stirling squadrons took it in turn to fly 55 glider loads to Wethersfield. The last operational sorties from Keevil were made by the Stirlings of 299 Squadron on the night of 6/7 October, when supply drops were made to the SOE on five separate targets. The Operations Watch closed at Keevil on the morning of 9 October as the last Stirling left. For their magnificent efforts in supplying the French resistance with arms, ammunition and

Spitfire PR XIs outside the Flight Test hangar at Keevil. (Vickers)

supplies the crews of Nos.196 and 299 Squadrons were later awarded the Croix de Guerre by the Free French Government.

Keevil was transferred to No.23 Group, but the theme of airborne operations remained. The next unit to take up residence was No.22 Heavy Glider Conversion Unit (HGCU), which was formed at Keevil on 20 October 1944. A satellite of the unit was established at RAF Fairford in Gloucestershire. No.22 HGCU was equipped with 46 Horsa and Hadrian Gliders together with 58 Albermarle Tugs. Its role was to give newly-qualified glider pilots conversion training onto heavier troop- and equipment-carrying transport gliders, and to keep them current on the types. This was to maintain the supply of replacement pilots to the front-line squadrons. The station was busy with the training of glider pilots throughout the rest of 1944 and well into 1945. In March 1945 the control of Keevil and No.22 HGCU were returned to No.38 Group. However, No.38 Group's need for the airfield ceased a few months later, when in June 1945 it transferred the HGCU to Blakehill Farm.

Spitfires had been in evidence at Keevil throughout its existence, as the flight testing of those aeroplanes manufactured at local factories had continued throughout the period. Some 600 Spitfires of various marks were assembled and flight-tested at Keevil.

Keevil Spitfires took part in fighter sweeps over occupied Europe, saw action in North Africa and Malta, and flew on operations in the Far East. Some saw post war combat in the Middle East. There are at least eight Keevil-built Spitfires still in existence, four of them airworthy. Several of them are still in the UK, the others being in the USA, Australia, Germany, Thailand and India. Four Keevil Spitfires were discovered in India in the 1970s, having been disposed of by the Indian Air Force and dumped on forgotten airstrips. Fortunately the sites were so remote that the aircraft escaped the attentions of the scrap dealers. The aircraft were recovered and have all since been restored, some to flying condition.

With the end of the war in Europe came a run-down in aircraft production, but work at the Spitfire facilities at Keevil carried on into 1947. As well as aircraft manufactured locally in Trowbridge, Keevil also received Spitfires from the Supermarine factory at South Marston. These were Mark 22s, and were transferred to Keevil for modification to Mark 24 standard, the last mark of the Spitfire. However, the last of the Mark 24s saw the end of Spitfire work and the Keevil works were no longer needed. The MAP site was finally closed on 30 January 1948 and the land returned to the owners from whom it had been requisitioned. The buildings that had been constructed, including the flight test hangar, were handed over with the land.

However, other Spitfires were to appear at Keevil. When No.22 HGCU moved out in June 1945, it was replaced by No.61 Operational Training Unit (OTU), which came in from Rednal, Shropshire. This was a fighter pilot training unit, flying Spitfire Vs and Mustangs, the latter later being replaced by the Spitfire LFXVI. The unit also had Harvards, Martinets and Tiger Moths on strength. The arrival of the OTU meant that operational Spitfires appeared in the circuit at Keevil for the first time since the departure of the US 153rd TRS in March 1944. No.61 OTU was to become the longest serving unit at Keevil, for it was to remain until September 1947, providing conversion training for newly-qualified pilots, and enabling them to make the step from advanced trainer to fighter. Re-titled in July 1947 as No.203 Advanced Flying School (AFS) it also proved to be the last flying unit to be based at Keevil as, when it moved to Chivenor in Devon a couple of months later, No.203 AFS was not replaced.

Keevil airfield was put onto Care and Maintenance following the departure of No.203 AFS, and some of the outlying domestic sites were sold off. In December 1955 the airfield was transferred to the United States Air Force for use by the 3rd Air Force as a standby base, and later as a reserve airfield for training use by US Airborne Forces. Keevil was handed back by the Americans to the Air Ministry in 1964. Since that time it has continued to be used for military training by the Services, and the airfield is still retained by the Ministry of Defence today. Keevil airfield itself remains much as it was at the end of the war, although many of the buildings have since gone. Some do remain, however, including two of the T2 hangars, which are still in use. Frequent visitors are the Hercules transports from nearby RAF Lyneham, which uses Keevil for tactical training and exercises. Flying also takes place at the week-ends, when the pilots of the Bath and Wiltshire Gliding Club can be seen intensively flying training circuits, or leisurely soaring in the blue summer skies, thus forming a tangible link with Keevil's past.

10
LARKHILL

National Grid Reference (184) 120450, 3 miles W of Amesbury

For many people the name of Larkhill conjures up visions of the pioneering days of British aviation. This Wiltshire airfield in fact goes back to the earliest days of flying in the UK and it became the first military airfield in the country. However, Larkhill is a difficult site to pinpoint as aircraft have flown from several different and general locations in the area, all using the same name.

The first flying at Larkhill was by balloon. Balloons had been flown operationally by the British Army since 1885 in the Sudan, and the Royal Engineers Balloon Section had been set up at Aldershot in Hampshire. The importance of balloons for observation was seen during the Boer War, when three balloon sections were deployed. After that war balloon courses were started on Salisbury Plain for officers of all arms, particularly gunners.

The first powered aircraft to fly in Britain was actually financed by the War Office. It was built at Farnborough, by the famous aeronautical pioneer, Samuel Cody, and named British Army Aeroplane No 1. The aeroplane first flew on 16 October 1908 from Laffans Plain, Farnborough, not far from the Headquarters of the Royal Engineers' Balloon Company. The main runway of the Royal Aircraft Establishment, Farnborough was later built on the spot of Cody's first flight. However, the flight did not lead to the widespread use of military aircraft by the army, and it was left to individual officers to follow their interests in flying and to develop this new activity.

Horatio Barber, one of the first flying enthusiasts in Britain, rented a site at Larkhill in June 1909. On this land he built a shed in which to keep his aeroplane. Located near the junction of Tombs Road with the

Packway, this was to lead to a series of events that would result in the formation of the Royal Flying Corps. Next to Barber's shed the War Office built another for the use of the Hon. C.S. Rolls (of Rolls-Royce fame) in the flying instruction of Army pilots. However, Charles Rolls was tragically killed in a flying accident on 11 July 1910. The shed was instead hired out to Captain J.D.B. Fulton, Royal Field Artillery, who used it to stable his Bleriot monoplane. Captain Fulton was one of the leading pilots at the time, and later went on to become an Instructor at the Central Flying School at Upavon. Another early aviation pioneer, G.B. Cockburn, based himself at Larkhill, renting another aeroplane shed near the others.

More buildings followed on the site, for the Army and the Navy. In June 1910 the British and Colonial Aeroplane Company (later to become the Bristol Aeroplane Company) leased 2,284 acres of land from the War Office to establish an airfield at Larkhill. They constructed two hangars in which aircraft such as the Bristol Boxkite could be built and also established a flying school there, where army and navy personnel were taught to fly. To qualify for their Royal Aero Club Flying Certificate each had to undertake three circular three-mile flights. The first to be issued by the Larkhill school was Certificate No.32, to J.J. Hammond on 22 November 1910. Until the Central Flying School opened at Upavon on 17 August 1912, the two Bristol schools (the company had another school at Brooklands) were practically the only military flying schools in Britain.

The British army was gradually getting round to the idea of taking aviation seriously and on 1 April 1911 the Air Battalion Royal Engineers was formed, with its HQ and No.1 Company (responsible for balloons, airships and kites) at Farnborough and No.2 Company (concerned with aeroplanes) at Larkhill under Captain Fulton. The first army trials in aerial reconnaissance followed shortly afterwards when Captain Bertram Dickson of the Air Battalion flew his Bristol Boxkite from Larkhill to observe manoeuvres on Salisbury Plain. The War Office soon announced a scheme whereby army officers were at liberty to train as pilots at civilian schools at their own expense, and after they received their Flying Certificate they would be granted £75 and posted to the Air Battalion. This was probably the first British military aircrew selection system!

A study into the future of military aviation in Britain resulted in the formation of the Royal Flying Corps (RFC) on 13 May 1912. This consisted of a Military Wing, a Naval Wing, a Central Flying School, a Reserve and an aircraft factory (to be known as the Royal Aircraft

Bristol Boxkite operated by the Bristol Flying School at Larkhill. (Aeroplane)

Factory). The Air Battalion was replaced, and No.1 Company (airships and balloons) became No.1 Squadron RFC at Farnborough while No.2 Company (Aeroplanes) became No.3 Squadron RFC at Larkhill. No.2 Squadron was formed to hold the Reserve Pilots at Farnborough.

On 5 July 1912 two members of the newly-formed Corps, Captain E.P. Lorraine and Staff Sgt R.H.V. Wilson, were killed when their 70-hp Gnome Engine Nieuport Monoplane side-slipped out of control and crashed close to the cross roads on the Stonehenge-Shrewton Road. This was the first fatal air accident on Salisbury Plain. A memorial stone was erected in the crew's honour, and the spot is still today referred to as Airman's Cross. Just over a year later, on 13 July 1913, Major Alexander Hewetson of the Royal Field Artillery was killed when his Bristol Monoplane crashed on the airfield at Larkhill during the test for his Aviator's Certificate. A stone was placed at the spot where he crashed, and a stone cross was later erected beside the Stonehenge-Shrewton Road. The two monuments can be seen today less than a mile away from each other.

To equip its new corps the War Office decided to hold a competition to find a suitable aeroplane design. This was held at Larkhill during the summer of 1912, a dozen temporary hangars being built to house the contestants. Twenty-one competitors entered a total of thirty-two aeroplanes in what was to become known as the Larkhill Trials. A panel of judges was formed, who would be looking at a number of requirements such as take-off and landing performance, payload and endurance. To be eligible to participate in the various tests, aircraft had to be at Larkhill by 31 July 1912. However, eight of the aeroplanes entered never actually reached Larkhill to start with! Nonetheless the trials took place over the next few weeks, during which time some of the contestants crashed or sustained damage to their aircraft in accidents. The eventual winner of the trials was declared to be the Cody Biplane, although many considered that the prize should have gone to the Royal Aircraft Factory BE2A, which had been banned from the competition because it had been produced by the Royal Aircraft Factory (it had been designed by one of the factory's engineers by the name of Geoffrey de Havilland). After the trials the War Office purchased two Cody Biplanes and five other competing aircraft – a Bleriot, two Deperdussins and two Bristol Monoplanes. The following year it purchased thirty-five BE2As!

During the period of the competition No.3 Squadron moved to Upavon, and on its return to Larkhill at the end of August the officers were accommodated in The Bustard Inn and the men at Bulford Camp.

With the development of Upavon and Netheravon nearby, Army aviation activity started to tail off at Larkhill. No.3 Squadron moved to Netheravon in June 1913, and although the Bristol Flying School continued to use the airfield for another year, they too moved on 2 June 1914, to Brooklands. Larkhill airfield was then closed. When war started later that year work began on building two hutted camps in the area, and soon hundreds of corrugated iron huts covered the former airfield as the barracks expanded. During its existence at Larkhill, the Bristol Flying School had taught 127 pilots to fly. Out of the total of 664 pilots that had been trained in Britain by the outbreak of the Great War, almost half of them had been trained by the two Bristol schools. The one concern that had done more than any other to promote the early development of British aviation was the British and Colonial Aeroplane Company, later the Bristol Aeroplane Company, with its schools at Larkhill and Brooklands. The closure of the airfield at Larkhill did not mean the end of flying training by the Bristol Company in Wiltshire. They returned to the county in 1936 to set up another flying school (see *Yatesbury*).

During the inter-war years aircraft using Salisbury Plain were based at Upavon, Netheravon or Old Sarum. Those taking part in army exercises usually flew from Old Sarum. During the late 1920s and early 1930s some aeroplanes used parts of the plain for field training experience, and increasingly they tended to use stretches of Knighton Down, north of Larkhill Camp. Several units used the area, including Nos.2, 4, 13 and 16 Squadrons. These were all Army Co-operation squadrons, initially flying the Bristol F2B, then the Armstrong Whitworth Atlas and later the Hawker Audax. From January 1936 the main site at Knighton Down became known as RAF Larkhill.

With the start of the Second World War, training on Salisbury Plain increased and Knighton Down became popular as an aircraft operating area. On 2 June 1940 the airfield received its first permanent residents when D Flight arrived. The flight was part of No.1 School of Army Co-operation at Old Sarum, and had been formed the previous February under Captain Henry Bazeley, Royal Artillery. It flew a variety of aircraft to investigate the use of the light aeroplane in army co-operation. The particular role of the unit was to develop the Air Observation Post (AOP) concept, where light aircraft could operate near the front to provide reconnaissance for field commanders and spot for the guns of the Royal Artillery. D Flight had gone to France earlier, during the summer of 1940, to trial the AOP concept in realistic conditions. Although they did not actually see combat, the personnel of the unit did learn some useful lessons. The flight returned to Old Sarum on 20 May 1940. From there it moved the majority of its activities to Larkhill a couple of weeks later.

The flight was accommodated in huts at the nearby School of Artillery and from Larkhill it continued to develop the methods and techniques of using AOP aircraft.

D Flight flew a variety of types, relying on aeroplanes that were requisitioned (or 'impressed') from their civilian owners. These included the Piper Cub, Stinson Voyager, and Taylorcraft D – all American designs. It was the Taylorcraft that was to prove the most effective and later the design was manufactured in Britain as the Auster and modified to meet the army's requirements. The Taylorcraft C and D were designed by the Taylorcraft Aviation Company in the US, and manufactured under licence from November 1938 onwards by Taylor-craft Aeroplanes (England) Ltd at Thurmaston in Leicestershire. The first aircraft were typical of those that were to follow – a braced high wing monoplane with fixed undercarriage, having a wing of composite wood and metal construction and a fuselage of welded steel tube. The whole airframe was covered in fabric. Seating was provided for two people (a third seat was provided in later models). The original engine of the model C (later to be known at the Plus C) was 55-hp Lycoming engine. The only difference between the Plus C and Plus D was the

Auster AOP Mk III shows off its low-level performance. (Aeroplane)

engine – the latter had a 90-hp Cirrus Minor 1 engine. Both versions became known as the Auster Mark I in British service. The initial twenty Austers for the AOP squadrons were impressed civilian aircraft, but these were followed in service by new production aeroplanes. Other than the addition of split trailing edge flaps to improve short field performance and later the fitting of DH Gypsy Major engines, the basic Auster design was to remain unchanged throughout the wartime period. Total production between 1939 and 1945 numbered over 1,600 aircraft.

General Browning held a conference of Artillery Commanders at Larkhill in June 1940 to discuss the lessons learned from the recent campaign in France. At the Conference Captain Beasley pressed the case for the AOP concept. They had to move on from basic Army Co-operation he felt – reconnaissance aircraft either had to be fast enough and well armed to be able to get the information they required and fight off opposition, or be smaller and slower to be able to see more detail of a particular area, and to avoid opposition rather than fight it off. Although the Lysander was a good design it was too slow and lightly armed to fight off determined opposition and too big to avoid detection, he said. As it turned out, the RAF went on from the straightforward Army Co-operation aircraft to the single-seat fighter for tactical reconnaissance, which was complemented by the army's AOP concept. Both approaches were to prove successful.

Work continued at Larkhill to develop AOP tactics and methods. A useful device produced during the summer of 1940 was the Merton Gridded Photograph. Devised by John Merton, a Royal Engineers Camouflage Officer, these were photographs produced in such a way that they were striated with vertical lines relating accurately to the map. These impressed the School of Artillery, and two Lysanders were provided by Army Co-operation Command, together with cameras, to establish a photographic research section at Larkhill. This later became the Army Photographic Research Branch, which subsequently carried out good work for all three services and the US Army.

Activities at Larkhill carried on throughout the summer of 1940 and into the next year with training, Radio/Telegraphy experiments, photography, anti-invasion exercises and co-operation with field medium artillery regiments. Motorcycles were devised as one of the most effective methods of movement and communications on the ground between AOP units and the HQs. Courses were run at Larkhill for Air Liaison Officers and Gunnery Officers in the role of the AOP squadrons and the use of gridded photographs. Great interest was

Piper Cub, as flown by 1424 Flight from Larkhill. (Author)

shown in D Flight by the US Military Attache, Col Bryan Conrad, who took copious notes on his visits as the US Army were trying to develop an AOP capability of their own. Other visitors included General Sir Robert Haining, the Deputy Chief of the Imperial General Staff, Lord Milne, the Master Gunner, and Marshal of the Royal Air Force, Lord Trenchard. By the summer of 1941 sufficient numbers of trained personnel were available from D Flight to form the first AOP squadron, and this came into being as No.651 Squadron on 1 August 1941. The squadron was actually formed at Old Sarum, although there was a lot of activity at Larkhill in connection with the unit's formation. Both No.651 squadron and D Flight took part in Exercise Bumper during the autumn of 1941. This was the largest exercise ever undertaken in Britain up until that time. Centred on Salisbury Plain it was under the command of General Montgomery. The AOP units acquitted themselves well, and following the exercise it was decided to form more AOP squadrons.

On 20 September 1941 D Flight was re-designated as No.1424 (AOP) Flight. It continued with the development of AOP work and also concentrated on the training of more AOP pilots to man the planned new squadrons. Among the activities looked at was that of observing for the guns of Royal Navy warships during assault landings or during a land advance along a coastline. Personnel of the unit also liaised with the Combined Training Centre that was training Commando and other

119

units of the three services in amphibious warfare at Largs in Scotland. Part of No.1424 Flight's task was to look out for new aircraft types that might be suitable for the AOP role. As well as the Cubs, Taylorcrafts and Lysanders, they also had DH Tiger Moths and Avro Tutors. To these were added at some stage at least one Douglas Havoc and a Handley Page Hampden.

The Stinson Vigilant, another US design, was seen as a promising AOP type for the army and one hundred were ordered by the Air Ministry. However, when the first one turned up at Larkhill following trials at A&AEE Boscombe Down, it was found to be too big and unwieldy. Although it had a very good take-off and landing performance this was because of its large wing area, which resulted in the aircraft being too big and difficult to conceal. Fifteen Vigilants were subsequently issued to No.651 Squadron at Old Sarum where they formed a Combined Operations Flight. Their size limited their usefulness for AOP work and the wider availability of the Auster made the Vigilant superfluous. One aircraft that was considered by the unit to be suitable was the Miles M38 Messenger. This single-engined triple-finned low wing monoplane was built by the company at the request of the army, specifically for AOP work. It had a spacious cabin, good performance and an excellent short-field capability. However, the aircraft was never ordered into production for the AOP squadrons, probably because the manufacturer was also building Magister and Master trainers at the time, which would have been seen as a higher priority for the war effort. Nonetheless, a few Messengers were later used in the communications role, including one that was Field Marshal Montgomery's personal transport.

On 1 October 1942 No.1424 Flight was disbanded and reformed as No.43 Operational Training Unit. This was to reflect the Unit's role, which had become more one of training pilots for the AOP squadrons. At the time of its formation the OTU had thirty-two aircraft on strength, mainly Austers and Tiger Moths. It had a mixture of flying instructors, with ten coming from the Army and three from the RAF. In November it was decided to move No.43 OTU to Old Sarum in order for them to be nearer to the AOP squadrons that were forming.

The airfield at Larkhill was handed over to the army following the departure of No.43 OTU. For the remainder of the war the airfield was little used, as AOP aircraft could land on any clear stretch of ground on Salisbury Plain. The odd Auster did drop into Larkhill over the next few years, but for exercises the AOP units tended to use unprepared fields as part of their training.

Following the end of the war helicopters gradually took over from the Austers in the AOP squadrons, and their need for prepared airfields was even less than that of the Austers. The Larkhill airfield at Knighton Down was at a convenient location for access to the School of Artillery, and it was used by the Sioux helicopters of various Royal Artillery Regiments while acting as support units for the school during the 1960s and 1970s.

Today there is no recognised airfield at Larkhill, but it remains as a general helicopter operating area for aircraft visiting the School of Artillery or exercising in the area. There is a marked airstrip that is used for exercises and displays that take place near the school, and fixed wing aircraft can still be seen landing at Larkhill, in the form of Hercules transports from RAF Lyneham.

Little remains today to show the important part that Larkhill has played in Britain's aviation history. The buildings constructed for the Bristol Flying School still stand in Wood Road, Larkhill Camp. They are today used as stores buildings but remain almost certainly the oldest aeronautical buildings in Britain. A plaque fixed to a stone nearby states that this was the site of the first military airfield in the country.

II
LYNEHAM

National Grid Reference (173) SU005785, 8 miles SW of Swindon, off the A420

Located to the south-west of Swindon, RAF Lyneham is situated on the edge of a plateau overlooking the valley of the Wiltshire Avon. The village of Bradenstoke is just to the north of the airfield, and that of Lyneham is alongside it to the east. Still very much an active RAF Station, Lyneham is unusual among today's front-line RAF bases in that it was not one of those opened or modernised during the 1930s Expansion Programme. The site was, however, surveyed in the 1930s and its potential was noted at the time. The area offered a large area of flat ground that was sparsely-populated, but was also close to good lines of communication. In due course, following the Munich Crisis of 1938, the land was requisitioned, and construction work began almost immediately. The layout of the buildings at Lyneham is distinctly non-standard for an operational station; this is because it was laid out as a Maintenance Unit (MU). The main complex is a central group of four hangars with associated supporting facilities placed around them. A further four groups of hangars were dispersed around the perimeter of the airfield, which was laid out on grass.

RAF Lyneham was opened on 13 February 1940, and on 18 May the first unit was formed. This was No.33 MU, established as an Aircraft Storage Unit (ASU) under the command of No.41 Group, Maintenance Command, which had its HQ at Andover. No.33 MU was responsible for the reception, storage, servicing and modification of aircraft. Initially these came on delivery from the manufacturers, but later came from other MUs or operational squadrons. The first aeroplanes to arrive were Bristol Blenheim and Vickers Wellington bombers, Percival

Proctor and DH Tiger Moth trainers and Westland Lysander Army Co-operation aircraft. Having been delivered from the production factories, the aircraft were inspected, then kitted out with whatever service equipment was not installed by the manufacturers but was required for the aircraft to undertake its role. For training aircraft this may only have been a first aid kit and flare gun, but for combat types it would also have included such items as machine-guns, radios and bomb sights. By early September over 150 new aircraft of various types were in stock at No.33 MU.

Throughout the summer of 1940 Luftwaffe bombers ranged over southern Britain, dropping bombs and attacking ground targets. Airfields were on their list of targets, and Lyneham suffered three raids during the period of the war. The first of these was on 10 September 1940, when a single German aircraft attacked the airfield with its machine-guns. There were no casualties. The second was on 19 September 1940, when a Heinkel He111 bomber attacked the airfield and dropped two high-explosive bombs on one of the central hangars. The one that they chose was still under construction at the time, and four workmen were killed. Probably as a consequence of the damage inflicted that day, the hangar was never completed to its full length, and today, as the Air Cargo Hangar (J4), it is considerably shorter than the other hangars. The last attack on Lyneham was in the early hours of 15 March 1941, and again involved a single aircraft. Four bombs were dropped, and the raider fired its machine-guns. There were no casualties this time, but two aircraft were damaged.

No.33 MU continued to build up its stocks, and these later included Bristol Beaufighter fighter-bombers and Supermarine Spitfire fighters. Because of a shortage of pilots being produced by the Flying Training Schools, user units were not being formed as planned, and so a backlog of aircraft stocks built up at Lyneham and the other ASUs. Soon the main site was full, and another storage site was sought away from the main airfield. A Satellite Landing Ground (SLG) was therefore opened, at Townsend near Yatesbury, to provide additional storage. Although the flow of aircraft eased a few months later with the formation of units requiring the aircraft, Townsend remained a useful facility to hold additional stocks. The aircraft were delivered to Lyneham by ferry pilots, usually from the Air Transport Auxiliary, or from one of the RAF Ferry Pools. These pilots also flew the aircraft on to the SLGs or, when needed, on delivery to the flying squadrons. Townsend was used by No.33 MU until September 1942, when it was replaced by Everleigh on Salisbury Plain.

The MU was joined by another unit on 16 August 1941, when No.14 Service Flying School moved in from Cranfield. Three days later the control of RAF Lyneham passed to No.23 Group, Flying Training Command, which became the main user of the airfield. No.14 SFTS flew Airspeed Oxfords, and its task was to train student pilots to fly multi-engine aircraft. Training was intense due to the urgent need to train more pilots, especially for bombers, with the stepping up of Bomber Command's role in the strategic air offensive on Germany. Unfortunately accidents were the inevitable result of this intense activity, and, as well as the resulting crew casualties, many aircraft were badly damaged or written off. After spending the rest of the year at Lyneham undertaking this work, early in 1942 it was decided to move the SFTS out of the area in order to make room for transport operations. No.14 SFTS moved with its Oxfords to Ossington in Nottinghamshire on 20 January.

With the departure of No.14 SFTS, Flying Training Command relinquished its control of Lyneham and handed it over to Ferry Command. This command had been formed in the summer of 1941 as the result of a requirement to move large numbers of aircraft across the Atlantic to satisfy the urgent need for more aircraft for the RAF and Fleet Air Arm. One of the first requisitions of these US types was the Lockheed Hudson, acquired as a patrol aircraft for Coastal Command. Despite misgivings in some areas, Lord Beaverbrook, the head of the Ministry of Aircraft Production, felt that the aircraft could be flown across the Atlantic, saving a three-month sea voyage aboard a cargo ship. The Atlantic Ferry Organisation (ATFERO) was therefore set up with its HQ at Montreal. Because of the limited number of experienced crews available it was decided to return them to Canada by air, rather than sea, in order to speed up the ferrying process. A two-way transatlantic air service by landplane was therefore put into operation, using the most suitable aeroplane available at the time, the US Consolidated LB.30 Liberator. During wartime, and when long-distance flying, especially during winter, was still seen as extremely hazardous, this was quite an undertaking. As time went on, ferrying across the Atlantic became well established, and, with the larger number of aircraft being made available by the US, it was decided the bring ATFERO formally into the RAF organisation. On 20 July 1941 ATFERO became Ferry Command.

RAF Lyneham came under No.44 Group of Ferry Command, and on 13 February 1942 Group Captain Cock arrived as the first Station Commander to be appointed. The first of several units then arrived,

WAAFS loading mail aboard a Liberator transport of 511 Squadron at Lyneham.
(Aeroplane)

and this was the Ferry Training Unit, from Honeybourne in Worcestershire. Formed in November 1941, its role was to train pilots to fly aircraft over long distances and to teach them the art of long-range navigation. The unit consisted of three flights, known as Nos.1, 2 and 3 Ferry Training Flights, equipped with a variety of twin-engined aircraft types, including the Vickers Wellington, Bristol Beaufort, Bristol Bombay, DH Dominie, DH Mosquito, Lockheed Hudson and Martin Maryland. It was re-designated as the Ferry Training and Despatch Unit from 28 March 1942.

Soon two more units followed. These were No.1425 Communications Flight with Consolidated Liberators, which flew in from Honeybourne, and No.1444 Ferry Training Flight (FTF), which flew its Lockheed Hudsons in from Horsham St.Faith. Shortly after these arrivals, on 27 February 1942 No.1445 FTF was formed at Lyneham with Liberator IIs. The Flight also had other four-engine aircraft on strength, including the Handley Page Halifax II and the Boeing Fortress IIA. The Flight also had at least one Hawker Hurricane! These flights were involved with the final ferry training of all aircrew and the despatch of aircraft overseas. Most of this training was done 'on the job', and the crews were screened (i.e. assessed) by their instructors

The Salvation Army Red Shield mobile canteen stopped at 511 Squadron's technical hangar. Liberator Mk II AM911 'St Just' is undergoing servicing. (RAF Lyneham)

while on actual ferrying operations. Aircraft for delivery to overseas units were prepared for their long flight by staff detached from the Overseas Aircraft Preparation and Despatch Unit at Kemble in Gloucestershire. Due to the proximity of the bases that the Luftwaffe had established in France, wartime flights from Britain to the Mediterranean were hazardous. British aircraft flying out to the area therefore took a circuitous route, swinging out into the Atlantic to avoid German patrols in the Bay of Biscay. This was demanding on fuel, and so aircraft departing from Lyneham would fly to RAF Portreath in Cornwall. There they would refuel and undergo final preparations courtesy of No.1 Overseas Aircraft Despatch Unit based at the Cornish station before heading out into the Atlantic. However, despite the meticulous preparations, many aircraft and crews were to be lost, due to enemy action, engine problems, or simply running out of fuel.

As well as ferrying, the Lyneham units also provided transport services. No.1425 Communications Flight had, since its formation at Honeybourne in November 1941, established and maintained a transport route between the UK and Gibraltar. Now based at Lyneham, the flight started the station's long and close association with air transport. Equipped with Armstrong Whitworth Albermarles, and later also Liberators, from its new base it expanded this service into the Mediterranean and along the coast of North Africa as far as Egypt. Passengers and freight were carried, along with ferry crews. The flight was brought up to squadron strength during the autumn of 1942 with twenty-five aircraft including a dozen Albermarles, and on 1 October became No.511 Squadron. In November a further route was added, from Gibraltar to Malta, and a detachment of Albermarles was stationed at Gibraltar to maintain this service. Another event at this time occurred on 3 November, when the Ferry Training and Despatch Unit was disbanded and merged with Nos.1444 and 1445 FTFs to form No.301 Ferry Training Unit.

On 13 January 1943 No.511 Squadron flew one of its more notable passengers, when they took the Prime Minister, Sir Winston Churchill, to the Casablanca Conference to meet President Roosevelt of the USA and President Stalin of the USSR. This was codenamed Operation Static, and for this No.511 Squadron provided VIP transport for the Prime Minister and his entourage during the conference. The unit had a Liberator comfortably fitted out for VIPs, named 'Commando', which they used for such trips. Other Prime Ministerial flights shortly afterwards included some to Cairo and Moscow. The squadron also assessed the Avro Lancaster at this time by flying two of the bombers, W4114 and PP780, on its routes. However, the aircraft was not found to be entirely suitable for the transport role at that stage, and the squadron decided to carry on with its Liberators and Albermarles.

In early 1943 Lyneham started to be used by the British Overseas Airways Corporation (BOAC) as its main UK terminal for passengers and freight. There had been a curtailment of civilian flying in the UK with the start of the war, but some airlines were allowed to carry on flying, particularly when this was seen as contributing to the war effort. BOAC was one of these, and it had continued to fly a restricted service to various parts of the globe. Their aircraft included military types such as the Liberator and Dakota, but they were flown by civilian crews and carried civilian registrations. They were, however, camouflaged, as they would have been seen as fair game by German fighter pilots. Civil and military transport aircraft were to continue to operate from Lyneham for the following two years.

By the time that BOAC had arrived at Lyneham hard runways had been built to cope with the frequent use of much heavier aircraft than the airfield had originally been designed for. Other changes included a

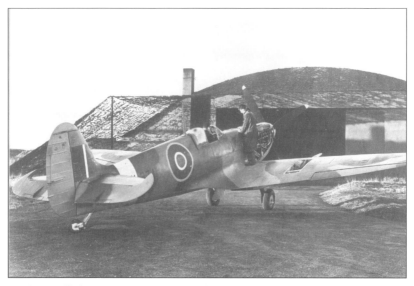

Civilian staff of 33 MU working on a Spitfire IXc outside the east end of D1 hangar at Lyneham. (RAF Lyneham)

change of command. A radical re-organisation of the RAF transport set-up led to the formation of Transport Command on 25 March 1943. The former Ferry Command was reduced to Group status, becoming No.45 Group, which now assumed responsibility for Lyneham under the new Transport Command.

The aircraft of No.511 Squadron continued to operate their scheduled routes, and it was on one of these that one of the unit's Liberators was lost on 4 July 1943. The aircraft was carrying General Sikorski, the Commander of Free Polish Forces, and several other VIPs, and it crashed inexplicably shortly after having taken off from Gibraltar, killing all on board apart from the pilot, Flight Lieutenant Prchal. Despite several theories, including sabotage, the cause of the crash has never been satisfactorily explained. A couple of Albermarles had also been lost off Gibraltar before this, and the place had a bad reputation amongst pilots during the war. The runway ran into the sea at both ends, so precise alignment for landing and takeoff were required. There was also turbulence from winds blowing around the Rock, and arriving aircraft were also often greeted by Spanish Anti-Aircraft fire. Although not always noted for accuracy, it is possible that Spanish gunfire may have had something to do with the aircraft losses.

The work of No.33 MU continued throughout this time, and by 1943 it was dealing mainly with the Vickers-Supermarine Spitfire. In May of that year a rationalisation by No.41 Group, which controlled the MUs, resulted in each MU assuming responsibility for particular types. This eased management of the aeroplane stocks, and the monitoring of their modification states. For No.33 MU this meant specialising in the Spitfire, and by mid-1943 the MU had over 250 Spitfires of various marks in storage. Later in the year No.33 MU also took on the extra responsibility for the preparation and storage of Hamilcar gliders. This meant receiving major components from the manufacturers, mainly furniture companies as the aircraft was made of wood, and assembling them. Over seventy of these huge tank-carrying gliders were assembled at Lyneham. They were put into storage, then issued to units that were preparing for the invasion of France. The Hamilcars were used for the training of aircrews and troops, mainly down the road at Netheravon. It was a very useful aeroplane, being able to carry a light tank or tracked carrier, and giving airborne troops armoured support on the ground, the like of which they never had before.

On 3 August 1943 No.1 Ferry Crew Pool was formed at Lyneham by redesignating the Ferry Crew Pool Filton. It flew the Vickers Wellington, DH Mosquito and Vickers Warwick. A new type appeared at the station the following month when No.511 Squadron received Douglas Dakotas. This aircraft was immediately put into service, taking over the Gibraltar and Mediterranean runs. The Albermarles were eventually withdrawn from use by the squadron in February 1944. Another new type came into service with No.511 Squadron in early November when the first Avro Yorks arrived at Lyneham. One of these, together with a Liberator, was used to provide special flights under the codename Operation Eureka. These took place out of Cairo to take Sir Winston Churchill and other VIPs to the Teheran conference of heads of state that started on 28 November. From Teheran, No.511 Squadron returned Churchill to Cairo for further talks with Roosevelt. At this time the squadron's routes were extended to Karachi in India.

In February 1944 No.525 Squadron was transferred to Lyneham from Weston Zoyland. This squadron had been formed at the Somerset station the previous September to operate the Vickers Warwick as a transport aircraft. The squadron had started operating a route schedule to Gibraltar in November 1943. Having resumed its operations from Lyneham the squadron extended its routes to various points in North Africa by March 1944. This was curtailed the following month when, following the loss of two Warwicks in quick succession, the aircraft were withdrawn from passenger service.

With the establishment of the front-line long-distance squadrons at Lyneham, it was decided to re-organise and move the remaining ferry units. On 16 March 1944, No.1 Ferry Crew Pool and No.301 FTU were disbanded at Lyneham, and were then merged to form No.1 Ferry Unit at Pershore.

As 1944 moved on No.511 Squadron was becoming more and more involved in special flights for VIPs, and the Squadron became the VIP Squadron for Long Range Transport. Liberator crews were detached to Montreal and York crews to Northolt for this purpose.

In May 1944 No.525 Squadron began receiving Dakotas, along with one Stirling to maintain passenger flying. It also resumed flying Warwicks but the aircraft were restricted to carrying freight. No.511 Squadron had in the meantime begun to receive Liberator VIIs, specially modified long-range unarmed transport versions of the aircraft, for their transatlantic and new Far East routes. The Squadron was reorganised with A Flight having 13 Yorks and B Flight 12 Liberators. Their Dakotas were then transferred to No.525 Squadron, which became an all Dakota Squadron in July 1944, flying four routes to the Mediterranean. By September the Squadron switched to Northern Europe, flying in supplies to support the Allied armies on the Continent. In October the squadron went back onto some of its longer-range routes, including to Karachi.

Meanwhile No.511 Squadron had extended its routes into Italy, and in September 1944 flew to the Soviet Union to support Nos.9 and 617 Squadrons, which had detached Lancasters there for attacks on the Tirpitz. A tragedy occurred the following month when, on 14 November, one of No.511 Squadron's Yorks, carrying Air Chief Marshal Sir Trafford Leigh Mallory and his staff, crashed into mountains near Grenoble. Everyone aboard the aircraft was killed. Sir Trafford had shortly before relinquished command of the Allied Expeditionary Air Force, and was on his way to the Far East to take up a new post as AOC-in-C, South East Asia Command.

On 11 October 1944 No.246 Squadron was formed at Lyneham from B Flight of No.511 Squadron, whose Liberators were transferred to the new unit. The squadron had earlier been a flying boat unit, and it was re-formed to operate from Lyneham as a long range transport squadron on the UK/India route. Initially the unit was heavily reliant on No.511 Squadron crews, not all of whom had transferred across with the aircraft. The squadron formed a Halifax Development Flight in December to investigate the ways in which the aircraft could be used as a transport. They were used on the route to Cairo with great success.

Avro York transport, as operated by 99, 206 and 511 Squadrons from Lyneham.
(Aeroplane)

At the end of 1944 the unit was transferred to Holmsley South in the New Forest. From there No.246 Squadron continued with its route-flying tasks until well after the war ended.

No.511 Squadron began concentrating on the Far East routes and on special VIP flights, and was wholly equipped with Yorks by January 1945. One of its main activities then became that of 'trooping', or carrying troops on postings or operational deployments, a task that the squadron was to maintain for a long while.

The personnel of No.525 Squadron had gradually changed over during the previous year, and by January 1945 the unit was predominantly Canadian. The squadron sent a detachment to the Crimea that month to fly personnel to the Yalta Conference. It was also flying covert support missions as well as maintaining about seventy transport services per month. These services were provided well into the summer of 1945, when schedules were changed in order to send troops to India. In the July No.525 Squadron was transferred to Membury, just across the county border in Berkshire, from where it continued its transport schedules.

Lyneham became the major staging post for overseas flights, and aircraft from other stations would often pass through for briefing, clearance and sometimes loading outbound, and for customs clearance, unloading and debriefing inbound. From June 1945 those RAF squadrons flying the Short Stirling V, an unarmed transport version of the four-engined bomber, began to use Lyneham as the UK terminal for their overseas services. These included Nos.46 and 242 Squadrons, flying to India. They carried seventeen passengers and staged through Tunisia, Libya, Palestine and Iraq, the journey taking twelve days. In August 1945 Stirlings began a service to the RAF base in the Azores from Lyneham.

Following the end of the war in Europe transport services carried on as usual for a while. Following VJ Day overseas schedules continued, not only to support occupying forces in the Far East, but also to repatriate Allied personnel. In October 1945 No.1409 Long Range Meteorological Reconnaissance Flight (LRMRF) moved in, equipped with the DH Mosquito IX and PRXVI and the Liberator VI.

The end of the war did not mean the end of tragedy, for on 23 November 1945 a Stirling approaching Lyneham in bad weather missed the runway and crashed into a group of buildings that included the operations building and a canteen. Fortunately both buildings were virtually empty at the time, but two people were killed on the ground. The crew of the aircraft escaped without serious injury.

With the run-down of the services following the end of hostilities there were many moves, reorganisations, disbandments and closures. Lyneham, because of its important international transport role, remained open and continued as a base for No.511 Squadron, No.33 MU and No.1409 LRMRF. In 1946 however, some changes took place. No.1409 LRMRF was disbanded on 13 May, and on 7 October No.511 Squadron too was disbanded. The latter was a temporary arrangement for, on 16 October, the squadron was re-formed at Lyneham by re-numbering No.246 Squadron at Holmsley South. No.511 Squadron continued to fly its Yorks on routes around the world, and it was joined by two other transport squadrons on 17 November 1947 when Nos.99 and 206 Squadrons were re-formed at Lyneham to fly Yorks.

With the end of the war there were twenty-two MUs in operation as ASUs, including No.33 MU. It was then the task of these units to deal with the vast quantities of aircraft that they had in store. Some types had been declared obsolete and destined to be scrapped. However, before they could be dismantled, engines, instruments and other equipment that was not then obsolete had to be removed for storage.

Hercules C Mk3 of the Lyneham Wing dropping paratroops during a demonstration at Larkhill in 2002. (Author)

Some types were ear-marked for sale to other air forces or to civilian concerns. The French bought 1,383 surplus combat aircraft from British stocks, including Spitfires, some of which would have come from Lyneham. Hamilcar gliders were still around at Lyneham in the early 1950s, but were eventually broken up and sold for scrap, mainly to local people. Hamilcar fuselages began to appear in local gardens and yards performing a variety of functions. One such fuselage performing as a shed in Chippenham was recovered in 1991 for museum display.

All three Lyneham York squadrons took part in the Berlin Airlift, which, from 24 June 1948, maintained the city of West Berlin, whose surface links had been cut by the USSR. For the Airlift Nos.99, 206 and No.511 Squadrons were based at the RAF base at Wunsdorf in West Germany. They were joined there by No.242 Squadron, which was moved to Lyneham the following year. The Lyneham squadrons spent a year helping to maintain the airlift, carrying a significant proportion of the RAF's lift of 281,727 tons of food, medicines and other supplies carried on 49,733 flights into the besieged city. Eight aircraft were lost during this operation, code-named Plainfare, including two Yorks from No.99 Squadron and two from No.206 Squadron.

After the Berlin Airlift the Lyneham squadrons continued flying until 1950, when Nos.206 and 242 Squadrons were disbanded. Nos.99 and

511 Squadrons carried on with the Handley Page Hastings, the York replacement. No.511 Squadron later flew troops to Korea and dropped paratroops during the fighting for the Suez Canal, along with Nos.53 and 99 Squadrons. Lyneham became the world's first military jet transport base in 1956 when No.216 Squadron re-formed at the station with the DH Comet C2, a military version of the first jet airliner. This resulted in a need for the main runway to be extended and two hangars to be demolished.

No.33 MU had continued to support the Spitfire after the war, and in 1953 still had seventy-seven Spitfires of various marks in cocooned long-term storage on site. At length these too disappeared, mainly scrapped, although some may have survived into preservation. The MU continued to deal with front-line combat aircraft, including the Meteor, Vampire, Canberra and Lightning. However, with a shrinking RAF No.33 MU itself was eventually no longer needed, and was disbanded in December 1967.

The Lyneham Hastings were later replaced by Britannias, which flew from the station alongside the Comets. In 1967 the first Hercules squadron, No.36, arrived at Lyneham. Later joined by Nos. 24, 30, 47, 48 and 70 Squadrons as well as the Hercules Operational Conversion Unit, the station has been the home of the RAF Hercules fleet since 1974. Today RAF Lyneham is the major tactical transport base for the RAF. It covers an area of over 2,500 acres, with three and a half miles of runways and 700 buildings accommodating 3,500 service personnel and some sixty Hercules. Since the war Lyneham's transport squadrons have taken part in almost every operation and emergency that has involved British forces, and many besides. In recent times, apart from such military operations as the Gulf War and Afghanistan, Lyneham's Hercules have been involved in numerous humanitarian operations, to such countries as Nepal, Cambodia and Ethiopia. The Lyneham Wing continues to uphold the best traditions of the RAF, and as the only operational RAF aerodrome in Wiltshire, it is something that the people of the county can be proud of. Long may it continue.

12
NETHERAVON

National Grid Reference (184) SU165493, 4 miles N of Amesbury,
off the A345

Netheravon can claim to be one of the oldest operational military airfields in the country, if not the world, having been in continuous use since 1913. The airfield came about purely by chance, when the newly-formed Royal Flying Corps (RFC) was looking for additional accommodation for its Military Wing in 1912. The hangars and camp buildings were completed at Netheravon early in the summer of 1913. Two landing areas were laid out, to the north and south of the aircraft sheds, which were positioned on an east-west axis.

During the summer of 1914 the whole of the Military Wing of the RFC, which then consisted of 700 personnel and 70 aeroplanes, assembled at Netheravon for a training exercise. Speed and altitude tests, tactical exercises and photographic trials were among the activities that took place. This was particularly timely, as a few weeks later war broke out in Europe. The airfield then became a centre for the preparation and despatch aircraft for France. Whole squadrons were also formed there as part of the reinforcement process for the Western Front. Later in the war Netheravon reverted to the flying training role as the need for replacement pilots rapidly increased. On 1 April 1918 the Royal Air Force was formed, by merging the RFC and the Royal Naval Air Service, and Netheravon then came under the General Officer Commanding South West Area, with its HQ at Salisbury.

Following the end of the Great War, Netheravon became the centre for the disbandment of a number of RAF squadrons. However, in 1919, No.1 Flying Training School was formed for the training of military and naval pilots. Although the school moved to Leuchars in 1931, it was to return a few years later.

A number of front-line bomber and fighter squadrons passed through Netheravon during the 1930s, some staying longer than others. On 23 May 1933 the airfield had a glimpse of its future when it became the venue for a world record parachute jump. Danish parachutist John Tranum used one of the resident Hawker Harts to set a free-fall height record, dropping from 20,000 feet and opening his parachute at 2,750 feet over the airfield.

When war came again in September 1939, security measures at Netheravon were heightened. Rudimentary ground defences were constructed, and these were manned by local units of the Wiltshire Regiment, who also started to patrol the general area of the airfield and the camp. Later the airfield defences were provided by No.2876 Squadron of the RAF Regiment.

Then No.1 Flying Training School, which had returned to Netheravon in 1938, had a mixed complement of Harvards, Hinds, Hart Trainers, Furies and Fairey Battles with which to train its pilots for the hostilities. Following a re-organisation of the flying schools, the unit became re-designated as No.1 Service Flying Training School on 3 September 1939. Its main role was to train pilots for the Fleet Air Arm (FAA).

The station's accommodation was not much changed from the First World War, and was starting to get packed because of the numbers of students being trained, as well as the large numbers of support personnel now needed to run the school. The airfield too was busy, so a number of Relief Landing Grounds (RLGs) were opened up in the local area, such as at Shrewton, a few miles away to the west, and brought into use. Some of the RLGs were also used for night flying practice. A popular character at Netheravon during this period was Sergeant Freddie Mills, the champion boxer, who was a Physical Training Instructor at No.1 FTS.

The end of 1941 saw a radical change to RAF Netheravon, when it was decided that the airfield was to be a centre for airborne forces. This was mainly because of its proximity to Salisbury Plain which, following the requisitioning of additional farmland, now had vast tracts of training land available for the use of gliders and paratroops. Until then the airborne units of the British Army and their RAF support squadrons had been scattered around the country, making co-ordination and communication, which was vital in setting up units for this new role, extremely difficult. A new formation, No.38 Wing, was set up at Netheravon under the command of Air Commodore Sir

Pupil pilots of the Glider Pilot Regiment are shown the instruments of a Hotspur glider. (Aeroplane)

Nigel Norman, Bt., to control RAF airborne support activities and to co-ordinate them with those of the 1st Parachute Brigade, whose HQ was already established at Bulford Camp nearby. The 6th Airborne Division was later set up with its HQ at Syrencote House, a mile and three-quarters to the south of Netheravon.

The first related flying unit to arrive at Netheravon was the Parachute Exercise Squadron, subsequently numbered as No.297 (Parachute) Squadron. It was followed by No.296 Squadron, which used Hart and Hector biplanes to tow its General Aircraft Hotspur training gliders. While No.297 initially had the de Havilland Tiger Moth, this was replaced with a much more suitable type, the Armstrong Whitworth Whitley, a twin-engined bomber then being withdrawn from front-line bombing duties.

The pilots of the gliders were seen as specialists, requiring their own particular training, so these men were recruited into a separate unit, the Glider Pilot Regiment (the GPR). They were to receive full elementary flying training, provided by the RAF on the DH Tiger Moth or Miles

Magister single-engine tandem two-seat basic trainer. They were then given glider training, initially on the Hotspur trainer, before they graduated to the Horsa, which was to become the main operational glider. However, the members of the GPR differed from other aircrew in one major way – having landed the glider, which was not going to be taking off again, they were expected to pick up their weapons and join in the battle. They were fighting soldiers as well as pilots, and this ethos was followed consistently throughout the regiment's existence.

The FAA had for some time been looking at alternative arrangements for the training of its pilots, particularly because of disruptions to its flying programmes due to the weather and to enemy air activities. The arrival of the airborne squadrons prompted a decision, and this was to move naval flying training, not just from Netheravon, but out of the country, to the USA. This followed an agreement that had been reached with the US Government. They moved out in the spring of 1942, and No.1 SFTS was formally disbanded on 7 March.

Sir Winston Churchill always showed a great interest in airborne forces. Indeed, following the success of German parachute and glider troops during the early stages of the war, he requested that a British airborne force be formed. In April 1942 a demonstration was laid on for the Prime Minister by No.38 Wing and 1st Parachute Brigade at Netheravon to show him the progress that had been made. Local units, including Nos.296 and 297 Squadrons, were to take part, flying in to a DZ and Landing Zone (LZ) set up at Everleigh not far away to the north-west of Netheravon. The demonstration was to consist of a drop by paratroopers and the landing of Hotspur gliders. The paratroops were dropped first, then the gliders came in. The Hotspurs had been released at 8,000 feet some distance away from the field, as it was hoped that the spectators would be surprised and impressed by the gliders' sudden appearance. Surprised indeed the spectators were, and in fact scattered, as the first three Hotspurs overshot the LZ and ran toward the crowd. The leader of the next formation hit some trees and deposited his passengers in disarray on the ground. It was not a very auspicious start. No-one recorded the PM's comments, but at least he didn't cancel the programme on his return to No.10!

As Nos.296 and 297 Squadrons became more proficient, it was felt that they should have some operational experience over occupied Europe. Because the airfield at Hurn near Bournemouth was closer to the Continent, both units were moved there from Netheravon. From Hurn both squadrons flew 'Nickelling' raids (dropping propaganda leaflets) over northern France by night, and a few months later took

Armstrong Whitworth Whitley dropping paratroops on a training exercise. (Aeroplane)

part in the tactical bombing of specific targets, also by night. During daylight they continued to train in the airborne forces role. Before leaving Netheravon, No.296 Squadron took part in Exercise Brigmerston on 11 July. Two sections of Hawker Hurricane IICs softened up the landing area, while smoke was laid by four Blenheims. Paratroops and containers were dropped by 25 Whitleys, followed by

139

three more towing Hotspurs, and another bringing in a Horsa. The final wave was a number of Hectors towing more Hotspurs. The exercise was a great success, and was viewed by the Rt.Hon.Sir Archibald Sinclair, Secretary of State for Air, and several very senior RAF and Army officers, including Air Chief Marshal Sir Charles Portal, Air Marshal Sir Sholto Douglas and Air Marshal Sir Arthur Barrett. All were entertained afterwards in the Officers' Mess.

Shortly after No.296 Squadron left, Netheravon received its only air raid of the war. This was on 27 July, when a single German raider ran in low over the airfield. It did not drop any bombs, but instead machine-gunned several buildings, including the WAAFs' and the officers' quarters, before hurriedly leaving the scene. There was some damage, but fortunately no casualties. The strength of RAF Netheravon was given in its Form 540 (which was the official record of the station's activities, the Operations Record Book [ORB]) a few days later as 1,247 officers and other ranks.

In August 1942, two new training units were formed at Netheravon. These were No.295 Squadron, which was to train pilots in paratroop and glider operations with its Whitleys, and the Glider Pilot Exercise Unit, which was to keep the pilots of the GPR in current flying practice.

Training had been taking place at Netheravon during November for the first British glider operation. Reports were received by British Intelligence that heavy water, essential in the production of atomic weapons, was being produced by the Germans at the Norsk Hydro plant at Vermok in Norway. As the factory was concealed in a steep valley, it was going to be hard to destroy. Given the codename Operation Freshman, the job was given to the Royal Engineers, and because of the difficult terrain, they were to be taken in by glider. Four of the best glider pilots were selected. The first glider was to be piloted by Staff Sergeant MF Strathdee and Sergeant P Doig of the GPR, to be followed in the second glider by Pilot Officer Davis and Sergeant Fraser, both of the Royal Australian Air Force. Two Horsa gliders were to be used (the type was new, and only just becoming available), and each was to be towed by a Handley Page Halifax four-engine bomber, which had been made available especially for the operation. Long-range tow training took place by the selected crews and aircraft out of Netheravon over several weeks, with the emphasis on night landings.

Eventually, at 17:40 hours on 19 November 1942, the force took off on what was to be one of the most daring and dangerous covert operations of World War II. The jumping-off point was Skitten, near Wick in Scotland. In addition to the two pilots each glider carried 15 sappers plus their equipment. The weather was foul following take-off, and the flight of 400 miles across the North Sea in such conditions was an epic one. Nearing the Norwegian coast, the crew of the first Halifax reported storm conditions, and when they arrived over their objective, they could not locate the landing area. Not having sufficient fuel to loiter in the worsening conditions, they had just decided to turn back when the tow-rope snapped. Strathdee did what he could to bring the glider down safely, but in nil visibility the Horsa crashed, killing eight of the men aboard and seriously injuring four. As the second combination neared the landing area, the Halifax lost power, and crashed into a mountainside, killing all aboard. Flying Officer Davis managed to release his tow-rope before the tug went down, and did his best to get his Horsa onto the ground. In the resulting crash-landing three men aboard the glider were killed and six injured.

The twenty-three survivors were in no fit state to evade capture, and were quickly rounded up by German troops and thrown into prison. Shortly afterwards, on the direct orders of Adolf Hitler, and against the Geneva Convention, in a criminal act of barbarity the wounded were strangled in their cells, and the remainder were shot. This was an extremely unfortunate start, but it did show that the Horsa was a capable design, and that the basic concept of using gliders for such operations was not only feasible, but had great potential, given the right conditions.

In January 1943, in order to provide technical support for airborne equipment, No.235 MU had been formed at Netheravon to recover and repair gliders, and No.3 Mobile Parachute Servicing Unit was formed at the station to repair the parachute drop equipment of paratroop units. No.3 MPSU was later sent to the Mediterranean, and No.4 MPSU was formed at Netheravon to replace it in the spring of 1943.

King George VI had visited Netheravon during the summer of 1942 to see progress on Britain's Airborne Forces, and visited the airfield again on 1 April 1943. He was met by Air Marshal Sir Arthur Barrett, Air Officer Commanding in Chief Army Co-operation Command, and inspected the No.38 Wing squadrons, all of which had gathered at Netheravon for the occasion, together with the MU and the Netheravon Station Flight, set up to provide light communications aircraft for liaison. The King also inspected three typical glider loads that had been prepared for him to view.

On April 17 three aircraft of No.295 Squadron, which had been re-equipped with Halifaxes, bombed a transformer station at Le Thieul. This was to be the last raid that the squadron was to mount from

Netheravon. On 1 May No.295 Squadron departed for Holmsley South in the New Forest, the majority of its personnel being transported in Horsa gliders. It was replaced at Netheravon by the Heavy Glider MU, which transferred from Hurn.

June 1943 saw another period of change for Netheravon, when Army Co-operation Command was absorbed by Fighter Command. With a view to the future invasion of the Continent, the 2nd Tactical Air Force was formed on this day as part of Fighter Command, with the duty of controlling the training and operation of all RAF units that were allocated for tactical support of the army. This included all of the units based at RAF Netheravon, and the rest of No.38 Wing.

An insight into station life at Netheravon during the summer of 1943 can be glimpsed from the entries in the Station ORB of the time. The fourth anniversary of the formation of the WAAF was celebrated at Netheravon on 25 June. Quotes from the ORB include the following:

'The weather was perfect, and a most enjoyable afternoon was spent, rivalry being keen for the Station Cup which, after a ding-dong struggle, was won by the 'Amazonian Athletes' of the Station HQ from the members of No.38 Wing. Picnic tea was served, then followed a thrilling netball match between No.38 Wing and Station HQ. Station HQ proved to be the victors – 13 goals to 12. The Victrix Ludorum Cup was won by LACW Rakall, P. A dance was held that evening.' Further entries later in the month attest to the 'brilliant weather' that June, and to the popularity of cricket, lawn tennis and swimming. The station cinema was also popular, with three different programmes being shown per week. Other popular entertainments included the Music Circle and the Recreational Library.

In March 1944 two more units appeared at Netheravon. The first was the Air Transport Tactical Development Unit (ATTDU), which conducted trials on a wide variety of airborne equipment, and flew a variety of aircraft ranging from the Halifax and Oxford to the Mosquito and Liberator. It was joined by No.1677 (Target Training) Flight, which flew Miles Martinets in order to keep up the No.38 Group Halifax tail gunners' standards of markmanship. During the summer of 1943 Netheravon became the centre for the many exercises that took place as part of the gradual build-up to the impending invasion of Europe. Exercise Snaffle, for example, took place on 10 August to evaluate the methods of supply of a bridgehead by parachute and glider. Field exercises also continued, sometimes in conjunction with paratroops. In late August airborne exercises included the involvement of Hamilcar heavy gliders, which brought in Tetrarch tanks and Bren Carriers.

For the invasion of France, codenamed 'Operation Overlord' (and known popularly ever since as 'D-Day'), there was to be an amphibious landing on the beaches of Normandy, supported by two major airborne landings to protect the beach-head from German attack. The west flank was to be protected by a US airborne landing, and the east flank by a British one.

Training for the British involvement in the airborne operations started in earnest in the spring of 1944 at Netheravon. Because of obstacles that had been placed by the Germans in French fields to prevent massed glider landings, British glider pilots trained for precision night landings in small groups, so that specific objectives could be taken. Eventually, nineteen major airborne exercises were to take place on Salisbury Plain to hone the participants' skills and build their confidence. Bridges were to be taken over the Rivern Orne and the Caen Canal to control entry into the east flank of the beach-head. Fields were identified beside each of the bridges that were without obstacles, as the Germans thought them too small to bother with. A field was found near Netheravon that was identical to that near the Caen Canal bridge. After the feasibility of landing three gliders into such a small area had been successfully demonstrated, it was into this field, by day and night, that the glider pilots hand-picked for the mission flew, again and again.

The King paid his last wartime visit to Netheravon on 19 May 1944 to view Exercise Exeter. Accompanied by Queen Elizabeth and Princess Elizabeth, he was met by Air Chief Marshal Sir Trafford Leigh Mallory, now Air Commander in Chief Allied Expeditionary Air Force, Air Vice Marshal Hollingshurst, General Browning and General Gale. Exercise Exeter was to be a demonstration of the aircraft, troops and equipment to be employed in the forthcoming invasion. All the operational units of No.38 Group were involved, along with many from No.46 Group. The majority of the GPR took part. Dakotas dropped 300 paratroops of the Canadian Parachute Training Corps on the northern airfield, while Halifaxes and Stirlings brought in 100 Horsa gliders to land troops on the southern airfield. This was followed by the arrival of Hamilcars that landed on the northern airfield bringing in Tetrarch tanks. By any standards it must have been an impressive display, with over 250 aircraft and over 2,500 troops demonstrating their capabilities.

Two days after Exercise Exeter another exercise was held, this time by No.46 Group, involving the landing of 75 Horsas on the southern airfield. This was the last major exercise at Netheravon before D-Day, the time after this being spent on final preparations of Horsas and

Halifax with Horsa in tow takes off for Normandy. (Aeroplane)

Hamilcars for the invasion, which everyone knew wasn't far away. Station strength at the end of May 1944 was 2,089 officers and other ranks.

Although on D-Day no missions were flown from Netheravon itself, the training that took place on the airfield there paid off. The three gliders that were to land beside the Caen Canal bridge, for example, did so with such precision that the nose of the first aircraft went through the boundary wire of the bridge's defences. Major John Howard, who led the attack, captured the bridge as planned, and despite determined counter-attacks by the Germans, held it until relieved by No.7 Para later in the morning. The deputy adjutant of No.7 Para that day was a young paratrooper named Richard Todd who, after the war, became famous as a film actor portraying such characters as Wing Commander Guy Gibson in *The Dambusters*, and, appropriately, Major John Howard in *The Longest Day*.

By mid-June 1944 a lot of used gliders were sitting around on the former LZs and battlefields of Normandy. As reserves of gliders in the UK were now sorely depleted, it was suggested that these Normandy veterans should be recovered and repaired for re-use in future airborne operations.

Work started on the recovery of gliders from France in early August. HQ 46 Group formed a Dakota Flight of six aircraft within No.1 HGSU specifically for the purpose of collecting airworthy gliders. They were to be recovered by the snatch method (not requiring the tug aircraft to

A sea of Horsa gliders in open-air storage at Netheravon in October 1945. (Aeroplane)

land) direct from the gliders' landing sites. Thirty-nine gliders were safely retrieved by this method by the end of August, the only mishap being to the first glider, which broke loose over the Channel (the two crew were rescued without injury). Other gliders that were unserviceable came back by landing craft.

The stocks of gliders retrieved and repaired by No.1 HGSU were to come into their own in September 1944, with the mounting of Operation Market Garden, the airborne carpet for the armoured thrust to the bridge over the Rhine at Arnhem. For Netheravon this was to be an anti-climax compared with D-Day, as most of the units and equipment were to depart from airfields in eastern England, closer to the objectives. When the operation started, on 17 September, it was hoped that similar follow-up glider recovery arrangements could be mounted to those that were so successful after D-Day. Unfortunately this was to prove impracticable, owing to the course of the ensuing battle. Apart from the fact that most of the LZs were to remain in German hands for some time afterwards, those gliders that were not wrecked on landing were systematically destroyed by the Germans to prevent their re-use.

In February 1945 the repatriation of liberated Prisoners of War along with wounded troops to the UK began when, on the 22nd, forty Dakotas arrived at Netheravon and disembarked 800 personnel before returning to the Continent.

Meanwhile, preparations were taking place for the final major Allied airborne operation of the war, Operation Varsity. This was to be a glider and paratroop landing in support of the crossing of the Rhine by

21st Army Group under General Montgomery. The airborne operation was to take place in daylight, and the airborne troops were to land to reinforce a bridgehead that was to be made by an amphibious crossing during the previous night. At Netheravon gliders that had been prepared for further use were wheeled out, connected to tugs and flown off to be delivered to the various 38 Group airfields in eastern England. Between 5 and 10 March 1945, 150 gliders were supplied in this way.

The invading force had mixed fortunes. US paratroops in the south overcame local opposition, knocked out several German tanks and linked up with British ground troops in the evening. US paras dropping to the north ran into heavy flak, and 22 C-46s were shot down in flames, fortunately after most of the paras had managed to jump. Many paras got hung up in trees, and several were killed by German soldiers and civilians while trying to extricate themselves. Other paras dropped into flak positions and defended areas, but the Germans were not expecting an airborne invasion after an amphibious assault, and were taken by surprise. The US and British paratroops fought bravely against heavy opposition and eventually gained the upper hand. The British 5th Parachute Brigade landed to the west, slightly off target, and had to re-group under heavy machine-gun and artillery fire. A battery of 88mm guns were causing them particular grief, so they decided that the only thing for it was to take out the German gunners with a bayonet charge, which they duly did. By mid-afternoon they had taken all of their objectives and linked up with British ground troops.

The Rhine Crossing was the last major airborne operation of World War II, and it was a glorious last fling. Ninety per cent of the gliders and paratroops landed as planned. However, of the British gliders which reached their Landing Zones, only 88 landed undamaged, the others being hit by flak and small-arms fire, 37 being burnt out. Of the British glider pilots, over one-third became casualties.

With the war in Europe at an end, repatriation of British and Allied troops started, and between 17 and 21 May, in the region of 3,000 soldiers of 6th Airborne Division landed at Netheravon in aircraft of Transport Command. The Command took over 38 Group in mid-1945, and the ATTDU was re-named the TCDU. Trials continued with various Transport Command types, including the Stirling, Halifax and Avro York, also flying types such as the Buckingham and Mosquito on regular schedules.

No.27 Squadron moved to Netheravon in June 1950, from RAF

The crest of the Royal Flying Corps is still proudly displayed above the main doors of the Officers' Mess at Netheravon. (Author)

Oakington. The unit took up the role of glider snatching, and displayed this at the 1950 Farnborough Air Show, one of the few public displays of the technique. There had obviously been a decision to radically re-organise RAF activities at Netheravon for, on 10 November 1950, No.27 Squadron was suddenly disbanded. This was the last RAF flying unit to be based at Netheravon. All No.38 Group activities and units were run down or transferred, and on 30 November 1950 the station was transferred to No.62 Group Home Command, and eventually became the Depot of the RAF Police. All aspects of RAF Police training then took place at Netheravon, including dog-handling. The depot remained for ten years, then in September 1960 moved to Debden in Essex. The RAF Police Dog Training Squadron stayed until the middle of 1963, when it too left for Debden.

This was to be the last RAF unit at Netheravon, for on 31 July 1963 the station was transferred to the army. The airfield was quiet for a while, but it was not long before the Army Free Fall Parachute Association started using it as the base for its two DH Dragon Rapides, and they were followed by the Southern Command Gliding Club and the Royal Artillery Flying Club. Netheravon has since become one of the major free fall parachuting centres in Europe, and has been the venue for national championships. Military aviation returned to Netheravon in 1966 with the formation of HQ 2 Wing Army Air Corps (AAC) at the station. The first AAC flying unit to appear was No.6 Flight AAC, equipped with the Westland Scout helicopter. Over the next few years the station became fully occupied, with new buildings being put up alongside the refurbished RFC and RAF ones. A succession of AAC units have since been based at Netheravon over the years, and today it is the HQ of No.7 Regiment AAC (Volunteers), flying the Westland Gazelle helicopter.

AAC and RAF units, as well as those of NATO nations, continue to make use of Netheravon airfield, particularly as a forward operating base for the Salisbury Plain Training Area. From its early beginnings with the Military Wing of the RFC to today's AAC, Netheravon's history has gone full-circle. It is to be hoped that, under the stewardship of the army, the fame of Netheravon as one of the oldest operational military airfields in the world shall continue for many years to come.

13
OLD SARUM
(Ford Farm)

National Grid Reference (184), SU153335 2 miles north of Salisbury

The name of Old Sarum has long been synonymous with land warfare because of its location right on the edge of army country – Salisbury Plain. The RAF School of Army Co-operation was set up there early on in the airfield's existence and this link with the army was to continue for a further 60 years. During that time too, its primary role was one of the training of army officers and RAF aircrew for the Army Co-operation squadrons. As such, the men who passed through Old Sarum were generally based there for relatively short periods, but the training that they received at the airfield was later put to use in action in many different parts of the world.

Old Sarum is one of the oldest airfields in the country that is still active. Situated two miles from the cathedral city of Salisbury, it covers 182 acres. Like Middle Wallop ten miles to the east across the county border in Hampshire, the actual flying field is in its original condition. The size of aircraft operated never justified the laying of paved runways. Instead the runways were marked out on the grass.

The original landing ground that was to become Old Sarum was established to the north of Salisbury in 1917 in a pasture between the Portway (an old Roman road) and Ford village. The War Department acquired land that was part of Ford Farm, and this was the name given to the new airfield until it was officially changed to Old Sarum in 1918. During the First World War, Old Sarum was a training station, producing bomber squadrons and crews for the Western

Lysander MkIs of 16 Squadron in formation over the Wiltshire countryside in 1939. (Aeroplane)

Front. After the war, it was one of few RAF stations to be retained.

The RAF School of Army Co-operation (S of AC) moved to Old Sarum in March 1920. The unit had been set up to improve the relationship between the Army and the RAF, particularly in operations where the two Services were working together. RAF units had been formed specifically to work with the Army by giving it reconnaissance and ground attack support, and these were known as the Army Co-operation Squadrons.

As the army expanded in size during the late 1930s more Army Co-operation Squadrons were needed. No.59 Squadron was reformed at Old Sarum on 28 June 1937 (it had been an army support squadron during the First World War). It was set up as a night reconnaissance unit for No.11 Corps and joined resident squadron No.16, which had reformed at Old Sarum in 1924.

In 1938 No.16 Squadron became the first squadron in the RAF to be equipped with the Westland Lysander. This aircraft was developed to replace the Audax and Hind in the army co-operation role. It was a single-engined, high-wing monoplane. Unlike the Audax and Hind the Lysander was an entirely new design. It had to be able to land in small fields close to army formation HQs, possibly bringing a message from a forward unit picked up on an external hook. Such a performance required a high-lift wing and a low stalling speed, but additional tasks included photography, visual reporting of the ground situation and ground attack of small-scale opposition forces.

When war was declared in 1939 the S of AC was operating Hectors, Lysanders, Ansons and Blenheims. With hostilities pending, the importance of artillery spotting and tactical reconnaissance was recognised, and the role of the S of AC was expanded. An element of the school was moved to Andover and reformed there on 21 October 1939 as No.2 S of AC. The remainder of the school at Old Sarum was re-designated No.1 S of AC on 20 December 1939.

One of the ideas that No.1 S of AC had developed was the use of light aircraft to aid communications and observation in the field. A variety of light aircraft were evaluated at Old Sarum during late 1939 and early 1940, including such designs as the General Aircraft Limited Cagnet, the Arpin A-1 and the Dutch Scheldermusch. However, it was the Taylorcraft Model D, a pre-war US design built under licence in the UK, which proved the most effective. Along with a single Stinson 105 Voyager that had been impressed (i.e. requisitioned from its civilian owner), an initial batch of eight Taylorcraft aircraft were provided to equip a trials unit, D Flight, formed in February 1940 at Old Sarum under the command of Captain Henry Bazeley. Trials were started to evaluate the idea of the Air Observation Post (AOP), the use of light aircraft for reconnaissance and artillery spotting.

Operational deployments from Old Sarum began in February 1940, when No.16 Squadron moved out, to Hawkinge, in preparation for deployment to France. The squadron arrived at Bertangles near Armiens on 14 April. When fighting began it was heavily engaged in tactical reconnaissance in the Le Cateau and St Quentin areas. Losses were heavy, but two German aircraft were claimed. After twelve days of fighting the squadron was withdrawn to Lympne in Kent, and from there flew tactical reconnaissance missions over Dunkirk, covering the evacuation of the BEF.

D Flight, meanwhile, was also sent to France in April 1940. They used the opportunity to mount a series of trials to test the AOP concept in a realistic situation, taking along three of the Taylorcraft and the Stinson Voyager, together with a ground support party. The flight crossed the Channel on 19 April, landing at Arras. They made contact with 1st Royal Horse Artillery and No.1 AA Battery for some pre-arranged familiarisation training. It also engaged in evasive trials with

Aircrews and groundcrews of B flight, 16 Squadron at Bertangles in northern France in 1940. (Aeroplane)

the Hurricanes of No.85 Squadron RAF. All went well for the AOP pilots, the fighter pilots finding it extremely difficult to bring an aim to bear on the light aircraft once they had been spotted. On 1 May the flight travelled to Sommesous airfield near Mailly-le-Camp. Here it trained with the French Army, planning to later move up to the front line in the Saar area to participate in artillery shoots against German targets. However, all plans were to change with the German invasion of the Low Countries on 10 May. D Flight aircraft were initially dispersed into the woods in case of enemy air attack, but after a few days it was decided to move the unit to the coast. At Dieppe they received War Office orders to withdraw. With the ground party travelling by sea from Le Havre, D Flight flew home to Old Sarum on 20 May 1940.

The first Royal Canadian Air Force (RCAF) unit to reach Britain, No.110 (Army Co-operation) Squadron, arrived at Old Sarum in late February 1940, with a dozen Canadian-built Lysanders. They started training and worked up with frequent army exercises and AA battery ranging. On 9 June 1940 they exchanged places with No.225 Squadron, an RAF Lysander unit, at Odiham. From Old Sarum No.225 proceeded to carry out dawn-to-dusk anti-invasion patrols along the south coast between Selsey Bill and St Albans Head. The squadron also provided

Lysander crews liaise with army staff at a forward HQ during a field exercise in the spring of 1941. (Aeroplane)

detachments of Lysanders for Air/Sea rescue duties. This carried on until the end of the month, when it moved to Tilshead, but the squadron's aircraft continued to fly in the area until July 1941.

Although Old Sarum had been identified by the Germans as a military target, it was largely ignored by the Luftwaffe for most of the war. There were, however, at least a couple of incidents. One of these occurred on the morning of Monday 21 October 1940, when a lone Junkers JU 88A-5 of KG51 bomber strayed into the Salisbury area. Unable to find its briefed target, the bomber strafed Old Sarum at low level and headed back towards its base at Villaroche in northern France. However, just before it was able to reach the coast, it was intercepted by two Spitfires of No.609 Squadron that had been scrambled from Middle Wallop. The JU 88 was shot down and it crashed at Manor Farm, Blackbush, near Milford-on-Sea, killing the four-man crew. The aircraft was the 100th victim to fall to the guns of No.609 Squadron. Another attack on Old Sarum occurred during the night of 11/12 May 1941, when an enemy aircraft dropped incendiary and high explosive bombs. One hangar was burnt out and the Sergeants' Mess and Signals Section destroyed.

During the summer of 1941, No.1 S of AC was evolving into two main areas – those of AOP and tactical reconnaissance. The latter called for fighter aircraft that were able to fly at speed to a target area, but be capable of defending themselves if attacked. No.41 Operational Training Unit (OUT) was formed by the school to develop this concept. It had an initial complement of 28 Curtiss Tomahawk fighters, plus Harvards, Magisters, and a number of target-towing aircraft. They made use of Salisbury Plain and its many smaller airfields, such as Oatlands Hill, for training. The OUT later received North American Mustangs. The remainder of the school continued to train aircrews and to assist the development of the AOP concept.

Although D Flight had proved the feasibility of the AOP concept, it carried on developing techniques and methods of using the aircraft. Finally it was decided to form a proper AOP Squadron, and some of the personnel of D Flight became the nucleus of No.651 Squadron on 1 August 1941. This was to be the first of twelve British AOP Squadrons formed during World War 2. The majority of these, no less than nine squadrons, were formed at Old Sarum – Nos.651, 652, 653, 654, 655, 658, 660, 661 and 662 Squadrons. The initial equipment of No.651 Squadron were eighteen impressed Taylorcraft Model Cs, later supplemented with, then replaced by, the Auster AOP I (a fully militarised version of the Taylorcraft). In due course it later had the improved Auster II, IV and V. No.651 Squadron's main activity, particularly during the first few months, was reconnaissance and spotting for the artillery. Nos.652, 653 and 654 Squadrons were initially equipped with Tiger Moths, but these were replaced by Auster Is. No.652 Squadron trained hard until it flew to Normandy on 8 June 1944 (D-Day +2). They saw action initially in the Caen area until the breakout from the beach-head in August 1944.

By the time No.653 Squadron flew to Normandy, in late June 1944, it had the Auster IV. From landing the squadron was continuously in action throughout northern France, Belgium and Holland, ending up in the Hamburg area in mid-1945.

No.654 Squadron was earmarked for Operation Torch, and landed at Algiers in North Africa in March 1943. In July 1943 the squadron moved to Italy with 30 Corps.

No.655 Squadron's first aircraft were Auster Is, which were exchanged for Auster IIIs before the squadron went to North Africa in August 1943. After seeing action there, it took part in the Anzio landings in January 1944 and was almost continually in action from then until the end of the war, supporting 13 Corps during the advance to Florence.

No.658 Squadron initially had Tiger Moths, then later these were replaced with Auster IIIs. For a year and a quarter the squadron trained in England and Northern Ireland in preparation for the invasion of France. It flew to Normandy on 18 June 1944, spending much of its time then spotting for the artillery. On 17 July the squadron commander, Major Lyell, conducted a shoot for 600 guns on a group of forty enemy tanks heading for Allied positions. Thereafter the unit operated throughout the campaign in north-west Europe, supporting the 2nd Army through France, Belgium and Holland. In March 1945 the squadron crossed the Rhine with the Allied armies, and ended the war in northern Germany.

No.660 Squadron formed on 1 July 1943. After a couple of months they moved with their Auster IIIs to Andover. In February 1944 the unit received Auster IVs, which it took to Normandy in July 1944. Landing on Juno Beach, the squadron's role was to support 2 Canadian Army Group Royal Artillery in the Caen area.

The penultimate AOP unit to be raised at Old Sarum was No.661 Squadron, on 31 August 1943. Equipped with Auster IIIs, it also moved to Andover, in November. Re-equipped with Auster IVs, it moved to Normandy in June 1944 to join 21st Army Group. It was soon in action, and took part in the battle for Caen. By the end of August the squadron had flown 930 sorties.

The last of the wartime AOP squadrons to be formed at Old Sarum was No.662 Squadron, on 30 September 1943. Equipped with the Auster IV, it flew to Normandy on 8 June. The day after arrival the squadron was in action, directing the fire of the main armament of the battleship HMS Warspite onto enemy positions in the area of the Bois de Verney. Over the next three weeks the unit's Austers flew 476 sorties, including 100 shoots.

With the invasion of mainland Europe being planned, Old Sarum took its part in the preparations. The station became the main concentration area for RAF ground units going with the sea-borne invasion force. Temporary buildings and tents were erected, increasing the living accommodation to take more personnel. It could then take 8,500 people. Hard standings were built for 1,650 vehicles. One of the tasks undertaken at Old Sarum during the build-up was the water-proofing of RAF vehicles for the invasion, under the codename 'Snug'. Every RAF vehicle that was to be involved in the amphibious landings went through Old Sarum for waterproofing. Don Evans, who had been posted to Weston Zoyland the previous year, volunteered for special duties at Old Sarum, and found himself joining the Snug Unit in

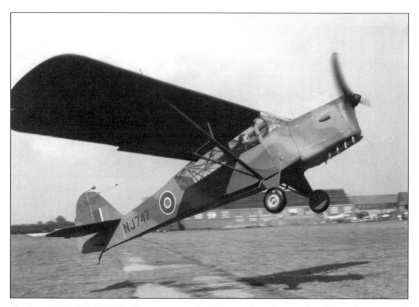

Auster AOP III NJ747 demonstrates its impressive short take-off performance in September 1943. (Aeroplane)

February 1944. As each vehicle had to be prepared for being driven through six feet of water, Don and his team had to apply Asbestos Waterproofing Compound to protect the vehicles' electrical parts. Breather pipes were used to extend exhaust pipes above water level. This preparation took up to twelve hours per vehicle, although for the more specialised types it took much longer. Occasionally, having completed a batch of vehicles the unit would take some of them to a lake near Blagdon in Somerset, to test the effectiveness of their work. As more and more vehicles arrived at Old Sarum, the airfield and surrounding roads filled up. Eventually there was just enough room in the centre of the airfield to land a light aircraft, but that was all. Before he left Weston Zoyland, Don had asked a friend on a US C-47 squadron that was based there to deliver his bike for him. The American said that it wouldn't be a problem. However, when the C-47 turned up at Old Sarum with his bicycle, it could not land for all the vehicles. After a couple of circuits the aircraft came in at low level and the Americans threw the bike out! Luckily the damage was not too bad, and Don managed to repair his bike and ride it again.

As part of the RAF surface invasion force, six Servicing Commandos were based at Old Sarum. At least four of these units had already spent some time in Wiltshire, having trained at Zeals in 1943. The Servicing Commandos (SCs) were formed to accompany the invasion and service aircraft on forward airstrips, but they were also trained for battle. One of the first of the SCs to arrive at Old Sarum was No.3209 SC, which moved in from Boxgrove in Sussex in May 1944. Soon, five more arrived; these were Nos.3205, 3207 and 3210 SCs, due to go in with No.3209 shortly after D-Day, and Nos.3206 and 3208, scheduled for a week later.

As the big day drew near, things started to happen. Fourteen days before June 5, originally scheduled for D-Day, all personnel were confined to camp. The whole airfield was marked out in taped lanes, and having had their vehicles suitably waterproofed and prepared, the out-going units were positioned on the airfield in Invasion convoys, lined up in order of departure. Eventually, on the morning of 1 June, the first convoys started to move off towards the embarkation ports. The following day it was the turn of the first of the SCs, No.3205, and their first stop on leaving Old Sarum airfield was in Castle Road in Salisbury, where a 10-man box of rations was heaved aboard each truck. Then they were on their way again, heading for the coast. The first convoys from Old Sarum were sent to the Marshalling Area at Fareham, but once the main Invasion force had left on 5 June, the remaining convoys were sent straight to the port of embarkation at Gosport.

On arrival off the Normandy coast, battleships were pounding the German defences with their 16-inch guns. Making their way past other craft firing batteries of rockets, the Tank Landing Ships (LSTs) moved towards the shore, and up the beach. As Victor Poynting, of No.3209 SC, explained, 'The LST's bow doors opened, the ramp went down and the trucks, already loaded with personnel and with their engines running, moved down the ramp and into the water, and made for the beach. One truck went into a shell-hole under water, and those that followed had to make a sharp detour around it. After a brief stop at the Assembly Point just off the beach where the vehicle waterproofing had to be removed, our convoy made its way amid small-arms fire to Villiers-sur-Sec, where our designated airstrip B2 (Bazenville) was being constructed, three miles inland.'

Although B2 Advance Landing Ground was only half-completed, aircraft were already making emergency landings there. Once completed, the ALGs were used as forward bases by the RAF fighter squadrons, which would arrive each morning from their bases in England. The SCs serviced, refuelled and re-armed these aircraft during the day, and they would return home to the safety of their home bases at night.

The four original SCs that went to Normandy were brought back to Britain at the end of July 1944. Eventually they all returned to Old Sarum for re-organisation and re-grouping, as it had been decided to send them to the Far East. The SC personnel drew their tropical kit, and left Old Sarum bound for RAF West Kirby, near Liverpool, in readiness for embarkation to India. The units arrived in India in time to play an important part in the war against the Japanese. They serviced and re-armed Hurricanes, Spitfires and Thunderbolts on jungle airstrips throughout south-east Asia, finishing up in Malaya and Indo-China at the end of the war.

In December 1944 No.1 S of AC became the School of Air Support, a tri-service organisation that brought in the Royal Navy and involve-ment with sea-borne assault. The unit was divided into two wings, the Offensive Support Wing and the Transport Wing. Its flying training role changed to one of battlefield demonstrations.

At the end of the war in 1945 Old Sarum became a very quiet place. There was very little flying going on, and in May 1947 the School of Air Support became the School of Land/Air Warfare. Post-war flying at Old Sarum mainly consisted of the Ansons, Dominies and Chipmunks of the Station Flight, and the gliders of No.622 Gliding School, Air Training Corps. The School of Land/Air Warfare became the Joint Warfare Establishment in 1963, working in liaison with the Joint Helicopter Tactical Development Unit that operated Westland Whirlwind helicopters.

Old Sarum was transferred to the Army Department in December 1971. The JHDU was disbanded in October 1976, but flying continued until November 1978 when No.622 Gliding School moved to RAF Upavon. The station was finally closed as a military base in 1979, but the airfield was retained as an unlicensed landing ground for light aircraft. The airfield was sold to the Edgeley Aircraft Company in 1981 for the manufacture of the Optica, a revolutionary new spotter aircraft. However, this ceased five years later after a disastrous fire destroyed two of the Belfast Truss hangars that Edgeley used for production.

Nevertheless, flying still continues at Old Sarum, as it has done since 1917. Apart from the war years, private aircraft have been hangared at Old Sarum ever since the 1920s, and have been flown in the evenings and weekends by their military or civilian owners. The most recent flying clubs have been the Wiltshire Aero Club and, since 1992, The Old Sarum Flying Club. Microlight and helicopter training also takes

In the early days, there was only one major obstacle on the aerodrome at Old Sarum, a thatched farm building with a windpump beside it. It was eventually removed, but not before several aircraft collided with it, including this DH6. (Dr Hugh Thomas)

place. There are many reminders of the past, as a memorial was unveiled to the AOP squadrons in 1993, and several former military Tiger Moths, Austers and Chipmunks are still flown from the airfield by their civilian owners. Today Old Sarum remains in good health, as one of the oldest and most active airfields in the UK.

14

PORTON
DOWN

National Grid Reference (184) SU210375, 5 miles NE of Salisbury

Porton Down has been the centre of research on offensive means and provision of protective measures for British Service personnel against chemical warfare since 1916. Although not a major airfield, the establishment had an aircraft landing ground, and it played an important role during the Second World War for all three Services, not least in the use of aeroplanes.

During the First World War chemical weapons were used on the Allied Forces for the first time on 22 April 1915, when 150 tons of chlorine gas were discharged by the Germans into the French lines across four miles of the Ypres front. Canadian and British troops were similarly attacked shortly afterwards. This led to the requirement for a means of retaliation in kind and to protect British forces from this new weapon: the British army was able to mount a gas attack on the Germans at Loos on 25 September, but this was a limited affair, and a more sustained approach to the problem was needed.

A research establishment was therefore set up in 1916 at Porton Down in Wiltshire in an attempt to provide a scientific basis for British chemical warfare. A site had been found, north-east of Salisbury and to the south of Salisbury Plain, that contained a natural bowl in the landscape, thus enabling work to take place in privacy. The new establishment came under the Trench Warfare Department of the War Office and was entitled the Royal Engineers Experimental Station. Work immediately started on studying the retaliatory capability. The method of delivery devised was the gas cylinder, but the Germans had already moved onto gas shells that were more effective. Work on shells with the Royal Artillery and research into other areas such as the design of effective respirators followed during the ensuing months of the First World War.

The first time that chemical weapons were used from the air by British forces was in 1919 when small chemical bombs were hand-dropped from RAF de Havilland DH9 aircraft on formations of the Red Army in northern Russia. No trials had in fact taken place at Porton Down beforehand but the need for aircraft to be involved in field trials for the delivery of chemical warfare agents and smoke was seen at the establishment in the mid-1920s. Following the use of an Avro 504 in trials in about 1926 it was decided to form a special flight to meet the requirements of the establishment. A landing ground was laid out on the range alongside the main scientific site, so that visiting aircraft could operate from the establishment, as well as providing a base for those aircraft involved in trials. However, there were no permanent facilities such as hangars.

The nearest RAF station at the time was Netheravon, and it was there that the Porton Experimental Flight was based, with four aircraft on strength, a Fairey Fox and two Hawker Horsley day bombers and a Blackburn Dart torpedo bomber. Spray tanks were originally fitted into the trials aircraft, with pipes and nozzles to emit smoke to detect dispersion patterns. Later a self-contained tank with its own discharge pipe and dispersal nozzle was developed. These spray tanks were able

Lysander, Harts, Whitley and Battle of the CDES Special Duty Flight in September 1938. (Dstl)

161

to disperse smoke operationally, and the designation Smoke Curtain Installation (SCI) was a useful security euphemism to disguise their major role in chemical warfare. The equipment was successfully trialled under the wing of a Hawker Horsley in 1928. Further trials demonstrated that it could be used effectively to disperse various agents at heights of up to at least 10,000 feet. The basic design of the SCI remained substantially unaltered throughout the many years of its subsequent existence.

The Porton Experimental Flight moved to Boscombe Down in February 1931 when suitable accommodation became available at the newly-reopened airfield. Shortly after its move the Flight was re-equipped with a Westland Wapiti and Hawker Hart two-seat day bombers, and was renamed the Special Duty Flight. These aircraft were updated as the aircraft types in front-line service changed, and at the outbreak of World War II the Flight had a Westland Lysander, Fairey Battle, Armstrong Whitworth Whitley and a Vickers Wellington on strength.

The work of the Porton Down scientists during the 1930s resulted in the anti-gas cape, chemically impregnated protective battle dress, gas detector paper and paint, decontamination liquid and procedures, gas identification sets, anti-gas covers for horses, mules and dogs, as well as respirators, not only for troops (and animals!) but also for the civilian population. As the result of the research and field trials undertaken at Porton Down during this time there were no better equipped forces in respect of anti-gas defence than those of the UK in the late 1930s. British military equipment was available to cater for all known chemical hazards. At the start of the Second World War the design of this equipment had changed very little, as there was no need. Equally there was little investment in offensive chemical capabilities, mainly due to political unease, with the result that there had been minimal British production of chemical agents or weapons. However, research had been permitted on the ways in which chemical warfare might be used against the British forces in any future war.

A new form of the SCI emerged just before the Second World War from Porton Down, which by now had been renamed the Chemical Defence Experimental Station (CDES). As it was a longer version of the installation it was of higher capacity, but was capable of being fitted inside an aircraft's bomb bay. In 1938 a Whitley Mk I was modified to carry one tank, with a discharge nozzle protruding through a port in the bomb bay doors. Later a Wellington bomber was modified to carry two of the larger SCIs in its bomb bay. The standard SCI continued to

B. 4 / 0 7   15. 5. 40.

Vickers Wellington being fitted with a large SCI by CDES technicians in May 1940.
(Dstl)

be used for smoke delivery as, being externally mounted, it was easier to replace the units for a quick turnaround on operations. Originally fitted to light bombers, the aircraft types on which the units were cleared for installation increased as aero engines increased in power, being eventually fitted to single engine types such as Hawker Typhoon and Tempest fighters.

When war started in 1939 the British chemical offensive stockpile was small compared with other countries. The RAF had limited stocks of mustard spray and bombs to be used by Lysander Army Co-operation aircraft and medium bombers to slow an invading army by contaminating landing beaches or strategic positions, and to mount counter-attacks.

A priority programme was therefore started by the Government to increase these stocks of chemical weapons and this resulted in the production of a substantial arsenal of chemical bombs and SCIs. The RAF took a major role in the distribution and storage of these weapons. Eventually, 60 RAF stations and 29 MUs were to hold large amounts of them. The RAF also had a decontamination organisation, with each station having squads to treat areas of contamination and a Gas Defence Centre.

Hurricane dropping smoke bombs developed by CDES during a ground defence exercise in November 1941. (Aeroplane)

It was feared that as a prelude to invasion the Germans would spray British airfields and military installations with mustard or other chemical agents. Any exposed aircraft, vehicles and equipment would be contaminated and therefore unusable for some time. On ordinary surfaces the agent would be difficult to detect, and would gradually vaporise, depending on the ambient temperature and its concentration, in the form of a toxic, if not deadly, gas. To give warning of such contamination, detector panels were positioned on airfields and equipment. The paint on the panels had been developed at Porton Down and was designed to react to any contamination by turning from a normal yellow colour to dark brown when spots of agent landed on it. Eighteen-inch squares of gas detector paint were also applied to aircraft upper surfaces, usually on wings and fuselage in positions that could be easily seen by the pilot or another member of the crew. Similar panels were fitted to military vehicles, and to the tops of pillar-boxes.

Many experimental weapons and munitions were developed and trialled at CDES during the war. Many were in response to service requirements for chemical weapons designed to attack particular targets, such as armoured vehicles, pillboxes or bunkers. Others were to improve the efficiency of mustard gas delivery by aircraft. Although several passed into service, none were actually used because of the Allied 'no first use' policy, which meant that such weapons would only be used in retaliation in kind against the Axis forces.

Smoke had been studied at Porton Down ever since the First World

War, for screening, signalling and marking purposes. The Second World War led to urgent operational requirements for new smoke munitions. These ranged from coloured smoke for signalling to smoke screens for hiding large industrial installations from air attack. The Royal Navy had a long-standing need for effective smoke generation by its warships. From 1941 onwards there was increasing co-operation between CDES and those concerned with planning amphibious operations, particularly regarding the use of smoke. At least one visit was made to Porton Down by Lord Mountbatten, Head of Combined Operations, to discuss the availability and role of smoke weapons in forthcoming amphibious operations.

Following the success of the daring commando raid on St Nazaire in March 1942, a more ambitious raid on a French seaport was devised, as a 'reconnaissance in force' to test the German defences and evaluate amphibious landing techniques. Dieppe was selected as the target as it lay only 70 miles away across the Channel and was within easy range for aircraft based in Britain. Plans for a combined operation by all three services were prepared calling for a landing by troops and tanks from ships and landing craft covered by naval gunfire with aircraft in support. It was named Operation Jubilee and the date was set for 18 August 1942. The tactical plan called for the capture of six heavy calibre gun batteries protecting the town, the destruction of harbour facilities and the capture of an airfield and divisional Army HQ nearby. The assault was to start at 04:50 hours and be completed by 11:00 hours followed by an orderly withdrawal from the beaches – all in all it was quite a tall order.

With a number of Luftwaffe airfields in northern France it was essential that heavy Allied air cover be provided to protect the landings. An unprecedented number of RAF and US squadrons were put under the control of Air Marshal Trafford Leigh Mallory, OC 11 Group, for the operation. Just for the day some 72 squadrons were committed. Their tasks included fighter cover (with 50 Spitfire Squadrons, including three from the USAAF), bombing and low level strafing (eight Hurricane and three Boston Squadron), reconnaissance (one Hudson and four Mustang Squadrons), and strategic bombing (one USAAF B17 Bomb Group). For the landings and the withdrawal, aircraft from two Boston and four Blenheim Squadrons were to lay smoke. Although they were aware of the fact that this was an important operation, none of the aircrew could know that they were about to be involved in what was probably the greatest single air battle of the Second World War.

No.226 Squadron moved to Thruxton, a satellite of Netheravon, with their Boston bombers in early August 1942, and began an intensive work-up with the smoke weapons developed by CDES. SCIs were fitted into the bomb bays of some aircraft, while others were to carry 100lb smoke bombs. They were joined by four more Bostons, two from each of Nos.88 and 107 Squadrons, and by Blenheims of No.13 Squadron. All were under the command of Wing Commander Surplice, OC of No.226 Squadron. Sixteen more Bostons of Nos.88 and 107 Squadrons were positioned at Ford on the Hampshire coast, to fly from there on the mission.

Bad weather on the morning of 18 August forced a delay, but after an agonising 24-hour wait the operation finally got under way. A fleet of 252 ships weighed anchor in their British ports and set sail across the Channel. Arriving off the French coast the landing force formed into thirteen different groups, each with its own objective. By 03:30 hours the landing craft were heading for the beaches. Meanwhile the Boston and Blenheim crews were readying their aircraft. Engines were started, and pre-flight checks carried out. The first aircraft to leave were six Blenheims of No.13 Squadron. Taking off at 04:15, each aircraft was loaded with 100lb phosphorous bombs. They were followed by the Bostons. The Blenheims had been given the task of blinding two AA batteries commanding the cliffs to the north-east of the beaches. As they arrived in the target area, they formed into line astern and, keeping as low as they could, dropped their smoke bombs. As they did so, they came under heavy AA fire, and one aircraft was shot down, several more being damaged. Having done their job the remaining Blenheims flew out to sea, but as they headed over the RN fleet, several ships fired on them, causing more damage.

Shortly afterwards the Bostons reached the area. They were to attack gun batteries on the cliffs. They spent 35 minutes over the batteries, dropping 156 hundred-pound phosphorous bombs and laying smoke from their SCIs to the rear of the guns from a height of about fifty feet. Ground fire was intense, and flying in the face of such murderous fire took steel nerves and considerable courage. Nine of the Bostons took hits, including one flown by Squadron Leader Digger Magill, which was hit in the bomb bay, igniting its smoke bombs. Nonetheless Magill managed to find his target and jettisoned his load of smoking ordnance. Despite the heavy flak the Bostons managed to lay a smoke screen between 800 and 1,000 yards long, which gradually drifted over the gun batteries, obscuring their views of the landings.

After setting their smoke screens the twelve Bostons headed back to base, although two did not make it all the way, crash-landing instead at RAF Middle Wallop. As other bombers arrived over Dieppe to bomb the batteries and strong-points, German fighters started to put in an appearance. Soon 20 or so Focke-Wulf Fw190s were in the area, firing on the bombers, and few escaped damage. Several bombers were shot down.

The raid did not go well, and the British and Canadian troops found themselves pinned down by murderous enemy fire. Casualties were heavy despite support from Allied aircraft and ships. As the troops were desperately fighting ashore, at about 11:00 hours four Bostons of No.226 Squadron mounted another smoke operation, along with eight Blenheims of No.614 Squadron, to screen the batteries. Two more No.226 Squadron crews followed them to lay a smoke screen along the beach, trailing it from a height of 50 feet for a mile or so. This action was particularly hazardous, as the aircraft had to contend with a cross-fire from the Germans on the coast and the RN at sea! Of this group, no aircraft were shot down over Dieppe, but two crash-landed on return to base, with casualties. The third wave of smoke layers consisted of two Bostons from No.88 Squadron, and one from No.226 Squadron. At 11:52 they came in over the harbour and flew to the cliffs about a mile distant, to cover troops on the beaches, who were by now starting to withdraw. The smoke screen was effective, but one aircraft was shot down into the sea.

More smoke sorties were flown to cover the withdrawal of the raiding force. Five Bostons of No.226 Squadron each fitted with SCIs and escorted by Spitfires of No.66 Squadron arrived over Dieppe in the mid-afternoon. They made eleven runs over the beaches. Defensive fire was intense, and one Boston was hit, diving into the sea.

The efforts of the smoke laying aircraft at Dieppe were highly satisfactory and gave more than the required protection to the invading force. Several aircraft were damaged, six badly damaged, and two were lost but one of the Bostons did manage to shoot down an Fw190.

The lessons learned from the Dieppe raid were taken onboard by all concerned, but one important result was that of the effectiveness of the SCIs and smoke ordnance carried by the aircraft taking part. The system was used regularly throughout the war, and was particularly successful during the D-Day landings. Nonetheless, work on refining smoke laying methods continued at Porton Down, but so did work on gas ordnance. Various aircraft were used for trials using simulated or actual chemical bombs in trials. On 29 July 1943, for example, a Boeing B-17 of the USAAF was flown from Boscombe Down on a chemical

The Hard Target on the Porton Down Range in 2002; still showing the scars of several impacts from airborne weapons. (Author)

bombing trial. Unfortunately some of the weapons would not release, and the aircraft was diverted to Thruxton, rather than let it return to Boscombe Down. There the aircraft was quarantined at one end of the airfield. Armed guards were placed around the aircraft, and the Station Gas NCO and a Decontamination Squad stood by. Gas detectors were positioned near the aircraft and regularly monitored. The following day a Wing Commander arrived from Porton Down, and after a check the aircraft was allowed to return to A&AEE.

At some stage during the war the 'Hard Target' was constructed on the Porton Down ranges. This massive reinforced concrete structure, some thirty feet high and forty feet wide, was built as an artillery target, but was also used by aircraft. The target still stands on the range in one piece today, although it does bear the scars of many ordnance strikes.

One important area of work at Porton Down during the Second World War was the development of protective clothing for all three services. Rather than provide an extra layer of protective clothing, CDES scientists came up with the idea of providing extra protection to the normal clothing worn by the troops. Experiments showed that a type of chemical could be used to impregnate fabric and give protection against toxic chemicals. This enabled an impregnated battledress uniform to be developed which, when worn with respirator and gloves, gave effective protection to the troops against mustard gas vapour. This was far better than encumbering troops with additional heavy oilskin protective clothing beyond the light anti-gas cape, which could be debilitating in use as well as adversely affecting the troops' physical abilities. The scientists produced a special impregnate in collaboration with the dry cleaning and textile industry and developed a process for use with service dress in a normal dry cleaning plant. Laundering destroyed the impregnate, so a system was developed by the Royal Army Ordnance Corps for the withdrawal and recycling of uniforms through special dry cleaning firms to ensure that uniforms were always in effective condition. The scale of this operation was huge, and it continued throughout the war. All British and Commonwealth troops that took part in the D-Day invasion, for example, were equipped with this clothing.

Porton Down's work for the services was extended to include health. Research on insecticides and repellents became important at CDES from 1943 onwards. The use of the insecticide DDT was studied, and the introduction of DDT-impregnated service shirts eradicated lousiness in the field army. The first large-scale production of DDT took place at Sutton Oak, Lancashire, in the production research facility known as the Chemical Defence Research Establishment. Other medical aspects of war studied at Porton Down during the period included burns treatment, the effects of underwater explosions, air purification in submarines, the development of aircrew masks and the hazards of fumes in gun turrets.

The title of the CDES support flight based at Boscombe Down had changed in 1942 to 'C Armament Test Flight' when it became part of C Squadron A&AEE. It changed again in September 1944, when all A&AEE units were re-organised. Support work for CDES then came under the new Communications and Special Duties Flight. As well as providing aircraft for Porton Down trials, the Flight also provided communications aircraft for both establishments. It operated a variety of aircraft at this time, including the Piper Cub, Auster, Fairey Swordfish, Republic Thunderbolt, DH Mosquito, Short Stirling and Avro Lancaster.

Towards the end of the war, the scientists at Porton Down were studying the effects of the tropical environment on chemical weapons and protection, as British troops were fighting the Japanese in the Far East. Following VE Day, however, they received a nasty surprise. In April 1945 German artillery shells were discovered bearing unknown markings. Examination of the contents revealed a highly toxic and largely undetectable compound that was lethal in small concentrations. This was Tabun, one of the new series of compounds that the Germans had discovered and named G agents or nerve agents. These compounds came as a complete shock to the Allies as stockpiles of shells and bombs containing the substances were found. It appears that the Germans had produced the stockpiles for defence, thinking that the enemy had similar weapons. If they had known that the Allies could not retaliate with nerve agents, who knows whether the Nazis would have used them as the Third Reich was dying? As the Russians had also discovered German stockpiles of these deadly weapons, nerve agents became the focal point for the work at Porton Down during the post-war years.

Aviation continued to figure in the work of the establishment at Porton Down after the war. The landing ground was later supplemented by a helipad, so that light aircraft and helicopters could easily be handled. However, the larger military aircraft required for Porton Down's work continued to operate from A&AEE Boscombe Down. From 1946 onwards aircraft have largely been provided by B Squadron for such work as chemical, biological, pesticide and meteorological trials. This traditional arrangement carried on from the late 1940s, when B Squadron provided an Avro Anson fitted with tanks and a rotary atomiser for an anti-locust trial, to the 1990s, when a Hawker Hunter fighter aircraft was flown with spray tanks to simulate chemical attacks on troops taking part in realistic training during the Porton Down 'Battle Run'.

The scientists and other staff of Porton Down continue to carry on the work today that was pioneered by their predecessors. Britain's ability to produce the best protective clothing and equipment for its armed forces in the face of increasingly sophisticated weapons of mass destruction is due in no small part to the dedicated scientists of this important and historic Wiltshire defence establishment.

15
RAMSBURY

*National Grid Reference (174) SU270703, 4¹/₂ miles
E of Marlborough*

This airfield was built in north Wiltshire during World War II , on high ground overlooking the River Kennet, and was named after the picturesque village of Ramsbury, which lies in the river valley to the north. Constructed as a training base for the RAF, the airfield was later used by the Americans for airborne forces training and deployment.

In early 1941 RAF Bomber Command was in the process of stepping up its campaign on Occupied Europe, and more airfields were needed in southern England for additional training and operational facilities for its squadrons. Membury, on the Berkshire side of the Wiltshire/Berkshire border, had already been established as such a base, and satellite airfields were needed in the area to support it. Ramsbury was one of these. The actual site selected by the Air Ministry was a good one, on a plateau to the south of the village. Construction work started in May 1941.

The area was mainly farmland and woodland, and once trees had been felled and hedgerows bulldozed, the runways and taxiways were put down. Three concrete runways were laid, in the standard pattern for a bomber station. Each runway was built to bomber standards, being 50 yards wide, but they varied in length, the main runway being 6,000 feet long. Twenty-eight pan-type hard-standings were constructed, running off extensions to the perimeter track on the south side of the airfield. Two T2 hangers were built (each one being 240 feet long and 120 feet wide), along with the control tower and the other usual operational and support buildings and installations. Living accommodation for the expected 2,400 personnel was built in the woods to the eastern side of the site. The airfield covered an area of some 500 acres.

When completed in August 1942 the airfield was handed over to No.92 Group, Bomber Command, for use by an Operational Training Unit. However, the RAF was not to be site's first tenant. With the arrival of the United States Army in Britain, it was decided to allocate Ramsbury to the US Army Air Force (USAAF), as they needed at least half-a-dozen airfields in the UK to establish themselves before commencing operations in Europe. The Americans started to arrive at the airfield towards the end of August, when the 64th Troop Carrier Group (TCG) flew in. They were equipped with the Douglas C-47 Skytrain (named the Dakota in British service). A week or so after the Americans had settled in, they received the attentions of the Luftwaffe, when a sneak raid was made. This went off, fortunately, without any casualties or damage (apart from a few craters on the airfield). The raid had apparently been forecast by Lord Haw-Haw (the British defector) in a broadcast on German propaganda radio, when he welcomed the 64th TCG to Britain and said that the Luftwaffe would be leaving their calling card.

Initially the C-47 crews spent their time flying supplies from the ports of arrival, such as Liverpool and Bristol, to and around the other USAAF bases in Britain. Training with paratroops started in September 1942, and this fuelled rumours that operations were about to start. By then it had been decided to delay the expected assault on the Continent, and instead start a second front in North Africa. Fitted with long-range fuel tanks, and following final kitting out, all fifty-one

Airspeed Oxford, as flown by 15(P)AFU at Ramsbury in 1943. (Aeroplane)

aircraft of 64th TCG took off from Ramsbury late in October for Cornwall. The Cornish bases of St Eval and Predannack were to be the jumping off point for the first leg of their journey to Algeria, where they were to take part in Operation Torch, the Invasion of North Africa. In early November 1942, following final preparations and flight briefings, the crews, together with the force of British and US paratroopers, boarded their aircraft, bound for Gibraltar. There the Wing waited for action. They flew on 11 November to Maison Blanche near Algiers, once the forward bases in Algeria had been secured. From there, the C47s of the 64th TCG flew paratroops to take the strategically important airfield of Bone, near the Tunisian border. The group then saw the campaign through to a successful conclusion, and stayed in the Mediterranean theatre for the rest of the war.

Ramsbury was very quiet after the Americans left. The airfield was transferred to No.70 Group, RAF Training Command, and on 7th December 1942 the advance party of a new unit arrived, from No.15 (Pilot) Advanced Flying Unit ((P)AFU). The role of this unit was to provide continuity and advanced training to pilots who had been trained under the Empire Air Training Scheme (EATS) in Canada, Australia, South Africa, Rhodesia, India, New Zealand and a handful of other British overseas territories. It was the job of the (P)AFU to familiarise the newly qualified EATS pilots with flying in the more constricted airspace of the UK, and particularly with the British weather. Equipped with twin-engined trainers, No.15(P)AFU also gave pilots the opportunity to convert from single-engine to multi-engine aircraft. The unit had been at Leconfield in Yorkshire, but facilities there were coming under pressure with the arrival of two newly-operational bomber squadrons, so it was decided to move the unit to the less congested south. RAF Andover in Hampshire was chosen as the new HQ for No.15(P)AFU, with Grove in Oxfordshire, Greenham Common in Berkshire and Ramsbury in Wiltshire as satellite airfields for flying training.

S Flight was allocated to Ramsbury, and their first intake of 25 pupils arrived on 5 January 1943. Training began in earnest. During its existence No.15(P)AFU was equipped mainly with the Airspeed Oxford. This aircraft first entered service during 1937 and became the RAF's principal twin-engined trainer. About 30 Oxfords were normally resident at Ramsbury at any one time. The unit also had several Avro Ansons and one in particular, N5262, seems to have been regularly used at Ramsbury during 1943. This aircraft was put to good use for navigational training and as a communications aircraft

173

regularly flying personnel, spares and equipment all over southern England.

Training units and accidents, sadly, often go together. The first fatality for the unit occurred on 2nd March, when Sgt R.C.M. Webster from the RNZAF was carrying out a solo night navigation exercise. His aircraft collided with trees on the downwind leg of a night circuit at 03:10 hours, and crashed. Another accident took place on 21 March, and both the instructor, W/O J.R.T. Hazleton, and the pupil, Sgt B.G.G. Francis, died when their aeroplane hit the ground while flying at low level. W/O Hazleton had survived one operational tour with Bomber Command before joining No.15(P)AFU.

Additional Flights of the (P)AFU arrived at Ramsbury during late July, having had to move out of Grove to make room for units of the expanding 9th Air Force, which was the US tactical air force then being set up in Britain.

Between February and September 1943 seventeen Oxfords were destroyed or badly damaged while operating from Ramsbury. Mid-air collisions were unfortunately not unusual. On 27 May 1943 two Oxfords collided and crashed near the airfield perimeter killing one of the pilots. Almost a month later on 25th June 1943 Oxford Is LX168 and V3955 collided in mid-air near Bishopstone, Wiltshire. All aboard both aircraft were killed. Another mid-air collision occurred on 20 July 1943, resulting in three deaths and one serious injury.

During August and September 1943 rumours spread around the camp that No.15(P)AFU would be moving out to make room for the USAAF. In October these rumours were confirmed and by the end of the month the unit had left. One part went to Babdown Farm in Gloucestershire and the remainder to Castle Combe in Wiltshire. The Americans took over on 1st November and the airfield became USAAF Station No.469. Although the RAF had officially departed, a small number of RAF personnel remained to act as liaison and to keep the airfield open, and they witnessed the arrival of the first group of American servicemen. Mr L Jones, then an NCO, remembers how pleased most of them were to meet the GIs. 'The Americans were very generous and I can remember being given cartons of cigarettes. Getting a lift to Hungerford Station was no longer a problem as transport would always be available for us. Their rations were also much better than ours but we disliked having all of our meal (main course and dessert) served on one sectioned tray. Because of this they allowed us to have two plates but we had to wash them up ourselves!'

During November 1943 a USAAF Station Complement Squadron

arrived to take over from the RAF, but it was December before the first flying units arrived. They were from the 434th and 435th TCGs of the US 9th Air Force, flying the Douglas C-47 Skytrain. They spent their time at Ramsbury exercising with locally-based companies of the 101st Airborne Division. Both groups later departed to Leicestershire. On 5 February the first aircraft from the 437th TCG flew into Ramsbury.

The 437th TCG was an element of the 53rd Troop Carrier Wing (TCW) of the 9th Air Force, USAAF. Each Group of the 53rd TCW was equipped with seventy-two C-47s, a type that had since proved to be so successful in the transportation role that it had become the mainstay for Allied work in this field. The wing was split into five groups, each group being sub-divided into four squadrons. The 437th TCG at Ramsbury was made up of the 83rd, 84th, 85th and 86th Troop Carrier Squadrons.

The 101st Airborne Division had arrived in England aboard two troopships in the autumn of 1943. From Liverpool they were transported through war-torn Britain to their camps in southern England. The 506th Parachute Infantry Regiment of the Division was assigned to several camps in the Marlborough area of Wiltshire, and the 3rd Battalion was allocated to Ramsbury Camp, not far from the airfield. The Regiment's training took place in local fields and woods. Robert Radler of Easy Company, 506th PIR (the exploits of which were later described in Stephen Ambrose's book *Band of Brothers*, and dramatised on television) remembers making tailgate jumps in Love's Copse near the Company's camp at Albourne, just to the north of Ramsbury. (Tailgate jumps were made at the back of trucks travelling at reasonable speed along country roads, when aircraft were not available, or it was considered too dangerous to jump into particular areas.) They would be out in the woods for several days and nights at a time, undertaking squad, platoon and company size manoeuvres. Live ammunition was often used, along with mines and live explosives.

It was realised that additional personnel in non-paratroop units would be required to parachute into action with the paras. These included doctors, chaplains, communications operators and forward artillery observers. To train these men the 101st Jump School had been set up in October 1943 under the command of Captain Walter Sobel, formerly commander of Easy Company. It was established in the grounds of Chilton Foliat Camp, a few miles to the east of Ramsbury. Ground training took place, but to qualify, five live parachute jumps had to be made by each man. For this, the men were driven up to Ramsbury airfield to embark on their training aircraft.

They were then taken up and eventually dropped into the grounds of the Jump School.

The 437th TCG started training at the beginning of March 1944 and carried on almost continuously in the months leading up to D-Day, subject of course to the vagaries of the English weather. As well as deploying troops by parachute, the role of the group was to deploy troops and supplies by glider. Initially emphasis was placed on getting the group pilots, both glider and powered, proficient in flying and towing the British Horsa glider. The controls and flying characteristics of this aircraft differed considerably from the US Waco CG-4A glider on which the American pilots had been trained in the USA.

Training consisted of formation flying, glider-towing and instrument flying (in preparation for operations at night or in bad weather). The group also practised paratroop dropping, both simulated and with troops. Emphasis was put on the marshalling of large numbers of aircraft on the ground, flying them off and getting them into formation at the required altitude as quickly as practicable. This was later practised at pre-dawn, the time when the forthcoming operations were planned to take place. At the end of formation-flying practices the aircraft and glider combinations returned to base where the gliders would be released, to come swooping out of the dawn sky and land on the grass. After the gliders had landed, the C-47s would return and fly past the control tower one at a time, dropping their tow-ropes to the ground for retrieval by the ground staff.

As with the tactical transport squadrons of the RAF, a secondary role for the USAAF C-47 units was to be that of casualty evacuation (or 'casevac'). Specialist medical personnel (mostly female) were provided for this role, in medical units attached to each group. In the case of the 437th TCG, this was the 814th Medical Air Evacuation Squadron (MAES). The personnel of the squadron had been trained together as a unit at Bowman Field, near Louisville, Kentucky, and consisted of one Chief Nurse (Captain), 24 Registered Nurses (1st Lieutenants), 24 Technical Sergeants and support staff. The squadron arrived at Ramsbury on 11 April 1944. At their new base the nurses started 'getting flight time', training for the missions ahead, and occasionally flying patients needing medical treatment.

Many parachute dropping exercises took place as part of the build-up to D-Day, the invasion of Europe. One of the final dress rehearsals was on Lambourn Downs on 11 and 12 May 1944. All of the planned D-Day departure airfields were used for this major exercise. It was an immense success, although there were one or two hitches. H Company

Captured Focke-Wulf FW 190 PN999 of 1426 (Enemy Aircraft) Flight on a visit to Ramsbury on 24 May 1944. (via Roger Day)

of the 502nd PIR dropped their parachutists over Ramsbury airfield by mistake. A number of them landed in the grounds of Littlecote House, the Divisional HQ, much to everyone's embarrassment!

On 24 May 1944 Ramsbury was visited by an unusual collection of assorted British, American and German aircraft. It was a 'Flying Circus' flown to Allied airfields, in the weeks before the invasion, to familiarise personnel with the main aircraft types that they would be seeing over the next few months. The German aircraft came from 1426 (Enemy Aircraft) Flight.

The invasion of Europe, Operation Overlord, was planned for early June 1944. That part of the plan calling for the initial assault phase of Overlord was code-named 'Neptune'. From the Americans this called for six massed glider landings – four from the 82nd Airborne Division coded 'Detroit', 'Elmira', 'Galveston' and 'Hackensack', and two from the 101st Airborne, coded 'Chicago' and 'Keokuk'. The 437th TCG were to take part in operations 'Detroit' and 'Elmira'.

At Ramsbury, soldiers of the 82nd Airborne Division, who would be among the first to go into action on D-Day, impatiently waited for the go-ahead. The moment that they had been training hard for over the preceding months was about to come. Now, on the evening of 5 June, final briefings were taking place. Jack Merrick, from the 84th TCS, who was to pilot the 51st and penultimate glider in the initial formation, remembers: 'We had been shown detailed maps of Normandy and briefed fully about our part in the operation. From that moment we were prevented from talking to anybody who was not taking part in the mission, and we moved about the camp in groups, escorted by armed guards.' Colonel Cedric E. Hudgens, who was to lead the first formation off that morning, read the Order of the Day from General Eisenhower. At last the crews and the paratroops were able to climb aboard their aircraft, where they nervously readied themselves for the journey across the channel to France.

At 01:59 the first of 52 tug and glider combinations moved forward in the moonlight to begin its take-off run. Within 30 minutes all 52 combinations had taken off. They released their gliders south of Cherbourg, their objective being to isolate the western end of the invasion beach-head. However, poor weather and anti-aircraft fire disrupted the formations, resulting in the glider and paratroop landings being more scattered than planned. Despite this the troops managed to get their bearings, and most Airborne units had reached their objectives by mid-morning. At 05:22 the first C-47s returned to Ramsbury.

Eighteen C-47s of the 85th TCS were temporarily detached to operate from Membury on D-Day, taking part in Operation Albany, transporting paratroopers of 101st Airborne Division to Normandy. They returned to Ramsbury later that morning. Later that day, at 19:07, the first of another 26 C-47s took off, towing 18 Horsa and 8 CG-4A gliders with supplies and reinforcements as part of Operation Elmira. As they crossed the channel on that summer evening the visibility was good, and the crews could see the enormity of Operation Overlord. Below them was the unforgettable sight of hundreds of ships in a seemingly endless stream heading all the way to the beaches of France.

At 04:39 on D-Day+1 (7 June), fifty C-47s of the 437th took off from Ramsbury towing 32 Wacos and 18 Horsas. This was part of Operation Galveston, which called for more supplies and reinforcements for the beach-head. The invasion had been a great success, but the Allied armies needed to be constantly re-supplied if they were to maintain their momentum against superior German forces. The 437th were called upon to deliver petrol, rations, clothing, blood plasma and, of course, ammunition, much of which came from Savernake, south-west of Ramsbury, where a vast forward munitions depot had been established.

On landing in France the aircraft were unloaded as quickly as possible. Nurses were carried on the outgoing supply flights to be on hand to tend to any wounded that would be brought back on the return flights. Back at Ramsbury the aircraft would be met by other personnel of the 814th MAES, and the injured would be rushed off to the nearest U.S.Army hospitals by ambulance. In fact casualties were not as heavy as had been feared.

On 12 July the 437th were informed that they were being sent to Italy to take part in another operation. This was except for four aircraft and their crews from each squadron, that were to remain behind at Ramsbury to maintain the re-supply task. The new operation was 'Dragoon', the invasion of the South of France. For the ferry flight out to Italy each aircraft was fitted with extra fuel tanks inside the cabin.

When they returned to Ramsbury on 24 August, the detachment found the airfield to be a lot busier than they left it. In their absence there had been a shuffle-round of TCG units, using Ramsbury as an air-head to maintain an uninterrupted flow of ammunition and fuel to France. The Group's remaining aircraft had been joined by the 98th TCS from the 440th TCG at Exeter, the 301st TCS from the 441st TCG at Merryfield, the 93rd TCS from the 439th TCG at Upottery and the 306th TCS from the 442nd TCG at Weston Zoyland. With the return of the main group from Italy, the visiting units gradually returned to their bases.

Like many other Allied airborne units, the 437th TCG was involved in Operation Market Garden, the daring plan conceived by General Montgomery to take the Allies into the German industrial heartland, in an attempt to shorten the war. A number of landings of British and US airborne forces were planned along a corridor through the Nether-lands, culminating in the capture of the Arnhem bridge over the Rhine.

C-47s of 437th TCG lined up at Ramsbury in preparation for Operation Market Garden on 17 September 1944. (via Roger Day)

179

Units of the 101st Airborne Division moved onto the airfield on 12 September to check and prepare their equipment. The aircraft and gliders were overhauled. On 15 September, the crews of the 437th were briefed. They were told that the mission would be taking place in daylight, and that they would be flying without co-pilots due to the shortage of trained glider pilots.

The operation was set for 17 September, and on that morning the weather was beautiful. Warm sun shone down on the troops waiting to board their aircraft. Seventy C-47 and glider combinations took off from Ramsbury at 11:00 hours that morning, to join the mightiest airborne force in history. Some 5,000 Allied aircraft took part in Operation Market Garden, including 1,400 transports that dropped 21,000 paratroops. In addition 2,300 gliders transported another 18,000 troops, while another 1,300 hauled supplies. It was the largest airborne operation of World War II.

Casualties were severe, with 124 transport aircraft and 132 gliders being shot down by enemy ground fire or crashing during the operation. The 437th lost more aircraft on that one mission than on all of their other combat operations put together. Carrying the 101st Airborne to Zon in the Eindhoven sector, they experienced heavy opposition. Six of the 64 C-47s that reached the German lines were shot down, and two Wacos collided over the Landing Zone. On the next day the 437th carried out a re-supply mission to Zon, but they followed a different route. This time no aircraft were lost, although several returned with damage from small-arms fire.

Following the Arnhem operation, the whole of the 53rd TCW reverted to the standard freight shuttle to France and Belgium, the 437th flying casevac on the return flights when necessary. Towards the end of 1944, a number of aircraft technicians from each of the group's four squadrons were assigned to B-24 Liberator bomber bases, to learn how to maintain the type. This arose because a number of Liberators that had been modified as transports to carry fuel, and re-designated C-109, had been received by the 437th. These aircraft were flown from Ramsbury, but were not very popular, for as flying petrol tankers they were extremely vulnerable, even to small-arms fire.

As the winter of 1944 came on, the weather became the main problem for the 437th. Aircraft might take off from base in bright sunshine, only to find themselves 'socked in' and unable to return from the Continent. These conditions could persist for several days. This weather was widespread in mid-December 1944, and on the Continent units of the Allied armies sat in their positions, waiting for conditions to improve. In the Ardennes region, troops of four US divisions were spread thinly along the Belgian border with Germany, preparing to make some sort of celebration for Christmas. Suddenly, at 05:35 on 16 December, an artillery barrage started from the east, and out of the mists and snows came the tanks and troops of 24 German divisions. The Americans were taken completely by surprise as over 250,000 German troops overran their positions. Startling inroads were made as the panzers moved forward, and eventually they created a salient up to 50 miles deep, giving the action its name – the Battle of the Bulge. The German aim was to reach the Belgian port of Antwerp, driving a wedge between the Allied armies. Situated at the centre of a road network on the line of the German advance was the town of Bastogne, Headquarters of the US 8th Corps. Allied Supreme Headquarters realised the importance of the town, so it sent in the US 101st Airborne Division to defend the area. The Germans moved forward, and by 20 December had encircled Bastogne. They called upon the Americans to surrender, and got the famous reply from Brigadier-General Anthony McAuliffe of the 101st Airborne, which was 'Nuts!'

Meanwhile, in England USAAF units were alerted to assist their colleagues on the ground. At Ramsbury, the 437th were put on standby, and tasked to fly supplies to the trapped 101st Airborne. Despite intense artillery bombardments and probing attacks by tanks and infantry, the 101st held their ground. However, there was no sign of a change in the weather, and no flying could take place. The aircrews sat around and waited helplessly, while a few hundred miles away in Belgium, the US paras were desperately fighting off the German attacks. Finally, on 23rd December, there was a break in the weather, when the dawn was cold but clear. The squadrons of the 437th took off from Ramsbury, and rendezvoused with groups from other British bases before heading for the Ardennes.

The first arrival over Bastogne that morning was at 09:30, when a lone C-47 towing a CG-4A glider appeared overhead. The glider was released and landed inside the US perimeter. It had brought in a pathfinder team to set up a drop zone and establish ground-to-air communications for the following C-47s. Shortly before noon that day the main force came over, ploughing slowly through the air at a little more than a thousand feet up. Out of their cargo doors tumbled the parapacks, suspended under parachutes of red, yellow, orange, blue and white. Although fighter escorts flew with the transports, to protect them from enemy fighters and to suppress ground-fire, some German flak guns did open fire, and several aircraft were hit. One of these was a

181

CG-4A gliders from Ramsbury being towed off the LZ by US troops using a captured German half-track during Operation Market Garden, for subsequent C-47 recovery. (via Roger Day)

C-47 from the 85th TCS, which was shot down. In the space of four hours, 241 aircraft dropped 144 tons of supplies to the beleaguered garrison in 1,500 packs.

The weather on the following day, Christmas Eve, also proved satisfactory, and the 437th again departed for Bastogne. Flying operations were cancelled on Christmas Day, as thick fog had descended. On 26th, however, flying was resumed, and aircraft of the 437th once again took off for Belgium. This was to be their last re-supply mission to Bastogne, for later that day the town was relieved by US ground forces. Over the five-day period 962 C-47s dropped 850 tons of supplies into the Bastogne pocket. On 26 December there were in addition eleven gliders, some of which brought in surgeons. During the five days the Germans shot down nineteen aircraft and badly damaged fifty more.

During January 1945 rumours started circulating that the 437th would be moving to the Continent. These rumours were to become fact the following month. As former Luftwaffe airfields in France were restored to operational condition, the 53rd Troop Carrier Wing started to move its groups across. On 25 February it became the turn of the 437th, and the Group left Ramsbury, its home for over a year, to move to an airfield known to the Americans only as A58, situated near the town of Coulommiers/Voisin, 20 miles East of Paris. Although all the American aircraft had left, the US Ninth Air Carrier Command still retained control of Ramsbury as a reserve base, with a rear echelon remaining until June 1945.

On 5 June 1945, a month after the end of the war in Europe, USAAF Station No.469 returned to RAF control once more. It was taken over initially by No.70 Group, Fighter Command. For some unknown reason, three days later the station was transferred to Transport Command, under No.4 Group. By the end of June the last Americans had left.

The RAF were now using Ramsbury in the same role as the Americans, for airborne forces training. In early July the airfield became a satellite of Welford, a Dakota base, and over the following few months RAF Dakotas were often to be seen at Ramsbury, flying circuits, or towing gliders. Training sometimes continued at night, and on one of these exercises on 19th October, Flight Sergeant Gooch flying Horsa glider TL937 became disorientated, mistook the street lights of Ramsbury village for the approach lights to the airfield, and made his approach. Realising his mistake in time, he managed to glide over a row of houses and land in a field behind. The aircraft landed in an allotment and severely damaged a chicken shed and the glider, but the local children did have an exciting new toy for a few days, until the RAF came to retrieve it!

On 29 October five Dakotas and five Waco Hadrian gliders of the Glider Pick-up Unit (GPU) arrived from Ibsley. The GPU's role was to retrieve gliders using the 'Airborne Snatch' method. The unit started training at its new base on 1 November, with three Dakotas making 12 glider snatches. However, the war with Japan now over, the use of the military glider was limited. The GPU was disbanded on 15 November.

At the beginning of 1946 Ramsbury became a satellite of Upavon, and Airspeed Oxfords of F Flight of No.7 Flying Instructors School (Advanced) arrived to take up residence, under the command of Flt Lt Green. This activity was to be short-lived, for it was decided that Ramsbury should be closed, and by the end of March No.7FIS(A) had returned to Upavon, and all flying had ceased. The last recorded military aircraft to use Ramsbury was in fact a Spitfire FR.22 (PK633), which force-landed on the airfield on 4 January 1947. By then the status of the airfield had been downgraded to 'Care and Maintenance'. With so many airfields under its control, and far more than it needed, shortly afterwards the Air Ministry relinquished Ramsbury to agricultural use.

In 1947 some of the airfield's domestic sites were taken over by the Wiltshire Agricultural Committee as hostel accommodation for the Women's Land Army, then still a very busy and important source of farm labour. Two dozen or so Land Girls lived on the site, working at local farms. In another group of former airfield domestic site buildings,

Lieutenants Becher, Clark, Norris and Gray of No.86 TCS being taken by Lt Col Lehr, OC of the Squadron. (Roger Day)

a camp for Displaced Persons was set up by Wiltshire County Council. These people were refugees, mostly from Poland or the Ukraine, who had been forced to flee their homes, first by the Germans, then by the Russians. Over the next few years more permanent homes were found for the newcomers. When, in 1950, the Women's Land Army was finally wound up, the Ramsbury hostel was abandoned, and the buildings soon became derelict.

By the mid-1960s much of the airfield's concrete had been removed, although a portion of southern perimeter track was retained as a public road to replace one closed during the war. Farm buildings were erected on the intersection of the two shorter runways, and remnants of the runways and perimeter tracks, reduced in width, are still in use as farm roads. The western end of the main runway has been used as an airstrip by local microlight fliers. The two T2 hangers were used by local farmers for storage for a few years after the war, but were dismantled in 1954. Most of the remaining airfield buildings were demolished by the early-1970s, but a few remain in place, including the station operations centre and several stores buildings.

Today, the site of Ramsbury airfield is again peaceful and quiet, a far cry from the historic activities that have taken place there, particularly during those hectic days of 1944. In the main square at Ramsbury, passers-by may rest on two seats donated by veterans of the 437th TCG, and in the church the veterans have erected a stone as a memorial

184

The Ramsbury Airfield Operations HQ, now in the garden of a private house.
(Author)

to their colleagues who gave their lives during World War II. The stone also serves as a token of friendship from them to the people of Ramsbury.

16

SOUTH
MARSTON

National Grid Reference (173) SU185882 1 mile NE of Swindon,
near South Marston village

Work on South Marston airfield started during the summer of 1940. The airfield was built to serve an aircraft factory that was constructed on the same site. Plans for the works and airfield went back to 1936 when the Air Ministry took the decision to set up state-owned reserve factories in the event of war. They were referred to as 'shadow' factories, as they were to run in parallel with the most strategically important factories and act as back up should the main production lines be disrupted by enemy action. The plan was initiated in 1938 following the Munich crisis, when it was realised that war was inevitable.

The site at South Marston was chosen because it was close to Swindon with its large skilled workforce and good lines of communication. The South Marston shadow factory was allocated to Phillips and Powis Aircraft Ltd, who manufactured training aircraft at their factory not far away from Swindon, at Woodley near Reading. In 1932 it took on the manufacture of aircraft designed by Frank G. Miles. Although the individual designs were prefixed with the name of 'Miles', contracts with the Air Ministry were actually with Phillips and Powis. The company was a prolific one – a greater variety of Miles types were flown during the Second World War than any other British manufacturer's.

Because of limited space at Woodley the new shadow factory was used to supplement the mass production of Miles Master advanced trainers produced by the company. The Master originated in the Kestrel, a speculative design by Frank Miles against a perceived need for a trainer with a good performance to match the new monoplanes that were coming into service with the RAF. The aircraft was named after the engine that powered it, the Rolls Royce Kestrel, which was also used in the Hawker Hart biplane bomber and the Fury biplane fighter. The Air Ministry was not interested at first, but after the failure of another design, they expressed an interest in a developed version of the Kestrel, to be called the Master. The Ministry awarded a contract to Phillips & Powis worth £2 million for 500 aircraft, then the largest ever awarded by the Air Ministry for training aircraft.

Work started on the construction of the shadow factory and airfield in January 1940 at the site alongside the Highworth Road near South Marston village. The site was levelled and work started, but first of all a railway spur was brought in via a cutting to transport labour and materials into the area. By July most of the buildings were well on the way to completion. The main assembly shop was one of the first buildings to be erected, but not to its originally planned size. When Ministry of Aircraft Production (MAP) officials saw the steelwork erected, they felt the building would be too large a target for enemy bombers, and ordered two-thirds of the steel stanchions to be removed. They were moved and rebuilt at two other sites nearby, half at Blunsdon, and half at Sevenhampton, to further disperse production.

Miles personnel were on site by July 1940 to start planning the setting up of production lines for the Master. By then the Rolls Royce Kestrel engine was no longer in production, but an alternative power-plant had been found. This was the Bristol Mercury XX radial engine, and fitted with it in November 1939 the aircraft became the Master Mark II. However, a shortage of the Bristol engine in turn meant that another engine was needed. The US Pratt & Whitney Wasp Junior was available in quantity, and this was chosen to power the next version of the Master, the Mark III. The production lines were laid down at South Marston in late 1940, in the spring of 1941 the first Master Mark III rolled out of the factory and, after testing, was delivered to the RAF on 13 March. By this time the supply of Bristol Mercury engines had improved, and the Mark II also went into production at South Marston, the first one being delivered to the RAF on 1 October.

Most of the early workers at the new factory were re-trained carriage and wagon craftsmen hurriedly transferred from the vast Great Western Railway works in Swindon. They soon learned their trade as

Master Mk III W8513 built by Phillips and Powis at South Marston. (Aeroplane)

airframe woodworkers and fitters, and coped very well. For the first eighteen months after production started the average output was fifty aircraft per month, and this reached a peak of seventy-seven per month between May and September 1942. Flight-testing of Masters at South Marston was limited as only a few company test pilots were available. They flew in from Woodley from time to time in the company 'taxi', a Miles Sparrowhawk, and flight-tested the Masters in batches. The last batch of Masters to be built at South Marston were 200 Mark IIs, and these were produced at a rate of only thirty-three per month as the production line was running down. The last Master to be manufactured was delivered to the RAF on 26 March 1943.

All of the 602 Master Mark IIIs produced were manufactured at South Marston by Phillips and Powis, as were 498 Master Mark IIs out of 1,698, the remainder being produced at Woodley. A total of 3,450 Masters of all marks were manufactured. Major users of the Marks II and III were the (Pilot) Advanced Flying Units, such as No.9 (P)AFU at Hullavington. It was also used as a glider-tug to replace the Hawker Audax and Hector. Many Master Mark IIIs were sent to the Flying Training Schools in South Africa. Other users included the Air Transport Auxiliary (ATA) who employed them as aircrew ferries (as did a number of front-line RAF squadrons), the Fleet Air Arm and the USAAF, as well as the Egyptian, Portugese and Turkish Air Forces.

During the summer of 1940 the Short Stirling four-engined bomber was in full production by Short Brothers Ltd in their two factories at Rochester Airport and Belfast. On 14 August the Belfast factory was bombed by the Luftwaffe, and the Stirling production line was put out of action. Five Stirlings were destroyed and a number of others damaged. The following afternoon the Rochester works was also attacked, and six more Stirlings were destroyed, and more were damaged. This was at a time that such valuable aircraft were sorely needed by the RAF. To avoid a recurrence of such a setback, the MAP dispersed production of the Stirling to Wiltshire. At the time the South Marston shadow factory was incomplete, so the damaged Stirlings were taken to the Gloster Aircraft works at Hucclecote, where Short's staff hurriedly evacuated there could complete them. New factory accommodation was therefore sought in the South Marston area, and the new dispersed production plants that were being constructed at Blunsden and Sevenhampton were allocated for Stirling production.

The fuselages were to be constructed at Blunsden, for fitting out at Sevenhampton. They were then to be transported by 'Queen Mary' aircraft road transporters through the winding Wiltshire lanes to South Marston airfield. The wings were assembled at South Marston in part of the Phillips and Powis factory. The various components of the aircraft would then be brought together in a pair of specially constructed erection and flight test hangars (known as FS2 site) on the airfield and assembled. Four Stirlings could be assembled at any one time in the hangars before being painted and finished in another hangar close by. They were then prepared for flight test. Activity in support of the Stirling production also took place elsewhere in the area. Pressing and machined items were manufactured in No.24 Shop of the Great Western Railway Works at Swindon, while small components were made in a large requisitioned garage in the town centre (later to become Skurrys Car Showroom). To accommodate the Stirling two concrete runways were built at South Marston airfield, both being 1,000 yards long and 70 yards wide. Both runways were later extended. A taxiway linked the end of one of the runways with FS2 site.

Production of the Stirling at South Marston was well under way by late 1941; during 1942 some sixteen aircraft were being manufactured per month. By then the wings were also being produced in the GWR

Joan Hughes was the youngest pilot ever to pass through the CFS. She went on to fly heavy bombers with the ATA, such as the Stirling from South Marston. (Photo courtesy West London Aero Club)

works, the major assemblies also being manufactured locally, such as the flaps and undercarriage units.

The first South Marston Stirling for the RAF was delivered in early 1942 by Flight Lieutenant Moreton, one of the works test pilots, who took the aircraft to RAF Marham. After this the ATA normally ferried completed Stirlings to the RAF (usually to a reception Maintenance Unit), the pilots usually coming from No.1 Ferry Pool at White Waltham. Lettice Curtis was one of these, being one of only twelve ATA women pilots who were qualified to fly four-engined heavy bombers. One day on arrival at South Martson she saw a Stirling on its nose at the end of the main runway. She later found out that this had been due to its elevator control wires having been crossed. This had been missed during an interrupted pre-flight inspection, and meant that when Test Pilot Tom Brooke-Smith was hurtling down the runway to take off, the aircraft would not unstick. When he made a final heave on the control column the Stirling's tail came up and its nose went down, the aircraft ending up ignominiously on the runway with its tail in the air at an angle of forty degrees! The first flying accident at South Marston had involved an ATA pilot when, on 18 June 1941, Puss Moth AX870 from White Waltham crashed on landing and was damaged beyond repair. Another accident occurred on 5 January 1942, and involved another visiting aircraft, this time Bristol Beaufort AX283 of No.217 Squadron, which crashed on take-off and was written off. A further visitor experienced bad luck on 25 March 1942, when Spitfire PRIV AB429 of No.1 Photographic Reconnaissance Unit overshot while making an emergency landing and was badly damaged.

As by then South Marston had become an important site, it was felt that its significance as a target ought to be disguised. The buildings were painted in disruptive patterns, and netting was erected from ground level to rooftops, both being attempts to disguise the size of the buildings and to break up their shape. The runway surfaces were sprayed with tar that was then covered in a coating of woodchips. This was then painted with camouflage colours. The grass was painted with dark patterns to simulate hedging and mocked up sections of hedges were made so that they could be drawn across the runways when they were not in use, to complete the effect.

Towards the end of 1942 plans were being made to phase out the manufacture of Stirlings at South Marston. To replace it a production line was proposed for the latest development of the Lancaster. However, before arrangements could be made for this production scheme, Supermarine stepped in and laid claim to South Marston with a more pressing requirement. The company needed to find more industrial capacity to produce the latest version of the Spitfire, the Mark 21. With the ending of Master III production by Phillips & Powis at South Marston in September 1942 (the last Master III was delivered on 26 September), Supermarine moved in. Responsibility for the factory remained with Phillips & Powis as the final batch of 200 Master IIs was still in production. These were completed on 26 March 1943. Supermarine officially took over South Marston on 1 April 1943, when the factory came under the parentage of the Castle Bromwich production division from its shadow factory near Birmingham, although still under the overall control of the MAP. The FS2 site was not needed by Supermarine, so MAP used it for the preparation and modification of US lease/lend aircraft. These came in from reception points in the UK and were installed with particular equipment, such as guns and radios, or worked on to bring them up to a particular modification standard in common with others of the same type already in service. Examples of aircraft received were Douglas Bostons and North American Mitchells. Sometimes a type would be modified to change its role, e.g. the Vultee Vengeance dive-bombers were converted to tow targets. Such work continued at FS2 until 1945.

Work by Supermarine at South Marston started with modification work to several batches of the Spitfire Mark Vb. For this the company took on staff formerly with Phillips & Powis, who provided a ready-made source of experienced employees, although the changeover from the Master to the Spitfire meant that they had to be re-trained to deal with metal rather than wood. Once the modification work was completed, the test-flying of the modified aircraft was the responsibility of Alex Henshaw, Chief Test Pilot at Castle Bromwich. He would fly down from Birmingham in the Company DH Dominie, often announcing his arrival by several low 'daisy cutting' passes before landing and settling down to the more serious task of testing Spitfires. He was often assisted in this work by Jeffery Quill, Chief Test Pilot of the Supermarine Flight Test Centre at High Post. While the modification programme was proceeding, tooling and production facilities were being set up in the former Phillips & Powis factory for the Spitfire Mark 21, which was to be the first Spitfire variant to be built at South Marston.

The Spitfire Mark 21 was the first of the type to be designed specifically for the Rolls Royce Griffon engine. It was a high-altitude fighter, and had a strengthened fuselage to take the Griffon 61 with two-stage supercharger (for improved performance at altitude), a five-bladed propeller, a re-designed wing, revised armament (four 20mm Hispano cannon) and a strengthened, wider-track undercarriage. An order for 2,962 Spitfire Mark 21s was received from the MAP in May 1943 as production was gearing up at Castle Bromwich and South Marston and the first prototype of the Mark 21, PP139, was constructed at South Marston during the summer of 1943. The first deliveries reached the RAF in December, but by then the air war had moved on, and most fighter operations were taking place at lower altitudes, with the emphasis on ground attack and support. Production of the Spitfire

Mark 21 was limited in the event to only one hundred and twenty-one aircraft. Initial deliveries went to No.91 Squadron, which was operational on the type by April 1945. They also served with Nos.1, 41 and 122 Squadrons, which flew them until later marks became available, when they were issued to the Royal Auxiliary Air Force. The Mark 21 was finally declared obsolete in May 1953.

The Seafire was also produced at South Marston, starting with the Mark 45, which was the naval counterpart of the Spitfire Mark 21. This was produced as an interim naval fighter, pending the availability of Seafire versions of the more advanced Spitfire Mark 22 and 24 that were in the pipeline. They were fitted with catapult and arrester gear fittings, but not folding wings. A total of fifty were produced at South Marston and Castle Bromwich. The Seafire F Mark 45 saw limited service with the Fleet Air Arm, as they were soon replaced by later mark Seafires, and the main role for a number of them was to act as ballast in aircraft carrier barrier trials. This meant the pilotless aircraft being catapulted into the barrier under power to check the effectiveness

View of the flight shed and paint shop at South Marston showing Spitfire Mk 21s being prepared, at least two having contraprops. (Vickers)

193

of the barrier and see what damage would be caused to the aircraft. One Seafire F45 did not take kindly to this sort of treatment, and when it was launched from a carrier in a steam catapult trial off the Isle of Wight, instead of obediently ditching into the sea, it took to the air. The aircraft then flew in circles around the carrier! After five minutes or so, guns were brought to bear to shoot the Seafire down, as it was flying in ever-decreasing circles around the trials ship. Before the first shot could be fired the aircraft flew into the sea, much to everyone's relief.

The Spitfire Mark 21 was followed by the Mark 22, which differed mainly in having a cut-down rear fuselage with a tear-drop cockpit canopy. While the last batch of these aircraft was being manufactured at Castle Bromwich, it was decided to close the factory. The parts for the remaining twenty-four Mark 22s were therefore transferred to South Marston in April 1946 for completion. The aircraft were eventually finished off as Mark 24s, the final version of the Spitfire, which embodied several detail improvements on the Mark 22.

The Seafire F46 was the naval version of the Spitfire Mark 22. Although the aircraft was not seen as an ideal naval fighter, as it did not have folding wings, its performance was so impressive that a contract for two hundred was awarded to Supermarine. However, the ending of the war resulted in the contract being cancelled after only twenty-four had been built at South Marston. The aircraft did not enter service, but were used for trials work, including the development of the next, and last, Seafire, the FR (Fighter Reconnaissance) 47. The first aircraft, PS944, flew for the first time from South Marston on 25 April 1946. Fitted with the Griffon 87 driving Rotol contra-rotating propellers, the aircraft also had folding wings. The first aircraft went to Boscombe Down for handling and performance trials in November 1946, but it was not until January 1948 that the first Fleet Air Arm unit, No.804 Squadron, began to re-equip with the type. Within a year, however, the entire production run, of a mere ninety aircraft, was completed at South Marston, and in January 1949 Seafire FR47 VR971, the last Seafire, and the last of the Spitfire family to be built, left the factory on delivery to the FAA. The Seafire FR47 saw operational service with No.800 Squadron, FAA, in Malaya during the 1949 Emergency, and flew strikes against North Korean targets the following year from HMS Triumph. In 1951 all Seafires were withdrawn from front-line service, although a number of FR47s served with RN Volunteer Reserve squadrons for several more years.

Following the end of the war there was a re-organisation of aircraft production facilities, and wholesale close-downs and disposals. South

Aerial view of the South Marston factory. The flight test hangars and airfield can be seen towards the top of the photograph. (Cambridge Collection)

Marston factory and airfield was sold by MAP to Vickers-Supermarine in October 1945 for £500,000. Post-war work at the South Marston factories included the conversion of Wellington bombers into T.Mark 10 trainers, to be used for the training of bomb-aimers and navigators at such schools as No.1 Air Navigation School at Hullavington. Spitfires continued to appear, coming in for repair and modification before being sold to overseas air forces such as Sweden and Thailand. Some aircraft were converted to two-seater trainers, and although the RAF were not interested, foreign air forces such the Irish Air Corps bought them. Walrus amphibians were refurbished for sale to the Royal Netherlands Navy and the Argentinian Air Force, and Sea Otter amphibians were similarly refurbished for the civil market.

In the late 1940s the South Marston factory and the Bradley Road factory at Trowbridge were the only two remaining parts of the Supermarine organisation in Wiltshire, and together they became part of the Vickers-Armstrong Supermarine Division. Production at both factories now concentrated on the Attacker, a jet-powered version of the Spiteful, the Spitfire derivative. This aeroplane had been developed for the RAF, but was turned down. Instead, the design was taken up by the Royal Navy as its first jet-powered carrier-borne fighter. The runways at South Marston were extended for jet operation in early 1950, and while this was being done, the first Attacker to be built at South Marston made its first flight from Supermarine's new Flight Test Centre at Chilbolton in Hampshire. Between 1950 and 1953 a total of one hundred and eighty-two Attackers were built for the Royal Navy and the Royal Pakistan Air Force.

These were followed in production by the Swift, a day fighter for the RAF, and this was in turn replaced on the South Marston production lines by the Scimitar, another fighter for the Royal Navy. The last Scimitar to be built in January 1961 was the final complete aircraft to be built at South Marston; following this the factory produced components for aircraft and other products of the Vickers Group, such as hovercraft and railway carriages.

Eventually, in the 1980s, the site was sold by Vickers to the Honda Motor Company. The original factory was demolished, and replaced by a state-of-the-art car manufacturing plant, and is now Honda's main European production facility. FS2 and Sevenhampton still remain, exactly as originally built, and are still in regular use. Today they represent the only remnant of South Marston, which, as an aircraft factory, was an important contribution by the county of Wiltshire to Britain's war effort, and later played a valuable role in the resurgence of Britain's aircraft industry post-war.

17

UPAVON

National Grid Reference (184) SU 153543, 1¹/₂ miles SE of Upavon village

Upavon is one of the longest-established airfields in the country, and probably the oldest active one. A site of 2,400 acres had been chosen for the airfield in the spring of 1912 as the location of the Central Flying School (CFS), to be established as part of the new Royal Flying Corps. Situated on training gallops stretching over Upavon Down on Salisbury Plain, the school was to be located to the east of the valley of the Wiltshire Avon, near the village of Upavon. The site appears to have been chosen more for its remoteness than its suitability as a flying field, in view of the army's concern over the attentions of the Press and the public regarding this new venture.

CFS Upavon opened on 19 June 1912 under the command of Captain Godfrey Paine RN. With hangars having been constructed for twenty-five aeroplanes, and along with all the necessary training, administration and domestic buildings, the school got off to a modest start, having a complement of only seven aircraft – two Farmans, two Shorthorns, two Avros and a Bristol Biplane. Nevertheless, the CFS slowly began to build up a reputation for thoroughness, efficiency and high standards that was to give it an international reputation in the years to come. Training started with the first training course on 17 August 1912, and one of its students was a Major by the name of Hugh Trenchard, later to become known as 'the Father of the Royal Air Force'.

By August 1914 the CFS had trained 93 out of the 664 British military pilots to fly, in addition to its task of improving the standard of qualified pilots. With the outbreak of the Great War, almost all of the school's aircraft and pilots departed for France and the CFS then became one of several flying schools that were required to churn out as many pilots as possible for the squadrons on the Western Front. The original airfield to the south of the Andover-Upavon road was expanded to include a second one, built on the north side of the road, increasing the size of the airfield to 3,324 acres. The original fourteen aeroplane sheds built on the airfield were later joined by three large 140-foot by 70-foot hangars.

One of the graduates of the CFS in 1912 was Robert Smith-Barry; he was not only a superb pilot himself, but he devised a method of training top class pilots that still forms the basis of flying instruction throughout the world today. Although Smith-Barry left the RAF at the end of the Great War, the RAF still continues to use his methods, later known as the 'CFS Pattern', as the basis of their flying training today.

The role of the CFS was expanded in 1915 when the Experimental Flight was formed at Upavon to evaluate and test prototypes of new aircraft for the RFC. Trials also included armaments, and with the expansion of the CFS in late 1916, it was decided to move the flight to a safer and more remote area. The Experimental Flight went to Martlesham Heath in Suffolk and was later to become the basis of the Aeroplane and Armament Experimental Establishment (see *Boscombe Down*). In mid 1915, the first Commandant of the CFS, Godfrey Paine, was promoted to Commodore and sent by the Royal Naval Air Service to Lincolnshire to set up a naval version of the CFS there. He established HMS Daedelus at Cranwell, and when the RNAS became part of the RAF in 1918, Cranwell became its college.

Following the end of the Great War RAF Upavon escaped the station closures that resulted from the wholesale demobilization that was sweeping the country. It remained a training station and the CFS was re-organised as a flying training school for flying instructors. On restarting its courses the reputation of the CFS returned and it became a byword for the excellence of its instructional standards. The high standards expected of its students resulted from a lot of hard work, and high spirits were not discouraged in order to counteract the effects of the associated stresses and strains. This resulted in rather bizarre behaviour by the flyers of the CFS, including hedge-hopping, train chasing and wing walking. On more than one occasion inexperienced student pilots flying from neighbouring No.1 Flying Training School at Netheravon would be shocked to come across a CFS aircraft flying in the area with one of its pilots dangling from the undercarriage or sitting on a wing reading the paper.

Upavon had a change of role in 1924, when the CFS was moved to

Wittering, and was replaced by two fighter squadrons, Nos.3 and 17. These squadrons provided night fighter defences for southern England, and were equipped with a variety of aircraft over the next few years, eventually receiving the Bristol Bulldog. In 1934 the fighter squadrons were moved to Kenley, and the following year the CFS returned to Upavon from Wittering.

By 1935 the CFS was equipped with a fleet of Avro Tutor and Hawker Hart two-seat trainers together with Hawker Fury fighters. To these aircraft, from 1937, were added Avro Ansons and Airspeed Oxfords for multi-engined training. In order to familiarise its students with other types of aircraft the CFS over the next four years gradually acquired a fleet of aircraft that represented every main type in service with the RAF, ranging from Miles Magister two-seat trainers to Vickers Wellington twin-engined bombers. The responsibilities of the CFS had by then expanded to include, for example, inspections of flying schools to ensure that the training techniques and instructors that they employed were up to the high standards laid down in the procedures which the CFS itself had pioneered (these duties were undertaken by the Examining Squadron).

The first Link Trainers appeared at Upavon in September 1937. This was a ground trainer (later to become known as a simulator) that provided safe, economical training giving students practice in instrument flying techniques. From late 1937 the Refresher Flight of the CFS was tasked to maintain flying standards for the civilian

Bristol Bulldog Mk IIs of 17 Squadron at Upavon in the summer of 1934. (Aeroplane)

199

instructors then being recruited to man the Elementary and Reserve Flying Schools (ERFTS) that were being formed all over the country as part of the Expansion Scheme of the RAF. Under this scheme in early 1938 work started on improvements to RAF Upavon. Although the original hangars had been replaced by two type A hangars in 1926 most of the buildings on the station were of World War I vintage. Therefore a new type C hangar was erected along with three barrack blocks, dining hall, workshops and married quarters. A Lorenz Blind Approach System was also built at this time for the airfield, at nearby Jenners Firs.

By the autumn of 1938 the number of flying training schools in the UK that the CFS had to provide instructors for had increased from two to ten, and the ERFTSs had increased from four to twenty-seven, which considerably increased the workload. The school's work now included the writing of Pilot's Notes, which were descriptions of the layout of the controls of each particular type of aircraft and their characteristics, rather like a car handbook. Before this there had been little information available on the flying of each individual type, but with the more advanced types then coming into service, far more detailed information was needed by the pilots. One of the driving needs for this was that squadron pilots had to be converted to the new monoplanes coming into service and something was needed to enable them to fly the new aircraft effectively. The Refresher Flight was expanded from April 1939, when it took over the newly completed C hangar. Every type of aircraft in service with the RAF went to the CFS to be flown and evaluated and for Pilot's Notes to be produced on each one. Despite the rebuilding of the station during 1938/39 flying training continued at the CFS along with its other tasks.

With the outbreak of the Second World War, all aircraft at Upavon were dispersed around the perimeter of the airfield and armed guards were mounted. More substantial airfield defences were constructed and manned by soldiers of the Wiltshire Regiment. Training went on, and many Reserve and Volunteer Reserve pilots were then taking part in courses, along with the first of the Air Transport Auxiliary pilots. These civilians included the first women pilots to be trained at CFS, amongst them Amy Johnson (record breaking long distance pilot), Winifred Crossley (who had given aerobatic displays with Sir Alan Cobham's 'Flying Circus') and the youngest pilot ever to pass through the CFS, 17 year old Joan Hughes, who went on to fly four-engine bombers later in the war and to instruct on them (see *South Marston*). Other pilots who arrived for assessment in 1939 included Douglas

Squadron Leader D'Arcy Greig, DFC, AFC, Chief Flying Instructor of the CFS, with some of the school's instructors at Upavon in mid 1938. An Anson, Harts and Tutors are in the background. (Aeroplane)

Bader who, having lost his legs in an air accident eight years before, had been invalided out of the RAF. As the RAF now needed trained pilots, he was re-assessed, and celebrated his first solo in eight years by flying an Avro Tutor upside down across the airfield! Passed as 'exceptional' Bader returned to flying and, following command of a Hurricane squadron during the Battle of Britain, became a high scoring fighter pilot before being shot down in 1942, becoming a prisoner of war and ending up in Colditz Castle.

The weather during the winter of 1939/40 was severe, and the whole of Europe was suffering under a coating of snow and ice. Flying at Upavon was curtailed, then stopped for several weeks in January. When it resumed in February the level of activity was limited. These conditions persisted into March, and on the morning of the 11th, the airfield was blanketed in fog, which came in suddenly at 10:15. Several aircraft that were airborne at the time had to land away at other airfields. A Fairey Battle from Netheravon was in the area when the fog came down, and attempted a landing at Upavon, but it crashed on the eastern boundary of the airfield.

The fall of France in May 1940 and withdrawal of British forces from the Continent resulted in Training Command Operational Order No.1, which called for training aircraft to be armed to repel a possible invasion. Upavon's North American Harvards, which the CFS was now flying, were to carry 20-pound bombs in this role. The troops of the Wiltshire Regiment enhanced Upavon's defences with more barbed wire and trenches to protect the station against paratroop attack, and they were joined by soldiers of the Royal Engineers, whose task was to repair the airfield following an air attack.

One of the roles of the CFS was to visit operational squadrons and assess their standards. Blenheim Squadrons were visited by CFS Refresher Training Squadron instructors in the spring of 1940, following a number of accidents on the type. It was found that pilots had been allowing the Bristol Mercury engines of the aircraft to idle before take-off, which resulted in the lower spark plugs of the radial engines becoming oiled up, so that they were prone to failure. Squadron Leader George Stainforth, World Speed Record Holder in the Supermarine S6B 1931, was on the staff of the Refresher Training Squadron, and visited squadrons at home and abroad to put the fears of Blenheim pilots at rest. He demonstrated the method of keeping the engines going by maintaining them on fast tick-over before take-off. He would then cut one engine following take-off, to demonstrate the good one-engine performance of the bomber. Stainforth's methods eradicated this type of accident and restored pilots' confidence in the Blenheim.

The Refresher Training Squadron investigated other problems such as an incident that occurred with a Bristol Bombay transport aircraft that nearly resulted in the aircraft's loss, following the movement of passengers in the cabin. The passengers walked down towards the tail of the aircraft while it was in flight, whereupon the bomber's tail flicked down, and the aircraft stalled. This was presumed to be caused by a change in the centre of gravity, but such a violent effect on the aircraft was surprising. Squadron Leader Jo Cox of the Refresher Training Squadron re-enacted the flight in a Bombay and volunteer pilots from No.216 Squadron. The pilots acted as passengers and at the appropriate time walked towards the rear of the aircraft. The tail flicked down, the pilots were flung to the rear of the cabin and the aircraft stalled. Cox fought to control the aircraft, as the passengers clawed their way back up the aisle to balance the centre of gravity. Eventually the aircraft was pulled out at a height of 400 feet. A report on the incident resulted in the requirement for all transport pilots to make out a detailed load sheet showing where the centre of gravity of the aircraft was, to enable it to be flown safely. This became standard practice in all transport squadrons and is used to this day.

On 14 August 1940 Upavon was raided by the Luftwaffe, when

Heinkel He111Ps of KG55 attacked the airfield. No damage is recorded, but one of the German bombers, G1+AA flown by Oberst Alois Stochel, Geschwader Kommodore, was shot down by ground fire and crashed into the ammunition depot at Dean Hill, to the east of Salisbury. No serious damage was sustained to the depot, but three of the bomber's crew were killed, including the pilot. Two members of the crew survived, however, and were taken prisoner.

As the demand for aircrews increased from August 1940 onwards so did the demands on the CFS. Courses were shortened and the output of trained pilots and instructors was increased. Both airfields at Upavon were in constant use by the Masters and Oxfords of the school during this time, and Relief Landing Grounds were opened at Overton Heath and New Zealand Farm to cater for the extra flying practice required and for night flying training. The CFS had already been using two other landing grounds in the area, Alton Barnes since 1936, and Manningford from 1939.

By 1941 forty students were being taken on every fortnight, and the Refresher Training Squadron staff returned to normal training duties to meet the extra demand. The heavy use of the airfield resulted in rutting of the ground surface, and so steel Sommerfeld track was laid in January 1942 to form a 3,000 foot runway. The role of the CFS and the future needs of the RAF flying training organisation were debated in the spring of 1942, and it was felt that the role of the CFS was still required, but in a different way. It was agreed that a central unit was required to be able to pool the vast amount of experience gained within the UK and the now fully-functioning Empire Air Training Scheme, and to ensure that instructional methods were kept up to date and in accordance with operational requirements. It was decided to set up a new organisation to take on this role, and on 12 March 1942 Group Captain Down of the CFS moved to RAF Hullavington, taking many of the school's staff with him, to set up the Empire Central Flying School there. The remaining staff at Upavon were under the command of Group Captain Holmes, and from 1 April 1942 found that they were now members of No.7 Flying Instructors School (FIS), although many of them felt that they were still the 'real CFS'.

No.7 FIS started its work with the introduction of four-week Operational Training Unit (OTU) courses, training instructors for the OTUs that were to take students on to their final stages of flying training, giving them specific guidance on flying a particular type of aircraft in an operational environment. For this work the FIS used Oxfords and Masters. Five months later, on 7 August 1942, the school

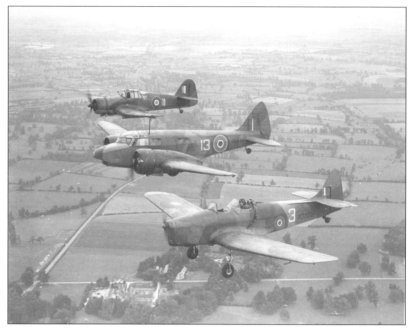

Magister, Oxford and Master of the CFS in 1942. (Aeroplane)

became re-titled as No.7 FIS(A), the new suffix meaning 'Advanced'. Courses accordingly became more intense, and were lengthened to eight weeks. Some of the Oxfords and all of the Masters were transferred to another FIS due to this change in activity, and they were replaced by Miles Magister tandem two-seat trainers.

Another runway, this time 3,750 feet long, had been laid out in Sommerfeld Trackway on the southern airfield during the summer of 1942, and this was supplemented by a tarmac taxiway in the August. Following this beefing up of the airfield surface, the number of minor accidents to 7 FIS(A)'s aircraft dwindled, but a Horsa glider did crash-land shortly after the taxiway was completed. A more serious accident occurred on 9 January 1943 when a Whitley of No.295 Squadron stalled while overshooting the main Upavon runway, and crashed, killing the crew.

In response to the demands for more flying instructors, courses at No.7 FIS(A) were increased in size. Beam approach training had also been taking place at Upavon, using the Lorenz Blind Approach System installed before the war. This system enabled pilots flying at night or in bad weather to find their way back and land at their base. This training

204

increased too in April 1943, with the formation of No.1537 Blind Approach Training Flight, using the Oxford. However, even using this type of equipment was not without its risks, and on the night of 22 December during a night landing in fog, Oxford LX595 crashed into one of the hangars and burst into flames.

A number of blister hangars were built around the perimeter of the south airfield to increase storage accommodation for aircraft, and by the end of 1944 there were two Type A hangars, one Type C, one Type L, ten blisters and a single hangar known as a Tunell.

No.7 FIS(A) carried on with its work at Upavon throughout the rest of the war, using its Oxfords for multi-engine pilot instructor training. The school remained after the end of hostilities. A review of flying training in the RAF was undertaken by the Air Ministry in 1946, and as the result of this it was decided to reform the CFS using No.7 FIS(A), the last remnant of the original CFS, as its basis. With the vast number of aerodromes available after the war, RAF Little Rissington in Gloucestershire was chosen as the location for the new CFS.

The CFS officially re-opened for business on 7 May. Following several more moves over the years, the HQ is today located at RAF Cranwell, Lincolnshire, alongside the RAF College that it had inspired in 1915. The CFS still forms an important part of RAF flying training, and its responsibility for the training of instructor pilots in the RAF continues. However, its roots in Wiltshire are not forgotten; included in the colours on the shield of the CFS crest are green to represent Salisbury Plain, and pale blue for the Wiltshire Avon.

Following the departure of No.7 FIS(A), Upavon became the home of No.38 Group, Transport Command, which literally moved up the road from Netheravon. The group was responsible for the control of the RAF's tactical squadrons, and the co-ordination of their work in support of the army. For the next few years, apart from visitors, the only aircraft to be seen flying from Upavon were those of No.38 Group Communications Flight, which did include an interesting variety of types, including a Wellington as well as Tiger Moths, Proctors, Ansons and Oxfords, but also at least one Spitfire, which must have been one of the few of such fighters flown by a Transport Command unit! In October 1948 No.2 Wing, RAF Regiment was formed at Upavon as HQ for two Light AA Squadrons and a Parachute Squadron. In February 1951, due to a high level reorganisation, No.38 Group was disbanded, but its place at Upavon was taken by its Command HQ the following April, when HQ Transport Command moved in from Bushey Park in Middlesex.

Tiger Moth, Magister and Oxford of the CFS on a visit to another RAF station in 1942. (Aeroplane)

No.38 Group appeared once again at Upavon when it was re-formed there in 1960, but due to a shortage of accommodation it moved almost immediately to RAF Odiham, a tactical helicopter base in Hampshire. In 1965 a new HQ building was opened at Upavon to accommodate No.38 Group, and the HQ was to remain at the station for some years, the formation itself being renamed Air Support Command in 1967. Further changes took place in September 1972, when Air Support Command was merged into Strike Command and its role was taken over by No.46 Group, re-formed at Upavon to control the strategic transport force, complemented by No.38 Group controlling tactical airlift. The two groups were co-located in November 1975, when No.38 Group returned to Upavon, as the largest group in the RAF.

Upavon continued as an RAF Group HQ until the early 1990s, when Strike Command at High Wycombe took over group responsibility for transport aircraft activities. There being no longer a need for Upavon as a Group HQ by the RAF, the station was handed over to the Army in 1993. Upavon today is an army HQ, and houses the Provost Marshal's Department, the Adjutant General's Department and the Army training organisation. A tangible reminder of the airfield's past exists in the form of the original CFS HQ building, which is preserved as a museum, known as the Trenchard Building.

The airfield itself, which is well-preserved along with a single Type C and two Type A hangars, is virtually unused today during the week, apart from the occasional visit by Army Air Corps helicopters or Hercules transports from RAF Lyneham on training flights. At the weekends it is a different matter, being busy with gliders being flown there by the Army's Wyvern Gliding Club and by No.622 Volunteer Gliding School of the Air Cadets, which moved there from Old Sarum in November 1978. Today at Upavon, as is the case with several other historic airfields in Wiltshire, aeroplanes carrying RAF roundels can still be seen giving future pilots their first experiences of flying training. In doing so the Air Training Corps is maintaining an important link between Britain's past and its future.

18
WROUGHTON

National Grid Reference (173) SU138788, 3 miles S of Swindon, off the A361

Situated on the northern edge of the Marlborough Downs, Wroughton is set in one of the finest locations for an airfield in the country, with splendid views across Swindon and northern Wiltshire.

The announcement that an airfield was to be built there was made by the MP for Swindon, Mr W.W. Wakefield, on 11 November 1938. The site had been chosen for an airfield some time before as the base for an Electrical & Wireless School and for aeroplane and equipment storage, but this was not the first time that it had figured in official plans. In 1917 the site had been surveyed as the location for an Aircraft Acceptance Unit, but it was never needed.

In early December 1938 compulsory purchase orders were issued that were to affect three farms in the area to the north of Barbury Hill Fort. Rectory Farm was acquired in its entirety, along with a part of Overtown farm. This acreage was to end up as the actual area of the aerodrome. The majority of Parsloe's Farm was also purchased, for a proposed RAF hospital. In all, the site was to cover 1,000 acres.

At the end of April it was announced that work on the aerodrome was to start. The original estimate for the project at that time was £800,000 for the aerodrome and £230,000 for the hospital. Rectory Farm House and its outbuildings were situated in the centre of what was to become the airfield, and they soon disappeared. The main technical area was positioned in the south east corner of the site with large Type C and D hangars for servicing and preparation work. Six smaller technical and operational areas were dispersed around the perimeter, each one having clusters of the smaller Lamella (L Type) hangars, which were designed mainly for storage. These hangars and the workshops were the only permanent buildings erected, the domestic and administrative accommodation being provided by wooden huts. These were later added to with corrugated iron Nissen huts.

By the spring of 1940 plans for the Electrical & Wireless School had been abandoned and on 1 April 1940, No.15 Maintenance Unit was established at Wroughton under the command of Wing Commander WC Farley as part of No.41 Group, Maintenance Command. The task of the MU was to receive aircraft from the manufacturers and from other units, store or modify them as required then prepare them for operational flying when required. An initial workforce of 30 civilians was recruited, to work under the direction of five RAF officers. Men of the 8th Battalion, Royal Welsh Fusiliers arrived to provide machine gun anti-aircraft defences for the airfield, but when the MU opened the aerodrome was not usable and only one hangar had been completed. It was decided to use a temporary grass landing strip one mile to the east of where the runways were to be, and this came into use on 3 April when five Westland Lysanders arrived, fresh from the Yeovil factory. However, aircraft operation was not easy because heavy rain had waterlogged the temporary landing ground and the only hangar available was flooded.

By the end of April the civilian workforce had risen to 200 in number, and a temporary canteen was provided for them. The next batch of aircraft to arrive, on 3 May, consisted of Bristol Blenheims, from the Bristol Aeroplane factory at Filton. These were to become the first of the No.15 MU deliveries; they were speedily prepared for service, and sent to No.107 Squadron at Wattisham on 19 May.

At the end of May 1940 the news from the Continent was very bleak, with the surrender of Belgium and the Germans pushing through to the French coast. On 25 May the first of the many Hawker Hurricanes arrived at Wroughton, and with the seriousness of the situation orders were to get them operational as soon as possible. The workforce laboured around the clock, and a shortage of available tools led to local factories being asked to donate tools to the war effort. Machine guns were fitted, then tested and harmonised at butts hurriedly constructed at the bottom of the northerly slopes of Barbury Hill Fort. The aircraft were towed to the firing point, where a gantry was used to lift the aircraft's tail off the ground and onto a trestle so that the guns would be pointing into the butts. The magazines were filled, and the guns fired into the bank of soil. Later a purpose-built stop-butts was constructed at a more convenient site on the edge of the airfield and sand bunkers used to contain the spent MG rounds.

With the arrival of the Hurricanes at Wroughton it was decided to use three of them to form a Battle Flight, the aircraft being flown by the unit's test pilots for defence against an air attack on the airfield. To confuse the enemy and divert attention away from Wroughton, a decoy airfield was laid out to the west of Barbury Hill. To add to the area defences a line of pillboxes was constructed in strategic positions around the airfield, with a number being built on the high ground to the west of the landing strip. A Home Guard unit was formed within the work force of the MU to man the defences.

With the fall of France German aircraft started to operate over Britain during the summer of 1940, and this activity built up with the onset of autumn. Raids started on Britain's defence systems, with airfields and radar stations being attacked, prior to the Germans' planned sea-borne invasion. This period of the war was later to become known to everyone as the Battle of Britain.

No.15 MU was heavily engaged during this crucial period and absolute priority was given to the preparation of combat aircraft for Fighter Command. Wroughton itself was to become involved in the battle on 13 August when a German raider dropped four bombs on the airfield, damaging two Blenheims. The following day bombs were again dropped in another attack, but this time they fell harmlessly into open countryside. On the 19th the Luftwaffe came over again, dropping bombs and strafing the airfield. One of the D-type hangars was damaged, as were some of the accommodation huts. Fortunately no one was injured. The Battle Flight was scrambled while the raid was in progress, but the Hurricanes could not catch the raiders before they left the area. The Hurricanes were scrambled again a week later as the airfield AA defences fired at a raider, but no contacts were made.

Following the attacks by the Luftwaffe on the airfield it was decided that the stored aircraft should be more dispersed to make them a more difficult target for the German pilots, and to minimise any losses should they be hit. Dispersal fields were planned, with small Robin hangars being built on each one to provide limited covered storage. The first dispersal was set up at Overtown Hackpen, a half of a mile away to the east. Four additional dispersal fields were then established near Barbury Castle, Burderop Park, Uffcott and Upper Salthorp Farm.

Aircraft production increased during the winter of 1940/41, despite the damage to factories during the German bomber offensive at the time. This meant even more aircraft being delivered to Wroughton, with the monthly intake increasing to 70 in the New Year. Long hours had to be worked by the staff to ensure that these aircraft were made ready for dispatch to the front line units. The aircraft were flown between the factories, the MUs and the squadrons by ferry pilots. These aircrew were trained to fly a variety of aircraft types on long-range cross-country flights. The original pilots were RAF, but they were later supplemented by the Air Transport Auxiliary, a civilian organisation formed in 1939 specifically to undertake the ferrying task. Eventually sixteen ATA Ferry Pools were formed to cover the country, and their ranks included a good number of female pilots, who soon demonstrated their prowess in the air.

The early months of 1941 brought falling temperatures and snow. This made work in the hangars very difficult and uncomfortable because of the limited heating available. It was at this time that the unit sustained its first accident, when a Mohawk crashed on take-off. The wintry weather probably contributed to the cause of the accident, and unfortunately the pilot died in hospital a few days after the crash.

Aircraft production steadily rose during the spring of 1941 and the output of No.15 MU increased in step with it. To cope with the extra work more staff had been recruited, and the labour force then consisted of 600 civilians and 150 service personnel. Work on the construction of the buildings had been carrying on during this time, and by April most of the permanent buildings were almost complete. Three large hangars were grouped together on the main site, along with the MU HQ building, workshops, civilian canteen, mechanical transport section and main stores. Six storage sites each with two or three permanent hangars and its own guardroom and canteen had been completed around the perimeter of the airfield. Most of the many accommodation and administration buildings, mainly huts, were also now up.

Like most other airfields built before or during the first year of the war, Wroughton had been laid out as a grass airfield. The heavy rain and snow of the winter of 1940/41 severely curtailed flying at Wroughton, with waterlogging of the main airfield causing delivery delays. It was therefore decided to lay permanent runways to alleviate the situation. Work therefore started in spring 1941 on the first of three runways that would be laid.

Because of its elevated, exposed location Wroughton suffered from strong winds which, because of their direction, sometimes made it too dangerous to attempt take-offs or landings. Plans had been made for a second runway, running from east to west, and eventually 3,700 feet long. It was ready for use in 1943, when a third runway, laid from north to south, was also then under construction. This was completed in the spring of 1944, and on 13 March it was declared ready for use.

211

A typical example of the work of 76 MU, a Harvard packed into its crate ready for shipment overseas. (Aeroplane)

It was the last major piece of construction undertaken at Wroughton.

In June 1941 another RAF unit arrived at Wroughton. This was No.76 MU, an aircraft packing unit that had been relocated from Cosford. The first vehicles arrived carrying the new unit's equipment on 14 June. They were allocated to No.2 site, which consisted of two type D hangars near Clouts Wood to the north-western edge of the airfield. The unit's task was to prepare aircraft for transport overseas. This entailed stripping the airframes down and packing them into large crates. The unit dealt with fighter, trainer, and general purpose aircraft. Only single-engined aircraft were dealt with by the MU as multi-engined aircraft were usually flown overseas (single-engine aircraft did not have any safety margin in case of engine failure in transit). Aircraft for packing by No.76 MU were flown to Wroughton by ferry pilots. Any snags that appeared on the ferry flight were noted down by the pilot and corrected by the MU staff after arrival. Before the aircraft were taken into the hangars to be dismantled, all fuel was drained from them into drums. Any armament was cleared of ammunition by armourers and electricians disconnected the batteries, which were taken out and separately packed. Radio equipment was also removed. Once in the hangar and cleared for dismantling the aircraft's propellers would be removed by engine fitters, who sometimes removed the engines as well. Riggers would take the wings off, and the tail unit, depending on type. If the tail was not removed the control surfaces (ie rudder and elevators) would be locked into position. The undercarriage would be retracted and locked; if the aircraft had a fixed undercarriage it would be removed and packed separately. All metal surfaces of the airframe would be painted or greased against corrosion, as would the cannon or machine guns. All loose ends of cables, leads, etc were sealed and wrapped in brown paper and adhesive tape. The aircraft fuselages would be packed in a wooden cradle, and this was pushed inside the packing case. The wings were then fitted into cradles fixed on the inside walls of the case. Each type of aircraft had a particular type of packing case into which the parts would be fitted in a particular way. When all the packing had been completed, the cases, which were painted a grey/blue colour, would be numbered and put to one side to await collection. When the time came lorries would arrive to take the crated aircraft to the various ports for shipment overseas.

Ernest Hawkins worked at No.76 MU throughout most of the

Armstrong Whitworth Albermarles. These aircraft were used by 15 MU for the test-flying of assembled Horsa gliders. (Aeroplane)

wartime period. He described working conditions on Wroughton airfield as 'being ideal in spring and summer for working inside and outside the hangars, but was governed by the weather when outside work was involved. The hangar was large, but one of the snags during mild, damp weather was that the concrete floor would sweat, and you had to watch out when wearing plimsoles. Winter time was harder. The heating systems in the hangars were practically non-existent, but we did manage to make two rest rooms (one male, one female) out of two large aircraft packing cases, and heated with them with wood burning stoves. The hangar doors had to be kept open – sometimes one end, sometimes both ends. The through wind and low temperatures did not improve conditions or tempers within the hangar. We used to wear extra clothing, including battle-dress blouses, scarves and gloves. If an aircraft had an engine test outside in the elements this called for balaclavas or woollen hats, particularly for anyone having to hold the tail down. When the ground was covered with snow a patch was cleared by the labourers with brooms, so that the anchor-men on the tailplane would not get covered with snow when the engine revved up.'

No.76 MU averaged an output of between 25 and 30 aircraft per month, and by the end of 1941 they had despatched 176 overseas. The unit started off by packing Miles Master trainers to go to South Africa for the Empire Air Training Scheme but later the majority of the aircraft packed were destined for war zones. A lot of Fleet Air Arm (FAA) aircraft were dealt with including the Fairey Swordfish, Fairey Albacore, Fairey Barracuda, Blackburn Roc and Supermarine Walrus. Some aircraft were packed for export to friendly, neutral countries such as Portugal and Turkey, and before being packed the aircraft were marked with the appropriate national insignia.

The highlight of 1941 was a visit from HRH the Duke of Kent, then Air Commodore on the Staff of the Inspector General of the RAF. Accompanied by senior officers from HQ Maintenance Command, he inspected No.15 MU on 15 November. A few months later he was to lose his life flying in a Sunderland of Coastal Command.

In mid-1941 No.15 MU had been looking for more Relief Landing Grounds for extra storage. On 22 November 1941 it took over control of the RLG at Everleigh on Salisbury Plain. It retained the RLG until September 1942, when it exchanged Everleigh with No.33 MU Lyneham for Townsend, near Yatesbury, which was much closer.

Early in 1943 No.15 MU was selected as one of the final assembly points for airborne forces gliders, as part of the widespread preparations for the planned invasion of occupied Europe. Components of the General Aircraft Hotspur training gliders initially arrived for assembly, but the majority were for the Airspeed Horsa troop-carrying glider. These aircraft were of all-wooden construction, and parts were delivered to No.15 MU from furniture factories and cabinet-makers located all over the country. When finally assembled, the gliders were test flown, being towed into the air by a powered tug aircraft. Initially Whitleys, these were later replaced by another Armstrong Whitworth design, the Albermarle.

FAA aircraft continued to arrive for preparation and modification, and these now included the Fairey Firefly, Supermarine Sea Otter, Supermarine Seafire and DH Mosquito. There were so many aircraft at Wroughton that they not only filled the hangars, but overflowed from the dispersals onto the airfield. By the end of May 1944 a total of 573 aircraft of various types were on site. In early 1944, a batch of Barracudas was flown in to No.15 MU for urgent radio and radar modifications. Many of these then took part in a raid on the Tirpitz, which was anchored in Alten Fjord, Norway. On 3 April, the battleship received fifteen direct hits from the Barracudas and never went to sea again.

During May 1944, with the lead up to the invasion, work on gliders became a priority. Horsas were destined to play an important part in Operation Overlord, the Normandy landings, the following month. These gliders were involved in the first action of the operation, when three landed beside the Caen Canal bridge, an important objective on the left flank of the beach-head. Horsas were also used in the invasion of southern France, the Battle for Arnhem and the Rhine Crossing, a nocturnal amphibious operation by units of 21st Army Group, followed up by a daylight landing by gliders and paratroops to link up with the ground forces and to consolidate the bridge-head. Not only did the Horsas prepared by Wroughton participate in the operation in large numbers, but the station's Albermarles did too, when the Glider Towing Flight was called upon to boost the attack force.

Work continued at Wrougton after VE Day. When the war finally came to an end, the Victory celebrations were tinged with apprehension as was the case at hundreds of similar sites all over the country, as there was speculation on what the future would bring. The Maintenance Units of Woughton had undertaken magnificent work during the wartime period. During that time an incredible total of some 7,000 aircraft had passed through the airfield amounting to no fewer than 62 different types, which by any standard is quite an achievement.

The number of aircraft handled by No.76 MU dropped dramatically after VE Day, and although it carried on working, the unit was put under review. No.15 MU, on the other hand, was as busy as ever, although its role was subtly changed to that of long-term storage and disposal.

No.15 MU then assumed responsibility for the Lancaster four-engine bomber. As bomber squadrons were disbanded at the end of the war, their Lancasters were flown to Wroughton, and by late autumn 1945 over 200 of these aircraft had arrived. A few Lancasters were later refurbished and re-issued to Coastal Command, but the remainder were scrapped on-site. These included at least two veterans that had survived over 100 operational missions.

It had been decided towards the end of 1945 to retain No.76 MU, but when even single-engined aircraft started being ferried out to their overseas locations, the packing task disappeared. The few commitments that remained with No.76 MU were then transferred to No.47 MU at Sealand in Cheshire, and No.76 MU closed on 30 September 1946.

No.15 MU's work continued during the late 1940s, and new types then arriving included the Avro Lincoln. The workforce stood at 400 in 1949, mostly involved in aircraft servicing and maintenance. In 1952 the last remaining Horsa gliders in store were scrapped, and the jet age arrived at Wroughton in the form of the Meteor. Most of these aircraft were received from the factory and prepared for issue to RAF fighter squadrons, but a number were also delivered to overseas customers, including the Dutch and Belgium. In 1953 the first Canberra jet bomber arrived, and supporting this aircraft was to be Wroughton's main occupation for the following 19 years.

More new types arrived in 1956 in the form of several First World War aeroplanes such as the Sopwith Camel and Fokker Triplane. These were part of the Nash Collection, which had been sent to Wrougton for storage, and were later to form the basis of the RAF Museum collection. During their years at Wroughton the aircraft were refurbished by No.15 MU staff, and their condition in the RAF Museum at Hendon today is a tribute to the MU's craftsmen. Also in 1956 the last Mosquitoes and Lancasters were withdrawn from service and sent to Wroughton for disposal.

In the mid-1960s the site was condensed, with the outer dispersals then being cleared of aircraft and no longer needed. They were sold to (or back to) local farmers. Fred White of Overtown, who had lost land under compulsory purchase and was paid between £20 and £30 an acre

Fairey Barracuda II of the type that passed through No.15 MU during an intensive modification programme in spring 1942. (Aeroplane)

before the war, had to pay the Air Ministry £300 per acre to get it back.

After having witnessed the scrapping of so many Lancasters, it was a pleasant change for Wroughton to be involved in the refurbishment of one. This was PA474, which had been overlooked because it was a research aircraft. It was decided to refurbish the aircraft, and it came to No.15 MU in 1963 for a complete refurbishment. After a complete airframe overhaul and the fitting of four low-time Rolls Royce Merlin Engines, the Lancaster emerged in September 1964 in an authentic wartime camouflage scheme. The aircraft later left Wroughton to join a Spitfire and a Hurricane in the Battle of Britain Memorial Flight, where she remains today.

Helicopters began to arrive at Wroughton in the late 1960s, and work on the Westland Whirlwind, Wessex and Sioux started to predominate. In 1972 the last Canberra moved out; this was because it was decided to transfer Wroughton to the Royal Navy under a rationalisation scheme. On 5 April 1972, No.15 MU was disbanded, and Royal Naval Aircraft Yard Wroughton was commissioned. Work on helicopters for all three services continued until, following defence cuts in the mid-1970s, it was announced that RNAY Wroughton would close on 1 April 1979. However, this decision was rescinded in 1978 and the RNAY continued to operate well into the 1990s before it finally closed.

Also in 1978 it was announced that the Science Museum was to use Wroughton as a store for its collection of aircraft and other large

Tiger Moths attending the Great Vintage Flying Weekend, held at the Science Museum Wroughton in June 2001. One of the aerodrome's massive C hangars provides a backdrop. (Author)

exhibits. They took over six hangars on the western side of the airfield. The first aircraft for the collection, a Douglas DC-3 Dakota, flew in, and it was soon followed by a DH Comet and Lockheed Constellation. In September 1980 the Science Museum Wroughton opened to the public for the first time. Today the Science Museum is the custodian of Wroughton, and keeps the airfield and its hangars in good condition. Flying still takes place during events organised at the airfield during the summer months, such as the Great Vintage Flying Weekend.

Little operational flying took place at Wroughton during its existence. Yet its role involved the MU in countless actions during the Second World War, from the Battle of France to the Rhine Crossing, by supporting the flying units in providing a constant supply of fully-serviceable, combat-ready aircraft to enable them to do their job. This was a mundane task, but an essential one, for without the aeroplanes the squadrons could do nothing.

19
YATESBURY

National Grid Reference (173) SU060705, 4 miles E of Calne

Yatesbury is another Wiltshire airfield that dates back to World War I. The site has played an important part in military aviation training during both world wars, and training at Yatesbury has taken place on and off from 1916 to 1965. Among other claims to fame, the schools at Yatesbury trained three airmen who later went on to win Britain's highest decoration for gallantry, the Victoria Cross – William Barker, Guy Gibson and John Hannah.

The site at Yatesbury originally consisted of a large field covering some 500 acres, divided roughly in half by a road running from the main Calne-Marlborough road to Yatesbury village. This in effect created two separate airfields, the parent station (Camp No.1) at Yatesbury West, and Camp No.2 at Yatesbury East. Several hangars and technical buildings were constructed on each airfield, along with offices and accommodation buildings. Yatesbury was opened as a flying training station in 1916. As well as training pilots, the airfield also provided training for squadrons. One of the foremost fighter squadrons of the RFC, No.28 Squadron, trained at Yatesbury in September and October 1917, when its pilots returned to England to convert to the Sopwith Camel. Lieutenant William Barker trained at Yatesbury and returned with the squadron to France. Later, he was awarded the VC for his courage in combat, and ended the war with fifty-two victories, the second-highest scoring British pilot.

With the Armistice in November 1918, the need for training at Yatesbury ceased, and the airfield closed in 1919.

Five years later, in May 1923, the Bristol Aeroplane Company (BAC) was awarded a contract by the RAF to run a flying school for reserve

219

'The model flying school at Yatesbury' – the main building of 10 E&RFS, shortly after being opened in 1936. (Aeroplane)

pilots. Known as the Reserve Flying School, it was set up at Filton. In 1935 it was renamed No.2 Elementary and Reserve Flying School (E&RFS), and that year it was decided to set up more such civilian-operated reserve flying training schools as part of the Government's Air Training Scheme, which was allied to the RAF Expansion Scheme. Eventually forty-four E&RFSs were formed. As part of this expansion the BAC was awarded a contract for a second school, and to accommodate it the company purchased the western half of the old airfield at Yatesbury. The school buildings and facilities constructed were of six types – hangars, mess and offices, accommodation, staff quarters, classrooms, recreation facilities and works facilities. New offices/mess and classrooms buildings were built and two of the three existing hangars were refurbished, along with other usable buildings. The airfield surface was restored and repaired. When all was finally completed the new school was widely acclaimed for its style, design and layout, and the BAC was commended by *Flight* magazine in November 1936 for producing 'a model flying school at Yatesbury, whose pattern few will equal and none will better.' From contemporary photographs the school certainly looks smart and business-like.

The role of the new school, to be known as No.10 E&RFS, was to teach students to fly, from basic to a good solo standard. Flying training took place on a fleet of Tiger Moths that were owned by BAC and were painted in black and silver house colours and civilian-registered. Hawker Audaxes and Hart Trainers were also flown later but these were in military markings. The initial training course lasted two months and required some fifty hours of flying time. As well as the purely practical flying aspects of the course, the students would be given a thorough grounding in the theory of flight, navigation, armaments, radio communication, engines and airframe construction, as well as more general subjects such as mathematics and aviation law. Throughout their course the students would be closely monitored, and their aptitude for either single or multi-engine flying would be noted.

The students would spend many hours 'flying' indoors in the Link Trainer. This apparatus would today be called a simulator, and consisted of an aircraft cockpit fitted out with all the controls and instruments needed to give the student the impression that he was flying a real aeroplane. It was linked to a control station, where an instructor sat. This had a map display, upon which a device called a 'crab' moved, faithfully reproducing the student's flying sortie. The Link Trainer saved many valuable hours of instruction in the air, as well as many lives and aircraft.

The student pilots would then go on to fly the Tiger Moths, and most went solo after between eight and ten hours' dual instruction. However, some took longer, depending on the weather and ability. After a while, if he didn't make sufficient progress, the student would be given the Backward Progress Test, a euphemism for the chop (some 30% of the students failed the flying training course). However, if the student's instructor was happy, he would hand him over to the Chief Flying Instructor (CFI), who would take the student up for a First Solo Test. At the end of the test the student hoped for the moment when the CFI would climb out of the aeroplane and say, 'Off you go – one circuit and landing'. The magical First Solo followed, when the student pilot found himself alone in the air, in sole charge of one of His Majesty's aeroplanes! Once the student pilots had gone solo, they were given the opportunity to improve and refine their skills by cross-country flying, both by day and night, forced-landing practice and aerobatics.

These measures were designed to boost the new pilots' confidence before they moved on to the next stage of training. Following the award of their Pilot's Wings, a regular RAF pupil pilot would be sent from Yatesbury to a Service Recruitment Centre to be issued with his uniform and receive basic military training before going on to further flying training at one of the Service Flying Training Schools. RAF Volunteer Reserve pupil pilots on the other hand would then return to their civilian jobs, but would later continue training at regular intervals during their spare time.

One of the first pupils to be taught at the school was 18-year-old Guy Penrose Gibson, who attended No.6 Course during the winter of 1936/37. Although he was an average student, Guy Gibson went on to an illustrious career in the RAF, culminating in his award of the Victoria Cross, as one of the RAF's youngest Wing Commanders after leading the Dam Busters' raid by No.617 Squadron in May 1943 (see *Boscombe Down*). Gibson was later killed leading a raid of 230 Mosquitoes and Lancasters over Germany in September 1944. He had asked permission to fly 'one last sortie', and was shot down over Holland on his return to base. Wing Commander Guy Gibson, DSO, DFC, was 26 years old when he died.

The flying training contract with BAC was so successful that the Air Ministry placed a further contract with the company in 1938 for the operation of a Civil Air Navigation School to train RAF observers to the same standards in navigation as the pilots. This was formed on 26 September 1938, and operated five Avro Anson Mk.I trainers to train its pupils. Courses at the school consisted of elementary map reading, followed by air experience and more advanced map reading. The pupils would qualify at the end of the course by navigating an Anson over a long and involved cross-country flight. Following their time at the CANS, the observers would proceed to bombing and gunnery schools to complete their training, before being posted to an operational squadron in Bomber or Coastal Commands.

More building started taking place at Yatesbury during 1938. A new accommodation block was built, and the mess/office buildings and classrooms were extended. The remaining RFC hangar was refurbished and a start was made on a new large steel-framed side-opening hangar, although this was not completed until after the outbreak of war. Ground defence buildings were also constructed, including lecture huts, a gas chamber and a 25-yard firearms range.

On 6 October 1938 Course No.15 started at 10 E&RFS with forty-one pupils from the Royal Navy. This was the first naval flying training course at the school.

In the meantime the RAF had been looking for a site to train ground radio operators, and it eventually decided on Yatesbury. Construction then started on a large training camp on the old eastern World War I airfield, which had been requisitioned from its owner, George Cowling of Manor Farm. Soon the site was covered in training and accommodation buildings, mainly being single-storey and of wood. Early in February No.1 Training Wing transferred to Yatesbury from Cranwell, and No.2 Training Wing was formed at the new school. This was followed a month later by the formation of No.3 Training Wing. Each Wing consisted of three officers and approximately one thousand airmen. The station was opened as No.2 Electrical and Wireless School (E&WS) on 1 December 1938. A few months later, in May 1939, the Bristol Wireless Flight (BWF) was established. Its job was to give airborne experience to student aircrew wireless operators from E&WS courses. For this the BWF had some twin-engine biplane DH Dragon Rapide aircraft, and later Percival Proctors.

When hostilities started in September 1939, there was a shake-up in the RAF training system. Some technical and flying schools were closed, while others were expanded, the net aim being to increase the numbers of trained personnel. The effect of this at Yatesbury was one of expansion. No.10 E&RFS was taken over from the BAC by Training Command, and became re-designated as No.10 Elementary Flying Training School (EFTS) on 3 September 1939. It was to concentrate on the basic flying training of student pilots, using its ground school and two-seat basic trainers. The school's Harts and Audaxes were transferred to Brize Norton and Shawbury. They were replaced by more Tiger Moths, transferred from other reserve schools that had been disbanded. No.10 EFTS's establishment of the aircraft increased from eighteen to fifty-four. This number reduced later in the year when the

Pupil and instructor in the cabin of a Dominie during airborne radio training. (Aeroplane)

223

original BAC Tiger Moths were shipped off to India, presumably to equip more schools there.

In October 1939 the E&WS set up two mobile radio sections to go to France with the British Expeditionary Force. On 1 November 1939 the Civil Air Navigation School was re-titled, and became No.2 Air Observer Navigation School (AONS).

Following the outbreak of war, defensive measures had been taken on the ground at Yatesbury. Seven air raid shelters were excavated and the concrete aprons and perimeter tracks of the airfield were coated in tarmac to tone down their light colouring. In addition the hangars were painted in camouflage stripes to break up their shape. Pillboxes were constructed in defensive positions around the airfield and several sand-bagged anti-aircraft gun positions were also built. A hutted Decontamination Centre was built for the treatment of personnel suffering from the effects of mustard gas or from contamination as well as conventional wounds.

John Hannah carried out his wireless training at No.2 E&WS in September 1939, and then moved on to No.4 Bombing and Gunnery School at West Freugh. After his final aircrew training at No.16 Operational Training Unit at Upper Heyford, Hannah joined No.83 Squadron at Scampton in August 1940 as a Wireless Operator/Air Gunner. Acting Sergeant Hannah started flying on operations in the squadron's Handley Page Hampdens, and was a member of the crew of aircraft P1355 (OL-W) on the night of 15-16 November 1940, when the squadron was sent to bomb German invasion barges at Antwerp. His aircraft took a direct hit from flak and caught fire. The flames were so bad that the rear gunner and the navigator abandoned the aircraft. Despite being badly burnt, and instead of taking to his parachute, Hannah disregarded his injuries and, with ammunition exploding in all directions, extinguished the fire. He then helped the pilot regain control of the aircraft, enabling their safe return to base. When the aircraft was examined by other aircrew back at Scampton, they were amazed that such a badly-damaged aircraft could have been flown home, and that a fire causing so much damage could have been successfully fought. For his heroic actions that night Sergeant John Hannah was awarded the VC. He was posted back to Yatesbury in September 1941 as an instructor with No.2 Signals School (as it had become). While not wishing to take advantage of his fame, he did make a request of the station commander, which was that airmen at Yatesbury should not have to salute when receiving their money on pay parades. This unusual request was granted, and it is believed that Yatesbury was the

Pupils at 10 EFTS assembling for a briefing in 1940. Behind the ranks of Tiger Moths, some Ansons and Dominies appear. (Aeroplane)

only RAF Station to receive such a privilege. John Hannah remained an instructor at Yatesbury despite the fact that his health was gradually deteriorating. On 10 December 1942, due to tuberculosis, he was medically discharged on full pension. John Hannah died in June 1947 at the age of 26, and remains the youngest airman ever to have been awarded the VC.

A new school was formed at Yatesbury on 18 January 1940. This was No.2 Radio School, and its task was to train Radio Direction Finder (RDF) Operators. RDF was the name given to radar in the early days of World War II. This training had previously taken place at RAF Bawdsey in Suffolk, and a nucleus of staff moved from there to Yatesbury to set up the new school. Training was given on all types of airborne radar sets such as the Air Interception (AI) for night fighters and Air to Surface Vessel (ASV) for Coastal Command aircraft. Training was also given to ground controllers, and four ninety-foot timber towers were built to carry the equipment used to give the pupils practical experience. Although the school had no aircraft allocated, it was to use the aircraft of other Yatesbury units when needed.

Great emphasis was placed on Morse code at the school. A speed of eight words per minute was set initially for sending and receiving messages, and this was increased by two words per minute each week, until a speed of eighteen words per minute was achieved by the students. During the course volunteers were invited for aircrew training. At that time wireless operators in RAF aircraft were also expected to man the guns, and the aircrew category was known as 'Wireless Operator/Air Gunner', or 'WOp/AG'. Those students that expressed an interest were given aptitude tests in a Dominie. The six-month course ended with an exam, and those volunteers that were successful were sent on an air gunnery course after a spot of leave.

With the defeat of France enemy raiders started to appear in some numbers during the summer of 1940. It was a concern that Yatesbury's unarmed trainers might encounter enemy aircraft during their normal flying training sorties. On 16 July 1940 almost a hundred ground defence personnel arrived at the station to take up aerodrome defence duties. The Luftwaffe appeared at Yatesbury shortly after this, when at 03:00 on 29 July a German raider dropped thirteen high-explosive bombs on the airfield. One of the bombs failed to go off, but the remainder exploded near the buildings of No.10 EFTS, with fortunately no casualties caused, the damage being minimal.

Yatesbury was used for aircraft dispersal during this time. Aircraft from No.10 Maintenance Unit (MU), Hullavington, and No.33 MU, Lyneham, which had yet to set up permanent RLGs, were parked at Yatesbury. These included Wellingtons, Bothas and Harvards. This continued until Townsend became available to No.10 MU following the departure of No.10 EFTS in September 1940, and other RLGs became available for storage in 1941.

As more radio operators and WOp/AGs were needed during the summer of 1940, No.2 E&WS was increased in size with the addition of a fourth Training Wing. In addition the school's training programmes were expanded to take more students. To assist in the process another E&WS was formed at Yatesbury on 10 June 1940. This was No.3 E&WS, flying Audaxes and Harts. However, it was not long before the increased pressure on the facilities at Yatesbury, with so many training units competing for space, provoked another re-organisation. On 26 August the two E&WSs were disbanded, and re-formed as Signals Schools. No.2 Signals School continued to operate at Yatesbury, while No.3 Signals School was moved to the ground training station at Wootton Bassett nearby. Flying facilities for both schools continued to be provided at Yatesbury, but other units were to move in order to make more room at the station. On 7 September No.10 EFTS moved to Weston-super-Mare, to continue its training from the airfield there. The school had trained 627 pupils at Yatesbury, in elementary flying training alone. On 14 December 1940 No.2 AONS was closed down, having trained 247 pupils on eight training courses. Its staff were transferred to No.2 Signals School.

Dominie and Proctor of No.2 Radio School overfly the side-opening hangar at Yatesbury. (Aeroplane)

During the early war years the Bristol Aeroplane Company still played an important part in the running of the Yatesbury school. The instructors that flew in the aircraft were employed by the company, and the aircraft were maintained by their staff. This was to change in 1942, when RAF instructors were brought in to replace the company's flying personnel. However, Bristol engineers continued to maintain the school's fleet of aeroplanes, which then consisted of sixty Proctors and thirty Dominies. These were later supplemented by Ansons, and to house this fleet of aeroplanes eleven blister hangars were built around the airfield perimeter.

Training continued into 1943, and, with more aircrew being required, the emphasis was on training flying personnel. In July 1943 the training of ground operators ceased at Yatesbury. Ironically, shortly after this it was found that the output of the Radio Schools was more than sufficient to replace the casualty losses on the squadrons. This resulted in a pool of personnel being set up at Yatesbury, to hold trained wireless operators until they were required for operational postings. This arrangement worked well, but it did result in a further training commitment as the numbers in the pool increased, in order to keep up the operators' standards, so that they could remain in currency.

Until December 1943 all wireless operators were also air gunners and wore a wing, or brevet, with the letters 'AG' on it. In December 1943 the Air Wireless Operator was also introduced, who was not a gunner. He wore a brevet that had the letter 'S' for signaller on it. Both the AG and S went on from the Radio Schools to advanced flying training, either in Bomber or Coastal Command. By October 1944 the Wireless Operator Pool at the station had increased to over 1,600 personnel (from 600 in mid-1943).

On the night of 18 November 1944 four Prisoners-of-War escaped through the wire of the POW camp at Devizes. They had no particular plan, and soon got lost anyway, so they laid up in a sheep pen during the following day. Having travelled eight miles or so from the camp the next evening, they found themselves at an aerodrome. It was in fact Yatesbury, although they did not know this at the time. The POWs hid in the bushes when it got light, and remained in hiding to observe. They soon realised that the airfield was used by training aircraft, and, as one of the prisoners was a glider pilot, felt that they had a good chance of stealing one. That night the Germans got into one of the Proctors and tried to start it, but without success. They got out, climbed into another aircraft and tried again, but could not start that one either. Fearing capture, they got out of the aircraft and left the airfield. However, the POWs were now cold, wet, hungry and disillusioned, and decided that they had had enough. The following morning they walked down the hill to the village of Cherhill, and gave themselves up to the landlord of the Black Horse. The publican telephoned the camp at Devizes, and when the guards later arrived at the pub, they found the POWs sat down to a hearty breakfast!

Although training at Yatesbury carried on into 1945, the demand for more aircrew gradually diminished, and in July 1945 the flying element of No.2 Radio School, including the Bristol Wireless Flight, was closed down. The school had trained 18,500 aircrew wireless operators to operational standards in 224,000 flying hours during the wartime period. The school itself carried on, and started the training of ground personnel once again. New courses were introduced, including the training of radar and guided weapons operators and technicians.

Flying continued when No.2 EFTS arrived from Worcester with their Tiger Moths. On 1 August 1945 the school started its first course at Yatesbury, No.74 Pre-Glider Course, for Army personnel. No.2 EFTS remained at Yatesbury for a couple of years, but was closed on 30 September 1947.

In 1951 the RAF Regiment started training its personnel at the station. A large number of RAF Regiment Squadrons were later formed at Yatesbury, along with Nos. 2, 5 and 7 Wings, RAF Regiment. The station was used as a holding area in August 1956 for RAF units involved in the Suez operation.

The closure of RAF Yatesbury was announced in 1964, and the air radio element of training was moved to RAF Cosford. Several aircraft had been maintained in the hangars for the ground training of technicians, and these were eventually moved to other schools of technical training, the last courses at No.2 Radio School passing out on 21 July 1965. Following this the station was put on a Care and Maintenance footing, parented by RAF Lyneham. RAF Yatesbury was finally closed in April 1969.

The hutted camp that had been constructed on the old eastern airfield was demolished by the Air Ministry before the land was sold off. This area has now reverted to farmland, and apart from the remaining gymnasium building, there is nothing to show that the RAF technical training school had been there. The airfield to the west, on the other hand, remains intact, with almost all of the buildings still standing. The site is a rare and almost unique example (the other being at Netheravon) of a complete World War I aerodrome that has survived with its hangars still in place. Moreover, the three RFC hangars are the largest group of their type left, and the outline of the original western RFC airfield that they served can still be seen. Within the World War I technical and domestic area the group of the 1935 Bristol School buildings also remain in a discrete group. The buildings are mostly in reasonable condition but derelict, and need to be repaired if they are to be seen for much longer. At the time of writing a haulage company operates from one of the hangars, and in another building aircraft restoration work is taking place – a tangible reminder of Yatesbury's past.

20

ZEALS

National Grid Reference (183) ST 780327, 1 mile N of village

Zeals was opened on 21 May 1942 as a forward operating airfield in the Colerne sector of No.10 Group Fighter Command. Situated on pastureland alongside Zeals Knoll six miles to the east of Wincanton, the site is just inside the county border between Wiltshire and Somerset. Construction of the 530-acre site had been started in mid-1941, although relatively little work was in fact required on the airfield itself, as it was predominantly grass with a tarmac taxi-way running all round the perimeter. The main construction effort involved building the nine hangars (eight Blister and one T1), the other operational buildings such as the control tower and fire station, as well as the station headquarters, barrack accommodation and other buildings of the domestic site.

The first unit to arrive at the newly-opened station was No.286 Squadron, on 26 May 1942. This was a regional anti-aircraft cooperation unit that had previously been based at Colerne and Lulsgate Bottom (see *Colerne*). Equipped with Defiant and Martinet target tugs, along with other types such as the Hurricane, it provided target-towing and gunlaying training for the AA defences in the south west of England. The squadron stayed at Zeals until 21 August, when it returned to Colerne.

The next occupants of Zeals were the squadrons of the Ibsley Wing, which arrived on 21 August 1942. They came on detachment for a few months from their base at RAF Ibsley in the New Forest. The Wing consisted of two squadrons, Nos.66 and 118, both flying the Spitfire Vb. Three days before their arrival, both squadrons had been involved in Operation Jubilee, the Dieppe Raid. The Spitfires of No.66 Squadron

The business end of a Whirlwind, showing its four 20mm cannon. (Aeroplane)

escorted the Bostons of No.226 Squadron on smoke-laying sorties over the landing beaches on the afternoon of the 18th to cover the withdrawal of the raiding force. One of the Bostons was shot down by flak, and No.66's Spitfires covered the return of the remaining bombers to base. On the way they were harassed by Focke-Wulf Fw190s, which shot down two of the Spitfires over the Channel, ten miles north of Dieppe. The combat was not all one-sided, and the Spitfires managed to shoot down one Fw190.

On arrival at Zeals, both squadrons' task was to provide escorts for Allied bombers operating over occupied France and the Western Approaches. The wing's first operation took them to Cherbourg docks, escorting Boston bombers of No.2 Group. Operations then continued for the next four months over northern France. During their time at Zeals the squadrons also took part in Rhubarbs, fighter sweeps over the Continent specifically to hunt for enemy fighters. For a brief period in September the two squadrons went to RAF Predannack in Cornwall for some coastal patrol work, and were replaced at Zeals by No.402

Squadron RCAF from Kenley and No.611 (West Lancashire) Squadron from Biggin Hill. Both Nos.402 and 611 Squadrons were among the first units to be equipped with the Spitfire IX, an improved version of the Spitfire V fitted with the up-rated Merlin 61 engine. This gave the squadrons the ability to fight the Focke-Wulf Fw190 on equal terms while flying high cover patrols and escorts. The Spitfire V had been found to be inferior to the Fw190 when the new German fighter first appeared.

On returning to Zeals the Ibsley Wing resumed their bomber escort work, supplemented by the occasional night patrol. No.118 Squadron had a high proportion of Dutch and Free French pilots in its complement, who were keen to get back at the Germans. On these escort missions Fw190s were frequently encountered and both squadrons often returned to base with a satisfactory score. As the version of the Spitfire that they were flying at this time was the Mark Vb any victories scored against the Fw190 were well-earned. Both Squadrons continued to fly from Zeals until 23 December 1942, when water-logging of the airfield was making safe operations too difficult. Because of this it was decided that the Ibsley Wing should return to its home base in the New Forest.

For the next three months the only occupants of RAF Zeals were the personnel of No.2835 Squadron RAF Regiment, who provided anti-aircraft and ground defences for the airfield. However, flying activity resumed at Zeals in March 1943 when No.132 Squadron with the Spitfire Vb flew in together with Nos.174 and 184 Squadrons with their Hurricanes. They had come to take part in exercise Spartan, a close-support exercise with the army. No.132 Squadron's task was to provide top cover, while Nos.174 and 184 Squadrons were to provide close ground attack support for the troops. No.174 Squadron was equipped with the Hurricane IIB fighter-bomber, whereas No.184 had the Hurricane IID, also known as the 'flying can-opener'. The latter were formidable aircraft, being fitted with a pair of 40mm cannon specially designed for attacking armoured vehicles. Like the Ibsley Wing these three squadrons were grouped into one formation, known as No.122 Airfield, for the duration of the exercise. The exercise was an early attempt at joint operations and involved the crews of the squadrons experiencing the same living conditions as the troops that they were supporting, by living and working in the field (although the tents were pitched on the airfield and not too far from civilisation!) Fortunately, the weather, which had not been too good, let up during the period of the exercise. As soon as the exercise had finished and the squadrons departed, teams from No.14 Works Area arrived on-site to try to improve the drainage of the airfield, and all flying was suspended.

It was about this time that some more RAF ground units arrived at Zeals. These were the Servicing Commandos, special units formed to support front-line tactical fighter squadrons in the field. They were trained along similar lines to the Army and Royal Marine Commandos, and their prime purpose was to accompany an invasion force to make captured enemy airfields serviceable for the operation of Allied aircraft, or to operate airfields newly-constructed by the Army Airfield Construction Companies. They were to service, re-arm and refuel combat aircraft, under fire if necessary, and to hold the airfield until it was safe enough for the RAF squadrons' ground crews to take over from them. The men of the Servicing Commandos (SCs) were therefore trained as combat troops as well as aircraft technicians. The first SC units were formed to take part in Operation Torch, the landings in North Africa. With the planned invasion of the Continent, more were needed.

Victor Poynting was an armourer at No.32 MU, RAF St. Athan in the spring of 1943, working on the repair of bomber gun turrets. He came from a large Salisbury family, and had two brothers in the navy, and two in the army. With himself in the RAF, 'we were a one-family combined operation,' he said. When he heard that volunteers were needed for special duties, Victor put his name down, and a few weeks later found himself getting off a bus at RAF Exeter, the airfield to the east of the city (now Exeter Airport). The station was the holding area for No.3209 SC, which had been formed there a few days before, under the command of Flight Lieutenant CE Wood. The unit had an HQ Flight and was divided into two squadrons, each formed from two further flights, with a total strength of 170 men. After a few days it was announced that the unit would be moving to RAF Zeals, and there on 9 May it joined Nos.3207, 3208 and 3210 SCs.

At Zeals a tough training regime started, with forced marches (which entailed marching then doubling, in alternate periods) and physical training. The men were taken to Salisbury for swimming lessons at the Town Baths, and those that could not drive were given lessons by British School of Motoring instructors in specially-provided Austin 12 saloons. Weapons training included the use of the revolver, .303 rifle, Bren gun, Sten gun and hand grenades. 'Musketry Practice' took place with the firearms on the ranges nearby. Classroom lessons were also given in a diverse range of subjects that included map-reading, first aid, radio communication, gas defence, field-craft and intelligence. To

Westland Whirlwinds were flown from Zeals by 263 Squadron in 1943. (Aeroplane)

this was added technical training in aircraft instruments, electrical systems, hydraulic systems and armament. Aircraft were made available for practical training, including a Spitfire Mk.V, Spitfire Mk.IX, Kittyhawk and Typhoon. As they were field units, they were issued with khaki battledress uniforms and boots – giving up their RAF shoes was a bit of a culture shock for some! Once the concentrated training had taken place at Zeals, sections were sent out to other RAF bases to gain experience. Victor went with a group to Middle Wallop initially. Later at Ibsley they found getting hands-on experience to be difficult, as the local RAF personnel were 'not having squaddies messing about with our aeroplanes!'

The airfield at Zeals was ready for use again in June 1943, and Whirlwind fighters of No.263 Squadron arrived. The Westland Whirl-wind was a twin-engined four cannon fighter with an impressive performance. No.263 had been operating the aircraft as fighter bombers for attacks on enemy shipping and airfields. The squadron stayed at Zeals for a month flying sorties over the French coast. In July they returned to their previous base at Warmwell in Dorset.

Also in July the SCs were given more varied training. On 3 July No.3209 SC left Zeals to travel to Scotland for amphibious operations training. It took three days to get their convoy of 3-ton trucks to Inverary. There, as part of Exercise Plonk organised by the Combined Training Centre, the troops and vehicles went aboard Tank Landing Craft (LCTs), from which they disembarked by scrambling nets and from the bow ramp in practice amphibious landings by day and night along the shores of Loch Fyne. Having gained some useful experience the unit returned to base on 16 July. A few days later the SCs were finally dispersed from Zeals to other airfields around the country. No.3209 SC, for example, went to Advanced Landing Ground 125, newly-constructed in the Romney Marshes, for operational training with Spitfire squadrons. The personnel of the SCs built up their expertise over the following months in the knowledge that they were to be part of the force that was to invade France. They operated all over southern England, providing working parties to assist other units for training, exercises and operations. They were to return to Wiltshire the following summer, during the build-up to the invasion itself (see *Old Sarum*).

In July 1943 Zeals was allocated for American use. It was selected to become an airfield of the 8th Air Force's Tactical Air Depot Area, then being established to support the large number of units expected to arrive from the USA over the following months. On 1 August personnel from the 66th Airdrome Squadron began arriving to set up the 1st Tactical Air Depot in order to support major maintenance, modification and repair of the C-47 transport aircraft. In October the base was transferred to the 9th Air Force, but it was soon apparent that the grass airfield was still prone to water-logging. No.4675 Flight, 5005 Airfield Construction Company, laboured to improve it, building hard standings and laying steel Sommerfeld tracking to reinforce the surface, but it was apparent that the airfield would not take the pounding that it would have to receive from heavy transport aircraft. The plan to use the airfield for C-47 support was therefore cancelled.

Nothing much happened for a while apart from the odd visit from a B-17 Flying Fortress bomber, and some glider trials. Then in December 1943 it was decided to set up the 5th Tactical Air Depot at Zeals to support the Republic P-47 Thunderbolt. Personnel started to arrive and soon 56 officers and 1,000 men were working there. The first batch of 50 aircraft arrived on 23 and 24 December. However, in the months that followed, with many aircraft coming and going, it was clear that Zeals airfield could not take sustained use of the heavy P-47. More metal tracking was laid but with the poor drainage combined with high rainfall that winter, conditions scarcely improved. It was eventually

The crew of a Mosquito night fighter prepare for another sortie in the winter of 1944.
(Aeroplane)

decided to transfer the 5th TAD to an airfield with tarmac runways, and Chilbolton was selected for this purpose. The move took place between January and March 1944. The last US unit to move out was the 21st Weather Squadron, which used Zeals as its HQ base during the time that the USAAF was there. This squadron provided meteorological information to the 9th Air Force and had small detachments at most of its stations in the UK.

The Station reopened under RAF management the following month, on 20 April 1944. Again it was a forward fighter airfield under No.10 Group, but this time the aircraft were night fighters. These squadrons were moved to Zeals as part of an effort to combat the increasing number of nuisance night raids being mounted by German bombers. On 11 May No.488 Squadron was the first to arrive, flying its Mosquitos in from Colerne. A RNZAF Unit, No.488 Squadron was originally formed in September 1941 at Rongotai in Australia, flying CAC Wirraways, before sailing to Singapore in October where it re-equipped with the American Brewster Buffalo. Based at Kallang it was not fully operational when the Japanese attacked. The first air encounters with the Japanese took place on 12 January and the squadron incurred heavy losses. At the end of the month No.488 Squadron withdrew to Australia, then returned to New Zealand. The squadron was reformed in the UK at Church Fenton on 25 June 1942 as a night fighter unit. Originally equipped with the Beaufighter it converted to the Mosquito XII and XIII. No.488 Squadron was later earmarked as one of the units to become part of the 2nd Tactical Air Force, the formation then being set up to take part in Operation Overlord, the impending invasion of Normandy. Having arrived at Zeals the squadron quickly got down to practising night flying from their new home. Although equipped with Funnel approach and Drem circuit lighting, systems installed to assist airfield landing approaches in the dark, night flying from Zeals was not easy because of the topography of the local area. There was a steep sided valley to the west and the airfield itself was on a slope away to the south east. In early June 1944 No.488 was teamed up with another Mosquito night fighter unit, No.604 Squadron based at Hurn, then Colerne, to become No.147 Wing. Together the two squadrons mounted operations over southern England and the continent as part of the build-up to the invasion. From the night of D-Day, 6 June, they put up nightly patrols over the beach-head.

On 18 June a second night fighter squadron arrived at Zeals. This was No.410 Squadron, a Canadian unit that had been formed in 1941 with Defiant gun-turret armed night fighters, before exchanging them for Mosquitos. By the time the squadron arrived at Zeals it was equipped with the Mosquito Mark XIII. The unit had previously been operating from Hunsdon in Hertfordshire and on arrival at Zeals went straight into action with No.488 Squadron. Soon each squadron was putting up an average of eight sorties per night and consistently making scores. During the month of June, No.488 Squadron alone intercepted and knocked down nine enemy aircraft.

By the end of June the aircraft of the two Zeals Mosquito Squadrons were ranging further afield in the defence of the Allied Armies on the Continent and on 8 July Squadron Leader March and Flight Lieutenant Eyolfson of No.410 Squadron in Mosquito MM570 shot down one of the new Messerschmitt Me410 twin-engined fighters over the outskirts of Paris. They also reported seeing Flight Lieutenant Huppert and Flying Officer Christie shoot down a Junkers Ju88 shortly before they themselves were hit by enemy fire and forced to bail out of their aircraft.

The tenth of July was an unfortunate day at Zeals, as two bad aircraft accidents occurred near the airfield. One involved Mosquito NFXIII HK500 of No.410 Squadron, which overshot the runway while trying to land at Zeals, possibly because of fog, and crashed at Pen Mill, Penselwood, to the west of the airfield. Both crew were, however, uninjured. A more tragic accident occurred the same day involving a Noorduyn Norseman communications aircraft of the USAAF. The aircraft is believed to have been in transit to Bristol when it requested permission to land at Zeals, possibly because of the weather conditions. However, Air Traffic Control refused due to the foggy conditions at the airfield. The Norseman orbited the area, then with great ill-fortune hit the tallest feature in the area, King Alfred's tower, an 18th century folly standing one hundred and fifty feet high on a hilltop in the corner of the Stourhead estate. The aircraft struck the pinnacle at the top of the tower, and crashed to the ground nearby. All aboard were killed.

A flight of No.604 Squadron with their Mosquitos joined No.147 Wing at Zeals in late July just before the whole wing was transferred to Colerne on 28 July 1944. Although their stay at Zeals was brief No.604 managed to shoot down a JU88 off Granville during the night of 26 July.

When No.147 Wing arrived at Colerne they displaced No.286

Dakota of the Glider Pickup Training Flight in spring 1945. (Aeroplane)

Corsair fighter, as flown by 759 and 771 Squadrons from Zeals. (Aeroplane)

Squadron, which then returned to Zeals. By now this unit was equipped with Oxford, Defiant, Hurricane, Martinet and Master aircraft, and were supporting AA Units across four counties. By September they were finding that the weather was making the ground conditions too difficult to operate effectively, and once room had been found for them at Weston Zoyland in Somerset they moved out, on 28 September 1944.

In October a detachment of No.3 Glider Training School was moved in from Northleach. This unit flew Master glider tugs and Hotspur Gliders, their main task being the training of glider pilots. Their aircraft became a familiar sight at Zeals over the next couple of months. The detachment moved out in early January 1945 to be replaced by another glider unit, the Glider Pickup Training Flight. The role of this unit was to train pilots to perfect a method of recovery when gliders had landed in sites that were inaccessible to powered aircraft. The snatch technique was originated by the Americans in Burma, and was developed by the Airborne Forces Tactical Development Unit at Netheravon. Its use involved the tow-rope being suspended between two poles and paid out in front of the glider. The towing aircraft was equipped with a hook and, flying low over the field, would engage the suspended tow-rope with this hook, snatching it and the attached glider off the ground. A reel was fitted inside the tug aircraft, and as the pilot applied full power to bring the glider off the ground, steel wire attached to the tow-hook ran off the reel to absorb some of the momentum of the tug aircraft and reduce the strain on the tow-rope with its attached now-airborne glider. Once the tug and glider levelled off, the tug rear crew slowly began reeling in the steel cable until the glider was within about 350 feet of the tug, and the combination then settled down for the rest of the flight. The PT Flight used 5 Dakotas and 15 US Hadrian gliders for this work. In March Ibsley airfield became available and the flight moved there to continue its training. During the unit's time at Zeals, on 19 February 1945, a visiting Dakota was involved in a flying accident near the airfield. The aircraft was from 107 Operational Training Unit, and had just taken off to return to its base after an overnight stay at Zeals, when it inexplicably crashed into a knoll not far from the airfield. All passengers and crew aboard the aircraft were killed. A copse of trees on the top of the knoll still has a gap where the aircraft went in.

The next tenant of the airfield was the Royal Navy. In early April the RAF handed over control of Zeals to the Admiralty, who required an airfield in the area to replace Charlton Horethorne, 10 miles to the south west, in Somerset, which was being closed. In line with the Royal Naval tradition that each shore station should be named and commissioned (just as ships at sea), Royal Naval Air Station Zeals became HMS Hummingbird, a training station within the Fleet Air Arm (FAA). The first FAA unit to appear at Zeals was No.760 Squadron. This had been an anti-submarine operational training squadron equipped with Sea Hurricanes. Disbanded in November 1944 it was reformed at Zeals on 10 April 1945 from the Corsair familiarisation flight of No.759 Squadron, part of No.1 Naval Air Fighter School at Yeovilton. Its task was to convert fighter pilots to the Corsair, prior to joining No.759 Squadron. Harvards were used to teach new pilots flying techniques that were peculiar to the Corsair, such as its particular landing method. Once the instructors were happy that the students had perfected this on the Harvard, they were let loose on the Corsair, which was a powerful and unforgiving beast in the wrong hands. Flying took place in the comparative peace of Zeals in order to relieve pressure on the Yeovilton circuit, which at that time was suffering an excessive number of accidents, some fatal, due to the crowded conditions and the inexperience of the pilots. The squadron also later received the Grumman Hellcat I, which it operated at Zeals from August 1945.

The following day, 11 April 1945, No.704 Squadron was formed at

Zeals control tower still stands, having been converted into a private house. (Author, courtesy Kevin Byrne)

Zeals as the Naval Operational Training Unit for the conversion of crews to the Mosquito. It flew the Mosquito FB.Mk.VI and a few examples of the dual-control trainer version, the T.Mk.III. In June four aircraft were detached to Thorney Island, where they were temporarily absorbed into No.703 Squadron for development work with the Antisubmarine Warfare Development Unit. The remainder of No.704 Squadron continued to train at Zeals until early September, when on the 4th of that month the unit itself moved to Thorney Island, where it reabsorbed its detachment. Another unit arrived on 14 April. This was No.790 Squadron from Charlton Horethorne. The squadron was attached to the Fighter Direction School at RNAS Yeovilton and it helped to train Fighter Direction Officers using Oxfords to simulate bombers and Fireflies acting as fighters. Shortly after arrival at Zeals the Squadron also received Spitfire Vbs and Seafire Is and IIs.

In July No.771 Squadron arrived at Zeals on transfer from Twatt in Scotland. This was a fleet requirements unit, and its job was to fly Corsair and Wildcat aircraft over the Portland Ranges, towing targets for RN warships to practise their target acquisition and AA gunnery. It also flew aircraft for the Fighter Direction School.

As autumn set in and the weather worsened the Royal Navy found the conditions at Zeals to be just as unpleasant as their predecessors had. To maintain their level of operations, one by one the squadrons were found new homes to go to. With the war now ended and other airfields becoming available, the FAA decided to withdraw from Zeals. By November 1945 only a small closing down party remained at the station and on New Year's Day, 1946, HMS Hummingbird was decommissioned. The site was reduced to Care and Maintenance and not long afterwards was de-requisitioned. A couple of local roads that had been closed when the airfield had been built were reopened and the whole area returned to agriculture.

Not much can be seen of Zeals airfield nowadays. The western airfield perimeter track still sees occasional use as an airstrip for crop dusters. Some buildings of the domestic site to the south of the airfield still remain, and the area is made use of for farm storage. The control tower survives, having been converted into a dwelling, and is known as Tower House. However, many local people still have fond memories of the gallant young men of different nationalities who passed through the station during the war years.

21
THE OTHER
AIRFIELDS

There were several airfields or airstrips in use within the county of Wiltshire during the wartime period that were not main airfields but subsidiary sites. Often they were not used continuously, just on occasions. Nonetheless these little airfields were important, as without them the main airfields would have become congested and been reduced in effectiveness.

Some of these smaller airfields were in use before the Second World War, having been established by the RAF or private landowners. The Automobile Association prepared a list of the civilian landing grounds for its members and published it in the 1930s as a handbook. Details of map references, landing runs, fees and facilities were given. In Wiltshire these included one at Marlborough (later to become Marlborough Relief Landing Ground (RLG)), at Melksham (half a mile south of the town between the canal and the railway) and at Trowbridge (one and a half miles north east of the town besides the A366, west of Semington).

RAF airfields were categorised as follows:

Parent Station – a self accounting airfield in any RAF Command. It may administer one or more satellite RLGs or ELGs. Its size is not standardised.

Relief Landing Ground (RLG) – an airfield administered by a parent station with accommodation for up to 100 personnel. Its function is to relieve flying congestion at other associated airfields by providing additional flying capacity.

Satellite Landing Ground (SLG) – an airfield administered by a parent station with little or no standard accommodation.

Emergency Landing Ground (ELG) – as SLG, but its purpose is to relieve flying congestion at other associated airfields and the landing area is to be used solely for forced landing practice and overshoot procedures.

The other airfields are as follows.

Alton Barnes

National Grid Reference (173) SU100620, 4 miles S of Avebury

Also known as Brown's Farm this field 4 miles north-west of Upavon was first used in 1936, as a practice landing ground by the Central Flying School, which was based at Upavon. Originally just a field with a windsock, it was used for circuit planning and forced landing practice by trainee instructors away from Upavon's busy and congested airfield.

The first aircraft to use the field were Avro 504N Biplanes. These were replaced by the more powerful Avro Tutors biplane trainers in 1937, and these aircraft used the field until late 1941. At the time, most landing grounds were difficult to find from the air, but Alton Barnes was different – flying from Upavon towards the White Horse at Milk Hill, the field was easily spotted between the Stanton St Bernard road and the Kennet and Avon Canal.

The threat of invasion resulted in construction of concrete gun positions beside the airfield in 1940 to protect it from air and ground assault. However, these did not prevent an air-raid on the night of 14 September when a German bomber dropped three bombs on the airfield. Following this, further gun positions were built around the perimeter.

As the war progressed, the demand for instructors to teach more aircrew increased, and with it the use of Alton Barnes. Transfer in the control of Alton Barnes came at the end of 1941, when the field came under No.29 EFTS at Clyffe Pypard, a newly-opened base 9 miles to the north. Under the active management of No.29 EFTS the airfield was upgraded to Relief Landing Ground standard following the construction of Nissan and Maycrete buildings along the Honey Street-Alton Barnes road. Blister hangars, ten in number, were built around the perimeter, and air-raid shelters were constructed. Instructional facilities later added at the airfield included classrooms and a Link Trainer building.

Night flying facilities were provided, and these included rendezvous lights on Milk Hill. These received unwelcome attention on the night of 16 April 1942 when an aircraft from a Bomber Operational Training Unit dropped a stick of small bombs nearby, having mistaken the lights for a night bombing range.

Extra care was needed when operating from Alton Barnes in bad weather, as the landing area softened badly after heavy rainfall. However, flying continued – No.29 EFTS operated Tiger Moths and Magisters, and the locals soon became used to these aircraft buzzing around the area. RN as well as RAF pilots were trained by No.29 EFTS, but in May 1942 the courses changed to include army personnel, on pre-glider training. No.29 EFTS consisted of four training flights accommodated at Clyffe Pypard, the students being trained at Alton Barnes travelling daily from the main site. In June 1942 the flights were increased to six, the extra two then being accommodated at Alton Barnes.

Up until this time there had been no flying control at the airfield, take-off and landings being a free-for-all on a loose priority system. Unfortunately the result was that luck played a great part in flight operations! With the congestion now occurring, it was decided to introduce an airfield controller to take control of flying operations. He maintained flying schedules and signalled aircraft to take off or land by Aldis lamp.

Glider pilot training was suspended in December 1942, and along with its continued elementary flying training, No.29 EFTS introduced grading courses instead. Heavy rain during the winter of 1943/44 re-introduced concerns over the state of the ground, so it was decided to lay metal Somerfield tracking as a perimeter track around the field and in areas particularly prone to water-logging.

In October 1944 RAF students were replaced by RN ones on the Grading courses, and these continued into 1945. The task of No.29 EFTS reduced with the end of the war in mid-1945 and on 7 July 1945 all the aircraft were flown back to Clyffe Pypard. A few days later the airfield was closed as an RLG and put under Care and Maintenance.

Very occasional use was later made of Alton Barnes over the next couple of years by aircraft from Clyffe Pypard for its original intention, that of practising forced-landings. However, the airfield was de-requisitioned in 1947 and returned to farmland. Today little remains apart from the Link Trainer Building, and a few air raid shelters and concrete bases. The Blister hangars (including the one that a disgruntled instructor successfully flew a Tiger Moth through in

The Avro Anson flew with several units that used the smaller Wiltshire airfields for training. (Aeroplane)

1944) have all gone. However, in recent years a couple of monuments have been erected at Alton Barnes by the Wiltshire Historical and Military Society. These commemorate the wartime use of the airfield and are dedicated to RAF aircrew that were killed there in flying accidents.

Everleigh

National Grid Reference (184) SU186556, 4 miles E of Upavon

Situated just north of the village of Everleigh on Salisbury Plain, this airfield was opened in 1940 as an RLG for the Central Flying School at Upavon. Originally consisting of a large flat grass field surrounded by trees, it was probably seen as ideal for forced-landing practice. To get an aircraft into such a field without hitting the trees required some thought by the pilot. The field was also used for circuit planning and general flying training away from the main airfield. Facilities at the

246

ground were basic, and consisted mainly of a temporary HQ building and a guard hut.

No.15 Maintenance Unit (MU) at Wroughton took over Everleigh to use for storage on 22 November 1941, and it became known as No.31 SLG. Its new owners laid out a new north-west/south-east grass runway and started work on concrete taxiways and dispersals. Hides in the trees were also constructed. Bad weather delayed progress, but gradually the field became usable, and by the end of March 1942 over a dozen aircraft were in storage on the site.

In April Everleigh was the venue for an airborne exercise organised by No.38 Wing and the 1st Airborne Brigade for the Prime Minister and a party of high-ranking Allied and Commonwealth observers. A demonstration was to be laid on for the VIPs, showing the deployment of parachutists and gliders in order to take an objective. However, the landing phase of the exercise did not quite go to plan. A Whitley that was to drop its paratroops ahead of the glider landing experienced a problem and had to make a second run over the Drop Zone (DZ) before it could release its troops. As the parachutists landed the Hotspurs were already making their approach to land, and, confronted with a field seemingly still covered in parachutes and running paratroopers, the glider pilots found it extremely difficult to find a place to put down. One paratrooper was unfortunately struck and killed by one of the Hotspurs, which then crashed into a hedge, fortunately without any further injuries. Another Hotspur crashed into a tree, and several more overran the Landing Zone, scattering some spectators. The Prime Minister's attention was drawn to the remaining six gliders that managed to land further away and successfully deploy their troops, but he was obviously not impressed with the overall display.

Work carried on at Everleigh in May 1942. Trees had been cut down to provide approaches for a new runway, but these were kept to a minimum in order to preserve the natural look of the area, for camouflage purposes. Facilities were provided for storing thirty-seven aeroplanes. These were of various types, and included Spitfires, Hurricanes, Lysanders, Blenheims, Oxfords, Wellingtons and Hotspurs.

When Everleigh was transferred to No.33 MU Lyneham on 30 September 1942 further expansion took place. Access tracks were laid into the wooded areas and dispersals were constructed to the north-west of the airfield in Everleigh Ashes, to the north at Cow Down and the east in Hog Down Wood. A sizeable RAF maintenance party and guard force had been in place at Everleigh, and these were replaced by a Ministry of Aircraft Production (MAP) working party and a small section of RAF police-dogs and their handlers.

Facilities at Everleigh were improved in early 1943 by the erection of a Super Robin hangar, which provided a useful facility for maintenance under cover. Following an inspection by the MAP, it was decided that Everleigh could be used for the storage of four-engined aircraft. In December a Short Stirling arrived from No.10 MU Hullavington, the first of many to be stored at Everleigh. The number of aircraft at the SLG gradually increased with the build-up to D-Day, and consisted mainly of Spitfires, Stirlings and Mosquitoes. This reached a peak of eighty-seven on site in July 1944. Numbers gradually decreased as the need for replacements went down towards the end of 1944 and into 1945, although Stirlings were in demand to replace losses following the Arnhem and Rhine Crossing operations. In May 1945 there were seventeen aircraft on charge at the SLG. With the end of the war came the end of the need for Everleigh, and the site was quickly cleared. Shortly after the last aeroplane left in November 1945, No.21 SLG was closed.

Today nothing remains to show that Everleigh was once a large aircraft storage area. One farm building in use on the site may be the original Super Robin hangar that was put there in 1943. Aircraft do, however, still appear there today. An Army Air Corps airstrip was laid out in the field next to the former Landing Ground, and the general area is regularly used as a parachute DZ for exercises on Salisbury Plain.

Manningford

National Grid Reference (173) SU 130590 2 miles SW of Pewsey

Situated in a large pasture known as Manningford Bohune Common, to the north-west of Pewsey Down, Manningford airfield was opened just after the outbreak of the Second World War. This was as a landing ground for the Central Flying School, which was two and a half miles away to the south. By the end of September 1939 the Avro Tutors and Hawker Hart Trainers of the CFS were busy at Manningford, practising take-offs, landings and circuit planning. The site had its limitations, which is why it was chosen, but this did mean that the occasional flying accident occurred. The CFS used the airfield for the next couple of years, until it moved. Its replacement, No.7 Flying Instructors School, did not need the landing ground for the type of training that it was undertaking, and so handed it over to No.29 EFTS at Clyffe Pypard on 21 November 1942. The school's Magisters and Tiger Moths used Manningford for forced-landing practice. However, No.29 EFTS did not make all that much use of it over the following two years.

In May 1946 Manningford was transferred to RAF Yatesbury, to be used by the Tiger Moths of No.29 EFTS until April 1947 when it was decided that there was no real need to keep the airfield on, and it was closed. There was never much in the way of facilities at Manningford, apart from a windsock, and today nothing marks the field's former use for RAF flying training.

Marlborough

National Grid Reference (173) SU 193678 one mile south of Marlborough, off the A346

This landing ground to the south of the outskirts of Marlborough appeared in the AA list, having been opened in 1935 as a private aerodrome by the Earl of Cardigan. He used the field to fly his Avro 504N from, which he kept in a hangar beside the main road. It was an unusual site for an airfield – apart from the fact that it sloped away sharply both north and south, it was positioned on top of a railway tunnel! Nonetheless it had a couple of decent landing runs of up to 1,800 feet. The Earl's Avro was soon joined by other privately-owned aeroplanes, and it became a popular location for local fliers.

In June 1936 the CFS started using the field during the week, for forced-landing training. This was, however, not without local opposition, staff at Marlborough College fearing that it would interfere with lessons (presumably because the boys would always be looking for aeroplanes out of the windows!). Nonetheless, use by the RAF continued, and the field was regularly visited by the CFS Tutors and occasionally other types from the school's fleet, including the Hawker Fury. A Fury unfortunately crashed on the airfield in 1939.

With the start of the war all private flying ceased, but Marlborough remained open as one of several SLGs maintained by CFS Upavon. Use of the SLG increased as flying training and the need for more pilots increased, but this did unfortunately result in more accidents. Nonetheless Marlborough remained in use with the CFS as a useful practice facility. When, in the spring of 1942, Overton Heath, which had been waterlogged, was re-opened as an RLG for Upavon, Marlborough was no longer needed, and ceased to be used. Marlborough was not re-

Opened after the war, but its hangar still stands alongside the A346 in testament to the field's important former use.

New Zealand Farm

National Grid Reference (184) 970505

This airfield was yet another used by the CFS, and was opened as Lavington RLG on 9 October 1940 on Cheverell Down in the north-western area of Salisbury Plain. Its name was soon changed to New Zealand Farm, and its main use was for night flying training.

A camp was set up in a large copse of trees which provided convenient natural camouflage cover. Huts provided messing and accommodation for the ground crews who operated the RLG. Parties would stay at the airfield for a week at a time, to lay flarepaths and refuel aircraft. The routine at the RLG started in the early evening when the Oxfords and Masters allocated for the evening's night flying arrived from Upavon. The flarepath, consisting of goose-necked flares (which were modified paraffin lamps) was laid out and lit as soon as it began to get dark, so that the night's flying could start. The ground party would then stand by, in case there was a change in the wind direction, and the flarepath needed to be re-set, or be extinguished if enemy aircraft were detected in the area.

Despite such precautions a raider did attack the RLG on 14 April 1941. A He111, attracted by the flarepath, attacked New Zealand Farm while flying was still in progress. It dropped ten bombs, but only one landed on the airfield, fortunately without much damage and no casualties.

To enhance the training facilities at the airfield, Beam Approach landing equipment was installed in the spring of 1942. This was a system that had been introduced on a limited basis into bomber and transport aircraft before the war, and was becoming more widespread in RAF aircraft. It was therefore important that CFS instructors should be proficient in its use. A similar system had already been fitted at the main base at Upavon. On 1 April New Zealand Farm came under a new parent unit, as the CFS had disbanded and been replaced at Upavon by No.7 Flying Instructors School (FIS). More staff were using the facilities at the RLG, so more accommodation was built in the copse to house them. Seventy-six personnel were based there in July 1942. The following month No.7 FIS became No.7 FIS (Advanced), the outward difference being that some of the Oxfords and all of the

Pupil having a last word with his instructor before climbing into a Master Mark I for another training sortie. (Aeroplane)

Masters were replaced by Magisters. Both types were used at New Zealand Farm.

In April 1943 No.1537 Blind Approach Training Flight formed at Upavon, and this unit was soon making use of the facilities at the Farm. A revision of the training syllabus for No.7 FIS(A) resulted in the need for each course to spend two weeks at New Zealand Farm for intensive night flying training. This scheme was successful, and training was proceeding well until 1 November 1943 when all flying was suddenly suspended. This was due to War Office plans for the nearby Imber Ranges, which were just to the south. The Army wanted to expand their use, which meant that the area occupied by the RLG became part of the danger zone. No.7 FIS(A) therefore had to move out, and New Zealand Farm was closed down, then transferred to the War Office on 17 December 1943.

After the war New Zealand Farm became an outstation of the Aeroplane and Armament Experimental Establishment at Boscombe Down, and was used for weapon trials. Strong-points were built in the area for photographic and visual assessment of the weapons' accuracy. Now returned to Army control, the site of the airfield has also been used as a DZ for parachute exercises, and today is still in use as an airstrip for military aircraft using Imber Ranges.

Oatlands Hill

National Grid Reference (184) SU 095405, 3¹/₂ miles W of Amesbury on A303

Oatlands Hill was not an ideal airfield, as it was sited on a hilltop, overlooking Stonehenge, which lay off to the north-east. It was opened as a satellite of Old Sarum in June 1941 for the training of Army Co-operation and AOP units in off-base operations. The airfield was pretty basic, with a few buildings providing accommodation being built under the trees around its edges. Four Blister hangars provided cover for aircraft.

The first unit to use Oatlands Hill was No.239 Squadron, which had been using Old Sarum on detachment from its base at Gatwick. The squadron flew Curtis Tomahawk Is, and was making the transition from Army Co-operation to fighter reconnaissance. From September the aircraft of No.41 Operational Training Unit (OTU), based at Old Sarum, used Oatlands Hill for training. This unit had been formed at No.1 School of Army Co-operation as a training unit for fighter reconnaissance pilots of Army Co-operation Command, and was equipped with Tomahawks, Magisters and Harvards. As part of its role the unit trained its pilots in field operations, and the very basic facilities at Oatlands Hill provided the right atmosphere for this! The Tomahawks and Harvards of No.41 OTU were regularly flying from the RLG by March 1942 and the following month another type of fighter appeared when the OTU started operating North American Mustangs. For these high-performance fighters Oatlands Hill was a challenging airfield to operate from, and there were a number of spectacular accidents involving Mustangs and Tomahawks during this time.

On 29 September the airfield was raided and two bombs were dropped, but no damage was done. No.41 OTU left the area in November and Oatlands Hill was then used intermittently by AOP and fighter reconnaissance squadrons undergoing field training. No.41 OTU had been replaced at Old Sarum by No.43 OTU, an AOP training unit, and they also used Oatlands Hill for field training. This pattern of use continued for the next month or so, until 17 February 1944, when the whole of No.43 OTU was moved out of Old Sarum and up to

Last remaining Blister hangar at Oatlands Hill, 2001. (Author)

Oatlands Hill. This was done because Old Sarum was to change over to preparations for the impending invasion of France, and all available space at the station was needed. The officers and men of No.43 OTU were not particularly happy at the move, being used to the comforts of the Old Sarum messes, and felt that Oatlands Hill could not properly accommodate a unit operating thirty Austers. The camp was inspected by Air Officer Commanding No.70 Group, and it was ordered that the squadron should move again as soon as suitable accommodation became available at Andover. This it did on 10 August 1944.

Although Oatlands Hill was put on a Care and Maintenance footing after No.43 OTU departed, it was occasionally used by units that had been moved into Old Sarum, to relieve the space constraints there. No.665 Squadron spent a month at the RLG in early 1945. Oatlands Hill continued to be parented by Old Sarum until 13 May 1945, when it was finally closed down. Today there is a little to be seen at the former airfield. Two airfield buildings remain (one being used as a dwelling house), and one of the four Blister hangars is still in place. The concrete bases of a few further buildings are the only other remains of Oatlands Hill's wartime past.

Overton Heath

National Grid Reference (173) SU 180657, 2 miles S of Marlborough, alongside the A345

Overton Heath was another SLG that was opened by CFS Upavon. The site had already been selected on the heathland of Clench Common overlooking the Vale of Pewsey, near Marlborough, in late 1939. Work went ahead to prepare the site, but it suffered badly from water-logging, and it was not until April 1941 that it opened. The airfield was considered as the base for a new training development unit that was being formed, but this work went to the Empire Central Flying School at Hullavington. Overton Heath was then proposed as a night flying RLG, but rejected, as water-logging was still a problem. Work started on redeveloping the site in February 1942, when No.5 Works Squadron laid two runways of Somerfield tracking and built seven Blister hangars around the airfield. Domestic buildings were also erected, with a mess, hutted accommodation and a stores being constructed in the southernmost corner of the site. Defensive pillboxes were also built. The unit had a complement of two officers and eighty-three men.

By the time that the airfield had re-opened, CFS had been replaced at Upavon by No.7 FIS, which then operated Oxfords and Masters. These aircraft soon became regular visitors, and some of the Oxfords became based at Overton Heath. With the closure of New Zealand Farm in November 1943, Overton Heath became more important to its parent unit, which had since become No.7 FIS(A), and was then flying Oxfords and Magisters from the RLG. No.1537 BATF had formed at Upavon earlier in the year, and its Oxfords also used the airfield. The largest aeroplane to land at Overton Heath arrived on New Year's Day 1944 in the shape of a USAAF Boeing B-17 four-engined bomber that force-landed on the airfield, fortunately without injury to its crew.

Training continued at the RLG throughout the rest of 1944 and into 1945. However, with the end of the war in Europe, and the take-over of Lulsgate Bottom by No.7 FIS(A) as an RLG in July 1945, the need for Overton Heath disappeared. The RLG was closed at the end of August 1945, but retained as an inactive site. In June 1948 the airfield was transferred to the Ministry of Agriculture and Food. The area is now farmland, with little to show of its past, apart from one Blister hangar still in use as a farm store, and at least one pillbox still evident.

Rollestone

National Grid Reference (184) SU 090440, 1½ miles E of Shrewton

This grass airfield on Salisbury Plain was first used because of its proximity to Rollestone Camp. There No.1 Balloon School had been set up in July 1916 to train crews and support personnel in the use of observation balloons. This equipment had been used for observing artillery fire by the British Army since the 1880s, and until 1935 students on Battery Commanders' Courses at the School of Artillery underwent training in the uses of balloons, and had to conduct shoots from them. The unit at Rollestone operated throughout the 1920s and 1930s, and after several name changes during that time became the RAF Balloon Centre in 1932. That year a large balloon hangar was erected at the camp to house two of the Type R balloons that were in use at the time. Beech trees were planted beside the hangar in the shape of the letter E to provide sheltered anchorages for further balloons. The Balloon Centre was re-titled as No.2 Balloon Training Unit in 1936, and in February 1939 was transferred to Cardington in Bedfordshire. Rollestone Camp was then closed for refurbishing and the building of additional accommodation, and in June 1939 was re-opened as the RAF Anti-Gas School, which moved from Uxbridge.

Throughout World War II the possibility of gas warfare with Germany was taken seriously by the Allies. RAF stations would have been among the first targets of such attacks, rendering any responses difficult if not impossible. Gas warfare was therefore a major preoccupation for RAF personnel, and formed an important part of their training. Topics covered ranged from initial training for all ranks (at trade schools or basic training centres), protection and decontamination of personnel and equipment (at schools of technical training), decontamination of aircraft and ground equipment (at schools of technical training, OTUs and stations) and station gas defence (at the stations themselves). The RAF Anti-Gas School was set up to train those RAF officers and Senior Non-Commissioned Officers who were to train other RAF personnel at the other schools and stations. This training carried on throughout the war.

Gas defence training and exercises were regularly carried out to ensure that the station could fight on if faced with a surprise German gas attack. A number of fields between the A360 and B386 were requisitioned in September 1939, and the area used to give students experience of gas attack from the air and how to deal with it. Aircraft from No.1 FTS Netheravon and from the Special Duty Flight at CDES Porton Down would fly over and spray the troops with a training agent to simulate a chemical attack. An airstrip was laid out at Rollestone so that aircraft could land to refuel or 're-arm'. The Special Duty Flight took over all gas-related aerial training from March 1940, but No.1 FTS continued to use the airstrip at Rollestone for night flying practice.

The Luftwaffe paid a visit to Rollestone early on the morning of 12 May 1941, when a raider dropped eight bombs on the landing ground before making a low run over the camp, machine-gunning the area. Windows were broken, but there were no casualties.

From 1943 the Glider Pilot Exercise Unit based at Netheravon started using Rollestone LG as an exercise area. With the end of hostilities, gas defence training courses reduced considerably, and in October 1945 the RAF Anti-Gas School moved to Sutton-on-Hull, where it merged with a fire-fighting school.

The LG was then in use by AOP Austers, and on 16 December 1945 No.657 Squadron arrived at Rollestone, where they remained for six weeks. On 25 July 1946, the LG was closed, and Rollestone Camp was given over to the army. They have used the camp ever since (apart from a spell from November 1980 to December 1981 when it was used as a civilian prison) for various military purposes. Flying took place for a while, from an airstrip laid out to the east of the camp in the 1950s. Rollestone Camp is still in place, with many of its original buildings, which are still towered over by the balloon hangar.

Shrewton

National Grid Reference (184) SU 076460, 1 mile north of Shrewton

Shrewton SLG was established by 1 Service Flying Training School (SFTS), Netheravon, in July 1940. It consisted of a large, roughly triangular area of land to the north of Shrewton village. As the SFTS at Netheravon was a very busy one, Shrewton SLG was extremely useful for the school's students to practise away from the main base. They would fly their Hawker Hinds, Hart Trainers and Fairey Battles in from Netheravon to practise circuit-planning, approaches, take-offs, landings and forced landings. By early 1941 the Shrewton RLG was a 24-hour operation, as the training by day extended into the evening, with night flying practice carrying on until the following dawn.

Army Co-operation units also used the Shrewton SLG, the Lysanders of Nos.16 and 225 Squadrons being regular visitors during exercises

Horsa crew ready for take-off during night flying practice in 1942. Several SLGs were used for this activity in Wiltshire, including Shrewton. (Aeroplane)

with army formations on Salisbury Plain. In June 1941 a detachment of No.225 Squadron Lysanders started night flying training at Shrewton.

The end of 1941 saw a radical change for RAF Netheravon (and its satellite airfields) when its role changed from flying training to a centre for the airborne forces. Squadrons based at Netheravon included the Glider Exercise Unit, which was soon re-titled No.296 Squadron. The unit was equipped with Hawker Hart Trainers and Hector glider tugs to tow Hotspur training gliders. These aircraft soon became a familiar sight at Shrewton and replaced those of No.1 SFTS, when it was disbanded on 7 March 1942. The first unit to be based at Shrewton was the Heavy Glider Conversion Unit, their role being to provide more advanced training to glider pilots who had learnt to fly the Hotspur, and take them on to the Horsa. The unit had Whitleys to tow the Horsas. However, it very soon became apparent that Shrewton was not suitable for them, and the HGCU moved to Brize Norton soon afterwards.

On 20 August 1942 the Glider Pilot Exercise Unit (GPEU) was formed from B Flight of No.296 Squadron, with the task of keeping trained glider pilots in current flying practice. Its Harts, Hinds and Hectors were soon at Shrewton towing Hotspurs, and a Night Flying

Flight of the GPEU was formed there to specialise in this activity. Flying gliders at night, often in minimal visibility, was difficult and dangerous work. One of the more unfortunate accidents that occurred was in November 1942, when Colonel John Rock, Officer Commanding the Glider Pilot Regiment, recieved fatal injuries following a night-time Hotspur crash at Shrewton.

During November Shrewton was also used by the Austers of No.43 OTU from Larkhill, but in December it was decided to close the SLG down while its facilities were improved, and the GPEU NF Flight went to Netheravon. Three Blister hangars were erected along the north east boundary of the field and a defensive pillbox was built nearby. Barrack huts and a mess were also built.

Shrewton was re-opened in March 1943 and used once again for glider flying training. The airfield was upgraded again during the summer and brought up to RLG standard. In the autumn of 1943 the GPEU returned to Shrewton, but then moved on to Thruxton where, on 1 December 1943, it disbanded to form the Operational and Refresher Training Unit (ORTU). The unit continued to use Shrewton as an RLG until March 1944, when the HQ moved to Hampstead Norris, in Berkshire. The Tiger Moth Flight of the ORTU moved to Shrewton and remained there until 11 November 1944, when it disbanded.

The RLG was little used until the end of the war when it was put on Care and Maintenance. Shrewton was retained as an Emergency LG for some time afterwards, and was sometimes used by A&AEE aircraft when using the Larkhill ranges for weapons trials. Today the only signs of Shrewton's part in World War II are some concrete building foundations and the remains of the defensive pillbox.

Tilshead

National Grid Reference (184) SU 021478, 1 mile W of village

Tilshead LG was established close to one of the many army camps on Salisbury Plain. Situated on downland to the west of Tilshead village, the LG was first used in 1925 by Army Co-operation squadrons during manoeuvres in the Salisbury Plain training area. Bristol Fighters first flew from the field followed over the next fourteen years by Atlases, Audaxes, Hectors and Lysanders.

Before the war the longest time that any squadron spent at Tilshead LG was one month; the first squadron to actually be based there was No.225 Squadron, which arrived with its twelve Lysanders on 1 July

1940. It set up a tented camp for its 28 officers and 355 men. Two anti-aircraft guns were set up, and the area became known as Tilshead Lodge Camp.

At its new base No.225 Squadron carried out anti-invasion recon-naissance patrols. Its Lysanders flew dawn and dusk patrols of every inlet and bay along the south coast between Selsey Bill and St. Alban's Head to check for signs of military activity or infiltrators. As well as patrolling the squadron was on stand-by to investigate reports of unusual activity made to the police, such as strange lights or bonfires.

On 13 August, a German bomber, a single Heinkel He111, appeared over the airfield. It made a wide sweep and flew off to the east before returning at low level from the south. It dropped five bombs as the gun-posts opened fire at it along with the rear gunners of two Lysanders that were parked on the airfield. Three tents were destroyed by one bomb, while partially-completed huts were damaged by another. The other three bombs exploded on the LG. Two Lysanders and a Tiger Moth were damaged during the raid, but fortunately there were no casualties among RAF personnel, who had taken cover in slit trenches.

By early summer 1941 the coastal patrol duties had ceased. However, a flight of Lysanders was sent to Pembrey, South Wales, in May to undertake Search and Rescue duties. More and more, No.225 Squadron was involved in army exercises, which meant being detached to many small airfields around the country. A large exercise in May 1941 involved a simulated invasion in the Weymouth area, and the squadron flew photographic reconnaissance sorties for the three days of its duration.

The airfield at Tilshead was acceptable for short-term deployments, but was hardly satisfactory for much longer periods. For No.225 Squadron, which had been there for almost twelve months, conditions at the airfield were getting more and more difficult by June 1941. It was therefore decided to move the squadron as soon as suitable accommodation could be found for them at an airfield nearby. In July space at Thruxton became available, so the squadron moved later that month.

Tishead continued to be used as an LG by aircraft on exercise detachments until the end of 1941, when it was given up by the RAF and absorbed by the army into the enlarged range area. One of the camps to the north of Tilshead was Airborne Camp, depot of the Glider Pilots Regiment, which, along with the Parachute Regiment, was formed in January 1942. At the end of January C Company of 2nd

Battalion Regiment was based at the camp for the raid on Bruneval, and they used the area for training prior to the mission. The GPR moved to Fargo Camp near Larkhill in September 1943. Today, nothing remains at Tilshead to give any clues to the wartime use of the site as an airfield.

Townsend

National Grid Reference (173) SU 070725, ¹/₂ mile NE of Yatesbury village

Townsend RLG was originally established in a large field to the north of Yatesbury airfield for forced-landing practice by the Tiger Moths of No.10 E&RFS. The single landing strip of the RLG was used by the school until it moved to Weston-super-Mare on 7 September 1940. Before this, however, Townsend had been earmarked as a dispersal airfield by No.10 MU, Hullavington. With increased enemy aerial activity over Britain during the summer of 1940 the safety of the stocks of the country's reserve aircraft was of great concern. Townsend was seen as an ideal site for dispersal, as it was large enough to land aircraft safely and also had good camouflage cover in the form of scattered woodland. The RLG was taken over by the No.10 MU shortly after No.10 E&RFS left Yatesbury, and, known officially as No.45 SLG, it was ready for its first arrivals. These were three Blackburn Bothas and a Wellington, which arrived on 29 November 1940. However, water-logging was a major problem, and because of this the airfield was not much used by No.10 MU. In September 1941 those aircraft that were in store were transferred to other sites and the SLG was closed.

In April 1942 Townsend was re-opened and control transferred to No.33 MU, Lyneham. Staff from RAF Lyneham arrived on 9 April, and they were joined by personnel of the Wiltshire Regiment, who were to provide local defence. Four Wellingtons were the first aircraft to arrive and by the end of May sixteen aeroplanes were on-site. In July 1942 it was decided that a second runway was required, and work started on this. Improvements were also made to access to the dispersal fields by the laying of tarmac, mainly to prevent propeller damage from stones and lumps of turf. In the process aircraft holding capacity was increased to seventy-six. Actual holdings of aircraft stood at thirty-three at the end of August, these being mainly Spitfires and Wellingtons.

Discussions were underway in the autumn of 1942 to expand the use of Townsend to take four-engined aircraft, and in September the RLG was transferred to the control of No.15 MU, Wroughton. However, shortly after this, despite all the improvements that had been made, HQ No.41 Group Maintenance Command ordered that Townsend should be closed. No reasons were given for this and room had to be found for the aircraft at other sites. By the end of October all aircraft in storage had been flown out, and the RLG was never used for storage again.

With the withdrawal of the MUs, Townsend was once again used as an RLG by the Yatesbury units for forced-landing training, No.2 Radio School regularly flying their Percival Proctors in for staff pilot continuation training. When it was re-formed at Yatesbury in July 1945 No.2 EFTS also used Townsend. Flying continued at the airfield for the next couple of years, but after No.2 EFTS departed from Yatesbury in 1947, it was no longer needed, and fell into disuse. Today the only signs of the wartime use of No.45 SLG Townsend are a couple of former RAF buildings in the fields near the village.

Wanborough

National Grid Reference (174) SU220820, 4 miles SE of Swindon

This airfield was set up as an RLG during the summer of 1940 by Flying Training Command, using a small grass field between Wanborough village and the estate of King Edward's Place. The airfield was alongside the Ermin Way, a Roman road running between Cirencester and the now-vanished town of Silchester. The surface of the field needed a lot of preparation work, but when this was finally completed in mid-1941 No.3 FTS, South Cerney, started to use it for forced-landing training in its Oxfords. In March 1942 the school no longer needed Wanborough and handed it over to No.3 EFTS at Shellingford, several miles away to the north, in Oxfordshire. The school's Tiger Moths used the RLG for the next eight months, flying endless circuits and bumps while training its pupils. On 9 March 1942 ownership changed again when Wanborough was passed to the School of Flying Control, based at Watchfield five miles to the north, in Oxfordshire.

The S of FC started a programme of improvements to the airfield to make it more usable. Huts were built at the south-east end of the site to provide accommodation for 110 personnel, including a combined Officers/SNCOs Mess. Four Blister hangars were erected on the southern and western sides of the field. The school started training two

261

flights of pupils as air traffic and approach controllers in August, the pupils being given their initial training at Wanborough before moving on to the main school at Watchfield. During this initial training pupils were given their first experience of aircraft operation and Air Traffic Control using Anson, Dominie, Oxford and Blenheim aircraft.

The school was well-established and just getting into its stride by December 1943 when it was decided that it should be moved to make way for another unit. This was No.3 Glider Training School, which needed another airfield to operate from, following severe water-logging of its main site at Stoke Orchard and its satellite at Northleach in Gloucestershire. The last of the personnel from the S of FC moved out of Wanborough on 18 December, just as the No.3 GTS advance party was moving in. The GTS soon got down to work, and a few days later its fifteen Hotspurs were on site, along with a dozen Master tugs. The first course at Wanborough started with an excellent instructor:-pupil ratio – there were twenty-three instructors and seventeen pupils!

With improved conditions back at their main base, No.3 GTS returned to Stoke Orchard in May 1944, and Wanborough returned to the S of FC. Airfield Controller courses recommenced, and once again the school's Ansons and Oxfords could be seen in the circuit and taxiing around the airfield. The gliders and Masters of No.3 GTS could also still be seen at Wanborough, as they continued to use the airfield until October 1944. US personnel attended courses at the school in June and July, and training continued into 1945. However, with the end of the war there was a rundown in training at the S of FC, and it no longer needed Wanborough's facilities. Wanborough was finally closed by Flying Training Command on 21 May 1946. Few outward signs of the wartime RLG now exist, with just the odd concrete hut base visible here and there. However, several buildings that are used by a riding school may have been part of the airfield's accommodation.

Landing Grounds used by the US Army

When the US Army came to Britain in preparation for the invasion it brought one and a half million troops and a vast array of equipment, including nine hundred light aircraft. These, mostly Piper L-4 Cubs, were mainly intended for air observation post (Air OP) duties with the field artillery, and operated either with infantry, armoured or airborne divisions, or with independent battalions. The L-4s were also used to

Piper L-4 Cub, as flown by USAAF units from Wiltshire 'Cub Strips'. (Author)

maintain communications between units and their HQs, and were flown by liaison squadrons of the 9th Air Force, which also used Stinson L-5 Sentinels. These aircraft could operate from short, unprepared airstrips, and although sometimes an established airfield would be used, most liaison and Air OP aircraft operated from improvised strips, called 'Cub Strips' by the GIs. The first were established in 1942, but over the next two years they multiplied. Most strips were on farmland, but public parks, golf courses, sports fields and even roads were also used. While a minimum length of smooth, even ground of 300 yards for the L-4 or 400 yards for the L-5 was required, the strips varied in size. Some could take only one or two aircraft, but others, such as the Polo Field at Perham Down near Tidworth, could take the ten L-4s and sixty personnel of an entire divisional air section. This strip was used initially by ten Cubs of the II Corps Air OP Training School in 1942 and later by the 29th Infantry Division when II Corps departed for North Africa. Other users included the HQs of the 2nd, 8th, 9th and 12th Armoured Divisions. Other established Cub Strips in Wiltshire included:

Bishop Farm – near Clyffe Pypard, used by various units.

Breamore – near Salisbury (7 miles south of the city, on the west side of the A338) – known as Butcher's Field. Situated near Breamore House, HQ of VII Corps, Third US Army. Used from July to August

1944 by L-4s of the Artillery Air Section of the HQ, Third Army. Another strip (3 miles north of Breamore House) was used by L-5s of the 153rd Liaison Squadron which also operated from Keevil. Both strips were also used by aircraft bringing visitors to HQ VII Corps.

Chitterne – used by L-4s of 978th Field Artillery Battalion.

Codford – used by L-4s of 119th and 228th Field Artillery Groups.

Erlestoke – used by L-5s of 153rd Liaison Squadron.

Godshill (2 miles E of Fordingbridge on B3078) – used by L-4s of unknown unit.

Hilperton – a field next to the Lion and Fiddle public house was sometimes used by the L-4s and L-5s of the 153rd Liaison Squadron.

Marlborough – probably at the 5th Armoured Division's Command Post at Chiseldon, then Ogbourne St George (7 and 4 miles north of Marlborough respectively). Used by L-4s of the Division and L-5s of the 14th Liaison Squadron.

Stonehenge – L-4s of various units stationed locally, including the 29th Infantry Regiment at Tidworth used a strip not far from the monument.

Tidworth – the Polo Field, Perham Down, was used by L-4s and L-5s of many units, including II Corps Air OP School, HQ 29th Infantry Division, HQ 2nd, 7th, 8th, 9th and 12th Armoured Divisions.

Tilshead – used by L-4s of 188th Field Artillery Group.

Trowbridge – used by L-4s and L-5s of 32nd Field Artillery Brigade.

Warminster – two strips were used in the area, at Knook Camp (L-5s of 153rd Liaison Squadron) and Sutton Veny Camp, on the south side of the B3095 (L-4s of 3rd Armoured Division).

Wylie – used by L-4s of units stationed in Salisbury Plain Exercise Area.

The US squadrons also used the airfields at Keevil, Larkhill, Rollestone Camp, New Zealand Farm, Oatlands Hill and Zeals.

22
SPITFIRE PRODUCTION IN WILTSHIRE

Of all the aeroplanes that have served with the Royal Air Force, none has achieved wider fame than the Spitfire. That fame has been well deserved. By combining a superb aerodynamically-shaped airframe with one of the best aero-engines ever produced, Reginald Mitchell and his design team created a thoroughbred that has become the stuff of legend. Never was there a better example of the right aeroplane being available at the right time, because the Spitfire was the first fighter that was able to tackle the seemingly invincible Messerschmitt Bf109. When the two adversaries met in the skies over Britain during the summer of 1940 in one of the epic battles of history, the result was the first major defeat for Hitler and a blow to his dreams for a Nazi empire. The Spitfire remained the RAF's premier fighter for the rest of the war and it came to symbolise freedom and the strong resolve of the British people to defeat Naziism.

The Spitfire was produced in more than 40 major variants, but served in only two major roles – as fighter and for photographic reconnaissance. The first production versions of the aircraft were fitted with the Rolls Royce Merlin engine, but this was later replaced by a

Spitfire prototype K5054 in flight over Southampton in 1936. (Aeroplane)

more powerful development, the Rolls Royce Griffon. A naval version of the Spitfire, the Seafire, was also produced. The prototype of the Spitfire made its first flight from Eastleigh in March 1936 and 13 years later, in May 1949, the last of its type, a Seafire Mark 47, was delivered to the Royal Navy, thus ending a production run of 22,749 Spitfires and Seafires.

Few aircraft have been so successful as the Spitfire, which entered service at the end of the biplane age, and was replaced in squadron service by jet fighters. The genius of Mitchell's Spitfire design and method of construction was demonstrated by its capacity for development. To keep pace with an ever-changing level of threats and requirements this continued well after Mitchell's untimely and early death in 1937 (at the age of 42) under the leadership of his successor, Joseph Smith.

Compared with the first prototype the final production aircraft had more than twice the engine power, and its maximum take-off weight more than doubled, from the two and a half tons of the Mark I to the five tons of the Seafire FR47. Its maximum speed was increased by a quarter from 362 mph to 455 mph, and its rate of climb was almost doubled. The aircraft's firepower had increased by a multiple of five.

The Spitfire was the only Allied aircraft to remain in continuous development, production and active service throughout the Second World War. It served with the RAF, the Fleet Air Arm, the USAAF, Commonwealth Air Forces and nineteen other overseas air forces. In British service the aircraft's operational career spanned twenty-one years from joining No.19 Squadron at Duxford in August 1938 to its last sortie in Malaya in 1959. Few machines of war have had the aesthetically pleasing lines of the Spitfire, but its delicate appearance belied its deadliness in combat. Although it was not the easiest type to fly, it was a pilot's aeroplane, liked by all who flew it for its manoeuvrability and all-round performance.

Reginald Mitchell, the Chief Designer of the Supermarine Aircraft Company of Southampton, who had been the creator of a series of high speed racing seaplanes, designed the Spitfire in answer to an Air Ministry specification of 1934 for an eight-gun fighter. It made its first flight on 5 March 1936. From the start it impressed everyone that flew it or saw it demonstrated. An initial order was placed in June for 410 Spitfires, and production started at the Supermarine factory at Woolston in Southampton.

The strategic importance of Southampton, together with its well-known location, meant that it was particularly vulnerable to German air attack. On 24 September 1940 a Luftwaffe raid severely damaged Supermarine's works at Itchen. The raiders returned two days later to drop 70 tons of bombs on both of Supermarine's factories, finishing off the works at Itchen and substantially damaging the Woolston works. Spitfire production was brought to a standstill.

It was decided to move the manufacture, assembly and flight-testing of Spitfires by Supermarine into five selected dispersed areas in southern England. As well as in Southampton these were Reading, Newbury, Trowbridge and Salisbury. Despite the weight of the raids, much of the production plant had been salvable, and this was dismantled ready for dispersal. So too were a quantity of damaged and undamaged Spitfire fuselages and wings, along with design equipment and essential paperwork. Gradually, from merely dispersing the production away from Southampton into the country, each area developed into its own self-contained Spitfire production unit. In Wiltshire Spitfire production took place in two main areas, Salisbury and Trowbridge. The team in Salisbury, under area manager Bill Weaver, got its act together fairly early on. Garages and motor showrooms were requisitioned in the city, and fuselage production was set up in the Wessex Motors Garage in Castle Street. These were then

The Wessex Motors garage in Castle Street, Salisbury in 1940. (Vickers)

transferred to the Wilts and Dorset Bus Company Garage further along Castle Street where the tail unit was fitted, then the engine, along with its piping, cabling and cooling framework. The main fuel tanks would then be fitted, together with all the electrical hydraulic and pneumatic systems. Wings were also built in the garage, then fitted with undercarriage units and systems. Another garage in Castle Street, owned by Anna Valley Motors, was used for the production of sub-assemblies such as the tail units and also for smaller items such as undercarriage doors, windscreens, cockpit canopies, and fuel tanks and, later, the arrester and catapult gear for the Seafires. Wing leading edges were also made there, although these had initially been manufactured in the Trowbridge area and sent across to Salisbury for embodiment into the wings at the Wilts and Dorset Garage. The main assemblies were then taken on special Queen Mary aircraft transporters or low loaders to airfields that had been taken over in the area. These were High Post, four miles to the north of Salisbury, and Chattis Hill, a little over ten miles to the east of the city, just across the county border near Stockbridge in Hampshire.

High Post was a flying field owned by the Wiltshire Light Aeroplane and Country Club and used by private aircraft owners until the outbreak of war, when all unauthorised civil flying in Britain was stopped. From September 1939 it was used by the RAF and in December 1940 Supermarines set up a factory unit at the airfield for the assembly of Spitfires and their flight testing. Activity at the airfield expanded later in the war and High Post became Supermarine's main flight test centre (see *High Post*). Another airfield for the flight testing of Salisbury Spitfires was set up at Chattis Hill near Stockbridge in Hampshire. The first Spitfires to be completed and test flown from the two airfields in the Salisbury area were Spitfire PRI X4497, which first flew from High Post on 12 January 1941 (only two and a half months after production had started from scratch in Salisbury) and Spitfire Mark IR7250 from Chattis Hill on 18 March 1941. Deliveries from the Salisbury area then took place at an average of six aircraft per week.

Day and night shifts were worked throughout the week and at weekends to maintain required levels of production and work carried on in the factories despite occasional raids by the Luftwaffe. One day early in 1941 German fighter bombers dropped a couple of bombs near Salisbury railway station and on another occasion a Heinkel He111 made a low run to the north of the Cathedral, dropping a few bombs and spraying the area with machine gun fire. However, production was delayed for another reason in the spring of 1941, when problems were experienced in getting sufficient numbers of trained personnel from Southampton. This was mainly due to insufficient housing being available in the Salisbury area. However, once this problem was overcome more experienced personnel arrived who were able to train new workers, and with the arrival of women in the factories there was a considerable increase in the number of employees.

Production at the time was concentrated on the Spitfire Mark Vb and Vc, but in early 1942 there was an urgent request from the MAP to all Spitfire production areas to concentrate more on the production of spares, which were in short supply, particularly overseas. At the time 19% of the southern area factories' production was in the form of spares and this proportion was therefore increased. During the third quarter of 1942, 46% of production was of spares, and this increased to 61% the following quarter. During the early part of the year conversion work also took place in the factories converting Spitfires into Seafires. These were the early examples of the naval version of the Spitfire that were fitted with catapult and arrester gear. In May two Spitfires were converted with folding wings and these became the first true Seafires. When the first purpose built Seafires were later manufactured at

Salisbury special modifications were incorporated into the aircraft on the production line, including additional strengthening of the fuselage to take the arrester hook, as well as the catapult fittings and folding wings.

In mid 1942 construction work started on new factory facilities in various areas, including Salisbury. Two new factory units were built, both just off Castle Road on the hill to the north of the city towards Old Sarum. The first was simply referred to as Castle Road Factory and was used for the production of fuselages. A second, and much larger, factory, known as Castle Road West, was used for the fitting out of fuselages and the production of wings. The two Castle Road units were opened in early 1943 and by the middle of the year were almost in full production. Nonetheless, production continued in the city's other units in Castle Street.

An area of concern during the autumn of 1942 was that of potential manpower shortages following from the increase in the calling up of the 25 to 30 age-group. Although there was a workforce of 8,260 in the region at the end of 1942, there were also 800 vacancies. During this time two new types of Spitfire were introduced, the Mark VII and Mark VIII. These were developments of the Mark V fitted with the more powerful version of the Merlin, the 60 Series. The Mark VII was a pressurised high-altitude fighter, while the Mark VIII was un-pressurised, and both were to lead on to the Mark IX, the most-produced of all the Spitfire variants apart from the Mark V.

The demand for Spitfires and their spares was unending, and new variants regularly kept appearing. To meet this demand new purpose-built factories were constructed, including the two in Salisbury and three in Trowbridge. Eventually there were sixty-five Supermarine units spread over southern England, of which forty-six were devoted to production, the remainder being support units. An additional factory was set up in Wiltshire at South Marston near Swindon. This was a MAP factory that was taken over from another aircraft manufacturer, not set up under the dispersal scheme (see *South Marston*). Although production was co-ordinated by the Supermarine Division of Vickers in Southampton, each area was autonomous under its Area Manager. In order that production within the dispersal scheme was to be efficient, different areas built allocated marks. Salisbury and Trowbridge both built Marks V, IX, XII, XIV; Salisbury additionally built the Seafire. Bringing new marks into production was not an easy task, as new jigs and tooling often had to be brought on-line and modifications, such as the new wing structure for the PR aircraft to include a leading-edge

The factory built on Bradley Road, Trowbridge, by the MAP for the production of Spitfires. (Vickers)

fuel tank, had to be introduced. Often there were several different marks of Spitfire in production simultaneously.

At the end of 1943 weekend working at the Supermarine factories was discontinued. In the spring of 1944 80% of the Spitfire production in the factories was for spares. In the second quarter 433 aircraft were produced, 450 were modified and 150 repaired. This was the time that the work force was at its height, of about 10,000 people.

At Trowbridge, as with the other dispersal sites, jigs and tooling were brought into the town from Southampton by low-loaders and lorries in October 1940. Production opened up initially at three requisitioned premises: at Fore Street Garage (later Boots) and Rutland Garage (later Isis Motors) in the centre of town, and at the Barnes steamroller works at Southwick, on its western outskirts. Fore Street was set up as the head office for the Trowbridge Area of the Supermarine Southern Region, under its Area Manager, Vernon Hall. Details and fittings were also produced there. At Rutland Garage the coppersmiths was established, where fuel tanks and pipe-work were made. At Southwick wing leading edges and sub-assemblies were fabricated. Shortly afterwards Knee's Garage (subsequently Kwiksave)

Spitfire Mark Is in production at Castle Street, Salisbury in 1940. (Vickers)

in the centre of Trowbridge was also brought into the picture for the production of fuselage and wing skins, and work began on a purpose-built MAP factory at Hilperton in the north-eastern part of Trowbridge to produce sub-assemblies. Cowlings were produced at another unit in the requisitioned Bolton Glove Factory in Westbury, a few miles away to the east of Trowbridge, with support activities such as stores and transport being located in other garages and showrooms. The assemblies and sub-assemblies produced in these units were shipped off to Salisbury and other Spitfire manufacturing areas for the first couple of years, as it was not until a large purpose-designed factory was built in Bradley Road that whole aircraft could be completed in Trowbridge. Wings and fuselages were manufactured at Bradley Road, and all the locally-produced sub-assemblies were brought together for installation into them. Once completed, the fuselage fitted with tail unit and engine, along with the wings, would be transported along the road to the recently-completed hangar at Keevil airfield. There the wings were mated to the fuselage, the propeller was fitted, and final preparation was made to the aircraft before flight test. As with the other areas, Trowbridge manufactured a variety of Spifire marks, including the Griffon-powered versions from 1944 onwards. Later that year, Trowbridge was also involved in making components for the Supermarine 371, the Spiteful, proposed as the Spitfire replacement.

Spitfire production continued in the Southern Region factories until the end of the war. Following the armistice some of the smaller Supermarine production units were closed down. In Salisbury the Castle Garage and the Wilts and Dorset Garage in Castle Road were closed, cleared and returned to their owners at the end of October 1945, followed by Anna Valley Motors in November and the Wessex Garage in December. Production of Griffon-engined Spitfires continued at the Castle Road factories until well into 1946, and both factories were retained until November 1947, when they were sold. Castle Road West still stands, and is today used by motor engineers Janspeed.

The Fore Street works in Trowbridge was the first in the area to be closed, being returned to its owners on 30 June 1945. It was followed by most of the remaining units in the town by the end of the year. The Hilperton factory was closed in April 1946 and later demolished, being replaced by housing. However, the Bradley Road factory was retained by Supermarine, and work continued on with the Spitfire Mark 24 and the Spiteful there after the war. Even when the Spiteful was cancelled in favour of jet fighters, the project carried on, and a batch of the aircraft, including the naval version the Seafang, was completed so that

Spitfire MkVs were produced in Trowbridge and Salisbury. (Aeroplane)

detailed evaluation could be made of the performance of the design's revolutionary laminar flow wing. Along with the South Marston factory at Swindon, the Bradley Road factory at Trowbridge became part of the Northern Area of Vickers-Supermarine Ltd in the late 1940s. Among other products of the factory were the jigs for the manufacture of wings for the Spiteful and the Attacker, and components for the Swift. It continued to serve the company until February 1959, when it was sold to the engineering company Hattersley Heaton Ltd. For many years the factory, still plainly showing its camouflage paint, was a landmark to the people of Trowbridge. It was referred to by them as 'the Spitfire factory' up until the day that it was demolished in the early 1990s to make way for a DIY centre.

Many Spitfires still in existence today have Wiltshire connections, having been either built in the county or based there. Of the 300 Trowbridge-built aircraft assembled at Keevil, for example, at least eight are still around. Four were discovered in India during the 1970s, lying abandoned on derelict airfields. These have been recovered and restored, some to flying condition. Four Keevil Spitfires are preserved in Britain, and one of these, one of the ex-Indian examples, makes regular appearances at flying displays. Although not built in the county, one of the most famous survivors with a Wiltshire connection is Spitfire Mark II P7350, which flies today with the RAF Battle of Britain Memorial Flight, and is the oldest airworthy Spitfire in the world. This aeroplane served with several front-line squadrons and saw combat during the Battle of Britain. Following an accident it was repaired and sent to No.39 MU Colerne in 1944 for storage. It was noted in records as being still in store there in March 1946, but the following year it was disposed of, being sold to scrap merchants John Dale Ltd. It was only because a member of the company's staff realised the historical significance of the aircraft after having examined its log-book that the aircraft was not immediately cut up. In a generous gesture of goodwill, John Dale Ltd offered P7350 back to the RAF, and it was accepted by RAF Colerne for its new museum. The Spitfire remained in the Wiltshire museum for the next twenty years, until it was restored to flying condition in order to take part in the epic film 'The Battle of Britain'. On the completion of filming the aircraft was transferred to the Battle of Britain Memorial Flight, and has been a firm favourite at the flight's displays ever since.

The dispersal of Spitfire production from Southampton to Wiltshire, Hampshire and Berkshire was a tremendous and imaginative under-taking that was made possible by foresight and detailed planning, the professionalism of the Supermarine engineers, the hard graft of the workforce involved and the splendid co-operation of the local people in whose towns the convoys appeared one night in October 1940. The county of Wiltshire made a significant contribution to Britain's war-fighting capability during the Second World War with its involvement in the production of the Spitfire fighter, along with that of Hampshire and Berkshire. Altogether, well over one-third of Spitfires manufac-tured were built in the factories of the three counties of the Supermarine Southern Region between 1940 and 1946: out of a total of some 22,700 Spitfires, over 8,000 were built in the region.

23
CIVILIANS AT WAR

At 11:15 on the morning of Sunday 3 September 1939, the Prime Minister, Neville Chamberlain, made a radio broadcast to the nation and announced that Britain was then at war with Germany. Although this was a shock, it was not really a surprise, as the international situation had been unstable for some time, and relations between Britain and Germany were at an all-time low.

In fact, Britain had been expecting war the previous year, and from the beginning of 1939 was effectively on a war footing. The Air Raid Precautions Act of 1937 had been invoked, a Civil Defence Corps had been formed, and air raid wardens, auxiliary firemen, ambulance drivers and other volunteers had been recruited. As the threat of poison gas attacks was of great concern to the Government, millions of gas masks (or 'respirators') were issued to the civilian population, and children practised gas mask drill in schools once a week.

What was not publicised at the time was that the respirators had been developed at the Chemical Defence Experimental Station at Porton Down in Wiltshire, where work on them had started as a priority project in 1934. The General Civilian Respirator was mass-produced from 1936, and was designed for adults and children down to five years old. A smaller one was designed for the use of younger children, and was painted in bright colours, so as not to look as fearsome as the standard plain black variety. A baby's protective helmet was also made. The development and production of the civilian respirator was a major achievement by CDES, and by the end of the war over 100 million had been produced. No other country was nearly so well equipped as Britain to protect its civilian population from gas attack.

By early 1939 thousands of Anderson domestic air raid shelters were being manufactured every week and delivered to towns and cities throughout Britain. They were of corrugated sheet metal and designed to be sunk several feet into the ground, then covered with soil or sandbags. Issued free of charge to households with an income of less than £250 per annum, they were named after the Government's Head of Civil Defence, Sir John Anderson.

Other precautions against air raids included the blacking-out of windows, either by painting over them or by putting up heavy curtaining, and putting tape across the window glass to prevent it shattering and causing injury. White paint was used liberally to assist movement in the blackout. With the headlights of their vehicles masked, it was difficult for drivers to see anything at night, so white lines were painted down the centre of the roads, and some kerbs, particularly those on corners, were also painted white. The edges of the front and rear mudguards of road vehicles were similarly painted so that they could be seen by other road-users. White bands were painted around trees and lamp-posts, and steps or other hazards or obstacles were also painted so that they would stand out in the gloom.

Public air raid shelters were built in towns, and public buildings started to assume a strange appearance as barriers of sandbags were built up against their walls in an effort to protect them against blast damage. The brilliant stonework of the new Wiltshire County Hall, started in 1938 at Trowbridge and completed in 1940, formed a landmark that could be seen for miles, so it was covered in a huge camouflage net. Some of the fixings for the net are still visible. Other measures in town and country included the covering of the tops of Post Office pillar-boxes in gas detector paint, as a warning of gas attack. Should a toxic chemical agent fall onto the box, the yellow paint would turn a distinctive dark brown.

The Air Raid Precautions (ARP) organisation's main function was to warn the public of impending air raids. In cities or large towns this would be by a wailing siren, but in smaller towns and villages wardens would cycle around the streets blowing short blasts on a whistle. If poisonous gas was suspected the warning would be given by a rattle,

The civilian respirator and baby respirator developed at CDES Porton Down. (Dstl)

similar to those used by football supporters, and the all-clear signal would be given by a hand-bell. The wardens found that their job would be accomplished more easily with the co-operation of the police, and this was easily arranged in Wiltshire since the Wiltshire ARP Controller was also the Chief Constable. The Auxiliary Fire Service was formed to assist the regular fire brigades in dealing with the expected fires resulting from air raids. Initially they had no uniforms and used equipment and vehicles loaned or requisitioned locally (such as saloon cars or builders' lorries). Later they became known as the National Fire Service and were issued with purpose-built fire tenders and pumps, along with appropriate uniforms and all the necessary equipment.

The Wiltshire Yeomanry, although not mobilised at the time, held their Summer Camp at the end of April 1939 with a view to preparation for war. This was at Corfe Castle in Dorset, and there was a good attendance, with over 600 men present. The regiment had 400 horses and a number of light vehicles and wireless cars. The Commanding Officer had called for new recruits to attend, and there was a good response. It was noted in newspaper reports that a pleasing feature of the camp was that 'the regiment continues to attract a great many sons of landowners and farmers'.

Blackout exercises were held during the summer of 1939. The one held over the southern half of Wiltshire, including Salisbury, on Saturday 13 May was typical. The blackout operated from 22:45 until midnight. Householders and all occupiers of premises were requested by the Chief Constable and Civil Defence Controller, Hoel Llewellyn, to co-operate in obscuring all lights that may be seen skywards. Streetlights were to be obscured by the Councils, and drivers were to drive on sidelights if they found it absolutely necessary to be out on the road. Wardens patrolled the streets of towns and cities, and RAF aircraft flew overhead to check that there were no unguarded lights that could attract the bombs of a potential enemy. The exercise in Salisbury went well, apart from two sodium lights being left on in the Salt Lane car park, and an opportunist burglary that took place during the blackout at the High Post Golf Club (the culprits were later arrested in Newbury). The blackout exercise was preceded by ARP exercises in Salisbury when, on 1 May, an air raid was simulated, as were also bomb damage, fires and mustard gas attacks.

The planned Empire Air Day still took place on Saturday 23 May, with displays at RAF Stations Boscombe Down and Upavon. This was advertised on the previous Wednesday, when a formation of nine Avro Anson aircraft from Boscombe Down flew over Salisbury. This was followed the next day by a massed formation of seventy-two Fairey Battle bombers, which flew around over the west of England, including most of Wiltshire.

On 24 August 1939 the Emergency Powers (Defence) Bill was passed in Parliament because of 'the imminent peril of war'. The new Act gave the authorities far-reaching powers. Houses could be entered and searched without reason or warning, property and land could be requisitioned for war use at will, people could be moved away from certain areas, the ports and railways were taken over by the Government, and bus and train services severely cut back. Under these powers the occupants of the village of Imber in the centre of Salisbury Plain were moved out and the area was requisitioned as part of the Salisbury Plain Training Area. The land was never returned. Also under these regulations identity cards were issued to everyone, but the requirement that they should be shown on demand to 'anyone in authority' caused so much animosity that the police and armed forces were ordered to request their production only for 'extreme reasons'. This was a far from easy time for civilians, with petrol rationing starting in September followed two months later by the first food rationing. Bacon and butter were rationed first, then sugar, ham, cheese and meat in the New Year. There were also shortages of fuel, sorely felt by the public during the extremely cold winter of 1939/40.

In mid-May 1940 the Local Defence Volunteers, later known as the Home Guard, were formed. Almost every village had its own volunteers, and soon the organisation began to make itself felt throughout the country. Their prime task was to deal with invading forces, and they took their duties very seriously. They manned roadblocks, patrolled their territory and checked on anyone moving around during the hours of darkness. Initially they had no uniforms or weapons, but made do with armbands, pitchforks and shotguns. They were later issued with khaki uniforms and obsolescent weapons, and organised into military formations. The Wiltshire Home Guard consisted of several battalions across the county, divided into companies in large towns, and platoons in smaller towns or villages. By mid-1942 the Home Guard numbered almost 1.6 million, but by then the threat of invasion had passed. However, they had developed into a well-trained force that was used as a reserve army, freeing up regular units for other military duties, until they were disbanded in 1944.

During the 1930s, an organisation called the Air League tried to draw people's attention to Britain's relative lack of interest in military

Heinkel HeIII brought down by British fighters in March 1940. (Aeroplane)

aviation. It formed the Air Defence Cadet Corps to arouse in youngsters an interest in aviation. This worked so well that the Air Ministry took an interest, and on 5 February 1941 took it over as the Air Training Corps. It was hoped that the new corps would provide a way of identifying suitable candidates for the RAF before they became eligible for military service. The corps was open to boys between the ages of 15 and 18, and within six months of its formation had a membership of over 200,000. Organisation was on the lines of the RAF, with wings covering counties, and squadrons being based on towns, with detached flights in villages. In Wiltshire a dozen squadrons were formed initially. A uniform was issued, based on the RAF one. Members of staff were sometimes ex-RAF, but usually adults who were prepared to give up their spare time on a voluntary basis to help out. Later they were given uniforms and taken into the RAF Volunteer Reserve.

The cadets were trained in drill, Morse code, small-bore shooting, navigation, theory of flight, engines and several other subjects, and as they progressed in their training and passed their exams, their success was signified by the badges on their uniforms. Aircraft Recognition was a popular activity, and air cadets were renowned for their skills in determining an aircraft, not only by its nationality, but also by its type and mark number. One senior officer is quoted as saying that the days of friendly fire would be over if every fighter squadron and AA unit had an Air Cadet on strength to teach them aircraft recognition!

Visits were made to local RAF stations by ATC squadrons to experience life in the service, and many cadets went flying on these visits. Such a visit by Warminster Squadron made on 1 July 1944 was recorded in RAF Keevil's Operations Record Book. Other ATC squadrons built up a good relationship with their local RAF station. As the result of such rapport, No.1011 (Amesbury) Squadron was adopted by A&AEE Boscombe Down in 1943. Cadets went gliding in ATC gliders, and they also found that the ATC uniform was a passport to more flying. Many were able to go along to airfields and scrounge flights in aircraft, almost at will.

One of the most successful cadets in this was Don March. Don's first flight was in a USAAF C-47 from Ramsbury, and this got him hooked. He would spend every hour of his spare time hanging around at the local airfields, waiting for a flight. Don's greatest claim to fame occurred on 12 July 1943, when he cycled to nearby Membury airfield, then occupied by the USAAF. He had studied the theory of flight and aircraft operation during his ATC studies, and was convinced that he knew how to fly an aircraft. On arrival at Membury with a fellow cadet, he decided that he would show his friend how well he could fly by demonstrating on an unattended Piper L-4 that they came across on the tarmac. Both cadets climbed in, and Don started the engine. He taxied away, took off and did a circuit. On landing the cadets were met by several irate US officers, who gave them a severe ticking off, before sending them off home! He thus became (probably!) the only ATC cadet to solo an American aircraft during World War II. Don March enjoyed many further flights throughout wartime Britain as an air cadet, and later joined the RAF to become a pilot.

Many air cadets contributed to the war effort before joining the services, by assisting the regulars during training at RAF stations, and by acting as runners for ARP and NFS units. Several were decorated for gallantry while still cadets and over 500 received gallantry awards as ex-Air Cadets, including one posthumous VC. By the end of the war nearly half a million cadets had gone through the ATC. Approximately 170,000 had joined the services, predominantly the RAF. Towards the end of the war, the Chief of the Air Staff, Air Chief Marshal Lord Portal, said: 'In maintaining the flow of men to the RAF, the Air Training Corps has made a decisive contribution to victory.'

As the war went on, further sacrifices had to be made by the British population. Clothing became rationed, and later fuel. 'Save' was the watchword, and everyone was exhorted to support the various national campaigns. Nothing was thrown away, as scrap metal, saucepans, rags, bones, rubber and waste paper were religiously collected for salvage and re-use in some way or another. Towards the end of 1941 railings were removed from parks and buildings, and public monuments were plundered for scrap. Items such as Napoleonic cannon displayed in towns disappeared, along with many First World War tanks that had been presented to towns as war memorials. The tank removed from the Memorial Gardens in Trowbridge in 1941 was but one of these. In November 1942 soap rationing was introduced (one tablet per person per month) and people were not to bathe in more than a five-inch depth of water in their bath. As an acceptance of the difficulties presented by the clothing ration, the Church of England in November 1941 ended its rule requiring that women had to wear hats in church.

The war brought much new construction, which caused disruption to local communities, but also brought employment. One of the first of these projects was the building of local defence positions across the country. The most distinctive remnants of this are the pillboxes, which

Pillbox at Old Sarum, with nature taking over, 2002. (Author)

284

can still be seen in various parts of Britain today. However, they are seen by some people as eye-sores, and many have been demolished over the years. Those that are left appear to have been placed randomly across the countryside, but this was not the case; they were in fact positioned according to a master plan developed by General Sir Edmund Ironside, Commander-in-Chief Home Forces.

Following the evacuation from Dunkirk and the fall of France in June 1940, the danger of invasion to Britain was brought sharply into focus. Ironside's plan called for the backing up of coastal defences by further ones inland, should a German landing be successful. The protection of London and the Midlands was to be by the GHQ defence line, with a series of command, corps and divisional stop-lines sited between it and the coast. The country was further divided by lines of defence that incorporated village and river lines in various directions. The idea was that, should an enemy landing be made, their advance inland would be contained by road blocks and pillboxes in the stoplines manned by the Home Guard and local troops. Mobile columns would then be brought up to reinforce the area, and prevent a breakthrough. Special units of Home Guard troops, with their local knowledge, would also harry the invaders. Churchill approved these plans on 25 June 1940, and work by hundreds of local authorities and civilian contractors then started on the building of thousands of pillboxes and anti-tank obstacles. The pillboxes were built in several sizes, according to standard designs. Anti-tank obstacles were of different varieties, including steel rails and concrete 'Dragon's Teeth'. From the start of the work, building contractors worked a twelve-hour day, seven-day week for five weeks, then at least another six weeks of normal working until the majority of the main defences were complete.

The GHQ line followed natural and artificial waterways, using topographical features where possible, to produce a continuous anti-tank obstacle. The pillboxes were positioned to overlook strategic points and to give cover to one another. These lines were impressive – part of the GHQ stopline that went from Bradford-on-Avon to Burghfield near Reading was fifty-eight miles long, and consisted of 170 pillboxes, fifteen anti-tank gun emplacements and five miles of anti-tank ditches. The line made good use of the Kennet and Avon Canal and rivers in the area. Wiltshire came under Southern Command, commanded by General Sir Alan Brooke, and Command defensive lines that crossed the county included the Salisbury stopline, which ran from Frome to Salisbury then to Odiham, and the Ringwood Stopline, running from Christchurch to Salisbury.

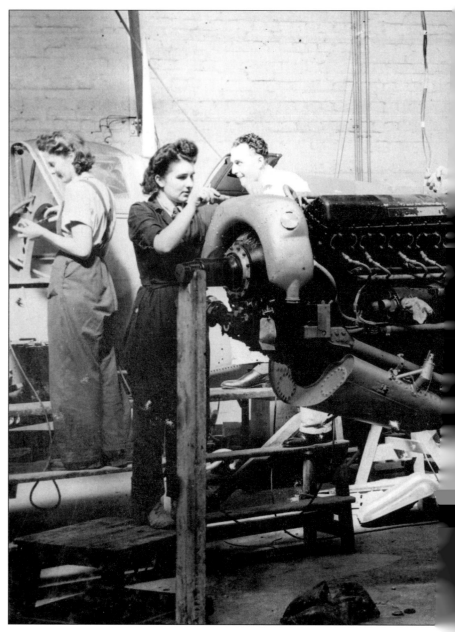

Women working on Spitfire fuselages at the Castle Rood factory in Salisbury. At least three people can be seen inside the fuselage. (Cambridge Collection)

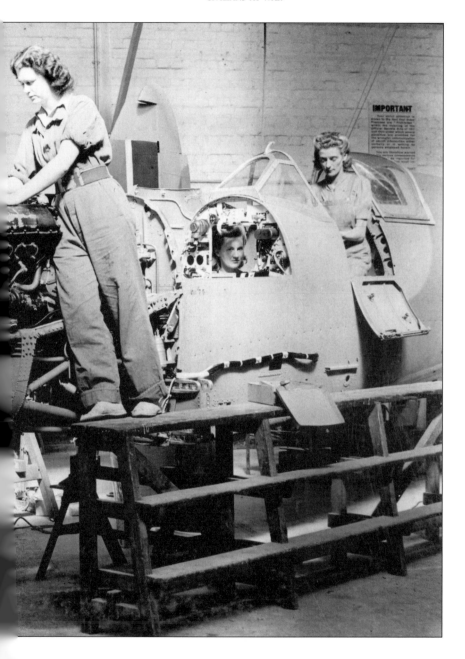

On 7 September the 'Cromwell' State of Readiness Order was sent out to Eastern and Southern Commands. Although it was only a rehearsal, it declared 'Invasion imminent and probable within the next twelve hours'. This caused confusion, with church bells being rung (they had been silenced, and were only to be rung as a warning if German paratroops landed) and in East Anglia several bridges being blown in accordance with a defensive demolition programme. Although causing unnecessary excitement, the event did bring a sense of urgency to activities, and the completion of unfinished defence works was accelerated! Other defensive measures included schemes for the flooding of water meadows in order to make them impassable for vehicles. Several such schemes were built in Wiltshire. At Castle Eaton near Swindon sluices were built to flood the fields alongside the River Thames. On the River Wylye, north-west of Salisbury, a series of a hundred small dams were built to raise the water levels enough to produce a tank barrier.

For almost the entire period of the war Wiltshire, along with the rest of the country, suffered one of the largest construction programmes ever undertaken in Britain – the construction of airfields. It was a massive project, and it has been estimated that it cost a total of some £1 billion. Scores of contractors were involved, both large and small, employing armies of construction workers along with fleets of heavy plant and machinery. They transformed the requisitioned farmland into airfields by moving millions of tons of earth and laying runways, taxiways and dispersals and erecting huge hangars and hundreds of other buildings. Many local people reckon that it was one of the major disruptions of the war, although, once completed, they did not seem to mind the sound of the aircraft taking off from the airfields.

With the war in full swing, everyone was expected to do their bit. The men were generally either in the Armed Forces or in reserved occupations if within the younger age-groups; otherwise they were working or retired. Women too could join the forces, which they were encouraged to do, or a voluntary service. The most famous was the Women's Voluntary Service, which had been formed in 1938. With uniforms of grey-green tweed skirt, red jumper and felt hat, the half-million WVS volunteers made a magnificent contribution to the Home Front. Often operating under difficult conditions, these ladies helped with the evacuation of children, aided the victims of air-raids, operated canteens, rest and reception centres for war workers and servicemen, and ran mobile canteens on airfields. No job was too difficult for the 'women in green' as they were known to everyone (but Widows,

Virgins and Spinsters to each other!)

A major change came at the end of 1942, when conscription for women between the ages of 20 and 30 years was introduced. Conscripts were given a choice of serving in one of the three women's auxiliary armed services, the civil defence or industry. Many women went to work for the first time, and most got to like it, or at least got used to it! The Essential Work Order had also been invoked by the Government to bring workers into the factories. This involved moving people from occupations not judged to be essential for the war effort into armament works, aircraft factories or shipyards. Coming from all walks of life, from milkmen and salesmen to waitresses and models, they were uprooted from their homes, friends and families and sent off to unfamiliar parts of the country. There they would live in lodgings and work in strange factories. However, this workforce, of which over half were women, undertook invaluable work to produce supplies and equipment that kept the Services operational. They were employed in many locations in Wiltshire, including aircraft factories in Salisbury, Trowbridge and Swindon, rubber tyre factories in Melksham, and armaments works in Swindon, as well as food processing companies across the county.

The Ministry of Labour had designated areas where war workers were to be dispersed, and, where recreational facilities were not widely available, War Worker Recreational Centres were set up. The Ministry paid for one such centre to be established in Trowbridge. This was located in Innox Road, and was popular with the local Spitfire production workers. As well as a main hall, the centre contained a bar, lounge, committee rooms and bathrooms – the latter a useful facility due to the shortage of baths in most lodgings at the time! Although Salisbury had two cinemas and many pubs, two floors of the largest department store in the city, Style and Gerrish (now Debenhams), were taken over by the Ministry of Labour and set up as a Recreational Centre.

Another institution that was popular at this time was the 'British Restaurant', or Community Feeding Centre. These were non-profit making and run by the local authorities with Government sponsorship, to provide a good hot mid-day meal for one shilling a head. By 1943 British Restaurants had become an established part of urban life, with over 2,000 in operation serving half a million meals per day. In rural areas there was the Women's Voluntary Service Rural Pie Scheme, which was set up in 1942 and provided over a million pies and snacks per week to approximately 5,000 villages.

Dragon's teeth beside the A419 near Cricklade in north Wiltshire, 2002. (Author)

Another important civilian organisation that came to the fore during the Second World War was the NAAFI (the Naval, Army and Air Force Institute). Besides having permanent canteens in many army camps and on RAF and FAA airfields in Wiltshire, the NAAFI also operated mobile tea wagons that brought refreshment to many of the crews working on lonely dispersed sites. Throughout the war, it was that 'cuppa' that was to keep up the morale of service personnel and civilians alike.

For years following the First World War, British agriculture had been in a decline, mainly due to cheap foreign imports. The industry needed revitalising, and with the outbreak of war, the Government was forced to take action. War Agricultural Committees were formed to direct farming activity. Organised on a national basis, each county was divided into districts, each one having its own committee. These committees were given far-reaching powers and could give farmers direction on types of crop to grow or animals to rear. Grants were available to encourage farmers to follow Government guidelines, but fines were also imposed on farmers who refused to co-operate. The committees' powers also extended to confiscation of land and farms in extreme cases of non-co-operation. Directives from the 'War Ag', as they were known, included such instructions that every farmer should increase his production of potatoes, and that dairy farmers should plough up a certain amount of their land for food production. All animals were registered with the committees, and numbers and types of beasts reared by the farmers were subject to their approval.

A major problem for the farmers was the shortage of labour on the land. Although farming was a reserved occupation, many farm-workers and members of farming families had volunteered to join the colours, and this exacerbated the situation. This situation was foreseen by Lady Gertrude Denham who, in June 1939, had formed the Women's Land Army (WLA). Like the WVS it had its own distinctive uniform, of green jersey, brown breeches and wide-brimmed brown hat. All members were volunteers, and they came from all walks of life. After a month's training, the girls were sent to one of the hundreds of hostels around the country (there were many in Wiltshire). There they were allocated to local farms, where they worked hard for long hours and little pay. Despite considerable initial suspicion from farmers, the women eventually gained their grudging respect, for their assistance was to prove invaluable to the farming industry. The WLA girls soon became a part of the country scene, and at its peak in 1943 the organisation numbered over 87,000. The WLA lasted until well after the war, being eventually disbanded in October 1950.

The British public on the home front suffered air raids, the blackout, the rationing of food, fuel and clothing, shortages of all kinds and total disruption to their lives for six long years. When Victory in Europe Day (VE Day, 8th May 1945) came, there was rejoicing in the streets, as well as a universal thanksgiving for victory, although the war against Japan was not to end for another three months. Most of the airfields of Wiltshire closed down fairly soon afterwards, and many of their personnel returned to civilian life. Several wartime Wiltshire airfields are still in use, but many others are now closed and forgotten by most people. It is only the memorials and monuments that are dotted about the countryside, and accounts such as this, that will remain to remind coming generations of the part that Wiltshire played during the Second World War.

BIBLIOGRAPHY

During the writing of this book I have consulted many sources, including documents and books, both published and unpublished. The following is a list of the main publications that I have used – I am grateful to the authors of these for their earlier work.

A History of the RAF Servicing Commandos, J. Davies and J.P. Kellett, Air Life, 1989
Action Stations No. 5 and No. 9, C. Ashworth, PSL, 1982
Action Stations Supplement and Index, B. Quarrie, PSL, 1987
Aircraft of the RAF since 1918, O. Thetford, Putnam, 1995
Ashley Walk, N. Parker and A. Pasmore, The New Forest Research and Publication Trust, 1995
Britain's Military Airfields 1939–45, D.J. Smith, PSL, 1989
British Aircraft at War 1939–45, G. Swanborough, HPC, 1997
British VCs of World War II, J. Laffin, Budding Books, 1997
CFS – Birthplace of Airpower, J.W.R. Taylor, Jane's, 1987
Deception I World War II, C. Cruikshank, BCA, 1979
Fields of Deception, C. Robinson, Methuen, 2000
From Royal Flying Corps to Army Air Corps, L. Campbell, self-published
Hurricane Combat, Wg. Cdr. K.W. Mackenzie, William Kimber
Lion with Blue Wings, R. Seth, Victor Gollancz, 1956
Lyneham, W. Pereira, Haynes, 1990
Mosquito Fighter/Fighter Bomber Units of World War II, M. Bowman, Osprey, 1998
Most Secret Place, T. Heffernan and B. Johnson, Jane's, 1982
Most Secret War, R.V. Jones, Coronet Books, 1979
Pictorial History of the RAF, J.W.R. Taylor and P.J.R. Moyes, Ian Allen, 1968
Pillboxes, H. Wills, Leo Cooper, 1985
Plain Soldiering N.D.J. James, Hobnob Press, 1987
Porton Down – 75 Years of Chemical and Biological Research, G. Carter, HMSO, 1992
RAF Yatesbury, Report compiled by Paul Francis of Airfield Research Publishing, 1998

Ramsbury at War, R. Day, Published by Roger Day, 1999
Secret Underground Cities, N.J. McCamley, Leo Cooper, 1998
Spitfire – a Test Pilot's Story, J. Quill, John Murray Publishers, 1983
Spitfire – Birth of a Legend, J. Quill and S. Cox, Quiller Press, 1986
Spitfire Odyssey, C.R. Russell, Kingfisher Railways Productions, 1985
Spitfire the History, E.B. Morgan and E. Shacklady, Key Publishing, 1993
The Beambenders: 80 Signals Wing 1939–45, L. Brettingham, Midland Publishing, 1997
The Dambusters Raid, J. Sweetman, Arms and Armour, 1993
The Greatest Air Battle, N.L.R. Franks, William Kimber
The Sky Suspended, J. Bailey, Hodder & Stoughton
The Source Book of the RAF, K. Delve, Airlife, 1994
The Fighting Grasshoppers, K. Wakefield, Midland Counties Publications, 1990
The Secret War B. Johnson, Arrow Books, 1979
The Secret Years, T. Mason, Hikoki Publications, 1998
The Squadrons of the Fleet Air Arm, Ray Sturtivant, Air-Britain Publication, 1984
The Squadrons of the Royal Air Force and Commonwealth 1918–1988, James J. Halley, Air-Britain, 1980
Wroughton Through to the 60s, written by Wroughton History Group, published by Wroughton History Group, 1997

INDEX

Squadrons

Other units

US units